N WEST
FOR
AIRCRAFT WRECKS

NORTH-WEST
AIRCRAFT WRECKS

New Insights into Dramatic Last Flights

Nick Wotherspoon

Pen & Sword
AVIATION

To Janet
In appreciation of her encouragement and support

First published in Great Britain in 2006 by
PEN & SWORD AVIATION
An imprint of
Pen & Sword Books Ltd
47 Church Street
Barnsley
South Yorkshire
S70 2AS

Copyright © Nick Wotherspoon 2006

ISBN 1 84415 478 5
ISBN 978 1 84415 478 4

Printed and bound in Great Britain
By CPI UK

Pen & Sword Books Ltd incorporates the Imprints of Pen & Sword Aviation,
Pen & Sword Maritime, Pen & Sword Military, Wharncliffe Local History,
Pen & Sword Select, Pen & Sword Military Classics and Leo Cooper.

For a complete list of Pen & Sword titles please contact
PEN & SWORD BOOKS LIMITED
47 Church Street, Barnsley, South Yorkshire, S70 2AS, England
E-mail: enquiries@pen-and-sword.co.uk
Website: www.pen-and-sword.co.uk

FOREWORD

As, rightly or wrongly, I am said to be one of the pioneers of aviation archaeology research, the author of this excellent book has asked me to write a foreword. Back in the 1960s, digging up aircraft wrecks was unheard of. However, investigating wreckage still to be found on remote high ground was sparked off by the acquisition of a bootleg copy of an official list of crash sites. Compiled by RAF Mountain Rescue Teams so as to avoid confusing new accidents with old incidents, it was riddled with errors and the aircraft types quoted were often wildly wrong. Systematic visits to the crash sites established, in most cases, the aircraft type but not much else. It also became obvious that the list was far from complete.

During the 1970s, the RAF's Air Historical Branch began to allow researchers to trawl their accident and aircraft record cards for information, and literally hundreds of 'new' high ground accidents came to light, as well as thousands on low ground. At the same time, aviation archaeologists in the south-east began to dig up the wrecks of the many aircraft of both sides shot down in the Battle of Britain. Soon, the recovery movement spread countrywide and was eventually regulated by the Ministry of Defence, because of embarrassing revelations about unrecovered human remains, unexploded bombs and other bad publicity.

Strangely enough, the further we get away from the war years, the more information is revealed, as shown in these chapters. Now the once anonymous pilots and crewmembers have names and even faces from photographs, and their earlier careers are detailed. The background to US Army Air Force crashes, obscure for decades, suddenly became available when copies of the official accident reports could be ordered for a small fee via the Internet.

Nick and the Lancashire Aircraft Investigation Team have researched many incidents and this book covers just a selection of them. The team has checked the official records, contacted fellow airmen and relatives, talked to local people and in some cases have dug up the aircraft involved. Nick has woven a mass of data very skilfully into enthralling human stories which will interest the enthusiast and layman alike. Their activities and the resulting book are a worthy memorial to those who died so tragically in accidents both operational or in training.

David J. Smith 2006

ACKNOWLEDGEMENTS

Firstly I would like to thank my good friend Mark Gaskell, whose meticulous research forms the basis for a number of the chapters in this book and whose aptitude for making sense of the listings of USAAF incident reports enables us to correctly identify many of the American crash sites in the North West.

To all those who have assisted us with our research and made our various excavation projects possible, we would like to offer our sincere thanks, as without the help of numerous individuals and organisations we would not be able to record and preserve the aviation heritage of our region and this book would simply not have been possible. As some of the research projects featured in this book stretch back over several years, sadly some of those to whom we owe thanks are no longer with us, making the acknowledgement of their contribution all the more important to us. Therefore we would like to offer our thanks to the following:

Barry Abraham, Airfield Research Group, Keith Atherton, BAD2 Association, Dick Baker, Mr F. Baybutt, Stanley C. Begonsky, Dave Blake, http://www.britains-smallwars.com, Staff of Bristol Public Library, Gareth Brown, Russell Brown, Mr. A. Bucknall, Jim Buie, Alan L. Clark, Stuart A. Clewlow, Neil and Ruth Cliffe, Commonwealth War Graves Commission, Ted Damick, Richard Danilo, Doug Darroch (Fort Perch Rock Museum & WWIG, Deceased), The Daughters of St. Paul, Boston, MA. United States, John Denehy, Family of the late T., Sgt. Howard E. Denham Jr., Mr. J. Duckworth (Estates Manager Bleasdale Estate), David W. Earl, English Heritage, Robin Farr, Aldon Ferguson, Craig Fuller (AAIR), Miss L. Fyles, Dave Gallimore, Family of the late 1st Lt. Charles Goeking, George Gosney (Deceased), Halton Borough Council, Maurice Hammack, Staff of Harris Public Library, Preston, Peter Haselden, Virgil Herek, Mr H. Heyes, Pat Holt, Lee Howard, Brendan Hughes, Karen Kirk, Knowsley Estate Office, B. Kroll (Ministry of Defence) Lancashire Record Office, Olivia Lawrence, Terry and Don Lovasik, Lytham and District Wildflowers Association, Robin McNair, Jay Manewitz, Mrs. R. Meadley, Members of RAF Millom Aviation &

Military Museum, Alan Mills, Kevin Mount (Deceased), Geoffrey Negus, Dave Parkin, Bob Pearson, Public Record Office, Wilhelm Ratuszynski, Edward Rawlinson, Mr. V. Richmond, Brian Rockliffe, Jean Rybaczek, Dilip Sarkar, Joyce Savage (nee Goulter), Dennis Sexton, Mark Sheldon, Tony Sheridan, Jerry Shore (FAA Museum), John Smallwood, David J. Smith, Grace Spring, Arthur Stewart, Gary L. Stone, Mike Stowe (US Crash Reports), Ray Sturtivant, Andrzej Suchcitz (Polish Institute and Sikorski Museum), Mr E. B. Turner, UK Armed Forces Personnel Administration Agency, United States Air Force Historical Research Center, Maxwell AFB, William Villani, Pavel Vancata, Mr J. Wareing, Staff of Warrington Public Library, Mr M. Wheatley, Janice White, Staff of Widness Public Library, Mr. W. Worswick, John Yates, Ruth Yates.

Inevitably many of the projects coverd in this book have involved may different individuals at the various stages of research, site investigation and actual excavation. Naming everyone is difficult, so to anyone I have inadvertently omitted, please accept my sincere apologies, but you can be sure your contribution was sincerely appreciated.

CONTENTS

Introduction   11

Chapter 1 – There's Something Wrong with Our Aircraft   15

Chapter 2 – Weekend Flyer   24

Chapter 3 – Thrown Out!   34

Chapter 4 – 'Unauthorised Aerobatics'   45

Chapter 5 – Fallen Eagle   51

Chapter 6 – One of Our Aircraft is Missing   60

Chapter 7 – 'Milk Run'   67

Chapter 8 – Hollow Victory   75

Chapter 9 – Almost Made It   84

Chapter 10 – When Luck Runs Out   91

Chapter 11 – An 'Old Warrior'   100

Chapter 12 – Enter the Jet Age   111

Chapter 13 – A Long Way from Home   123

Chapter 14 – Berlin Airlift   129

Chapter 15 – Abandon Aircraft!   139

Chapter 16 – Failed to Return   148

Chapter 17 – Out of Fuel and Out of Time   162

Chapter 18 – Bombers in the Marsh: The Warton Invaders   171

Appendix 1 – Aircraft Incidents   188

Appendix 2 – RAF Millom Aviation and Miliary Museum   243

Bibliography   245

Index   247

INTRODUCTION

The Aeronautical heritage of the North-west of England dates back to the earliest days of manned flight, with the first balloon ascent in the region taking place in Manchester in 1785, only two years after the Montgolfier brothers. It was James Sadler, who had become England's first 'Aeronaut' the previous year, who took off from the city and ascended to 13,000 feet and, eventually landed at Pontefract. The site of his departure was afterwards named Balloon Street and the event is commemorated to this day by a blue plaque.

By the dawn of the 19th century, ballooning had become a popular entertainment and no local fair or event was complete without at least one ascent. Despite the danger, however, there were surprisingly few fatal accidents, though the regions first aeronautical fatality occurred when William Windham Sadler, the son of James Sadler and the first person successfully to cross the Irish Sea in 1817, ascended from the Gas-works, Bolton on 29 September 1824 for a flight to Blackburn. During the flight, the balloon's passenger basket struck a mill chimney at Church near Accrington and he was thrown out and fell to his death; the site of this tragedy being commemorated by the naming of Sadler Street.

Continuing in the showman tradition, the famous pioneering aviator 'Colonel' Samuel F. Cody (1861-1913) was demonstrating his man-lifting kites to amazed crowds in the North-west as early as 1899 and claimed that the inspiration for this invention came to him whilst performing with his Wild-West show in Lancashire.

With the emergence of heavier-than-air powered flight, Blackpool became home to the first officially recognised (by the Royal Aero Club) aviation meeting to be held in Britain in October 1909, when over 200,000 spectators gathered to watch many of the great pioneers of the day demonstrate their machines. Amongst the many memorable sights was Hubert Latham's 'Antoinette' monoplane flying in gusts of 40 mph, typical local conditions, in which until then aviators had believed it impossible to fly safely.

Additionally, aircraft production has always been important to the economy of the North-west with one of the first factories being that of

A.V. Roe and Company established at Brownsfield Mills, Manchester in 1910, starting a tradition that would see the region playing an important part in both World Wars and continuing to the present day. It was during WW1 that the strategic importance of the industrial areas of the North-west first caught the attention of the enemy and the region saw two significant Zeppelin raids, the first in September 1916, with bombs falling in the Rossendale area and on Bury, and the second in April 1918 over Bold and Wigan. Though there was some damage and a number of casualties during these raids, on both occasions the raiders were in fact completely lost and believed that they had bombed different targets. Although Liverpool was singled out as a target and initially the German's believed they had successfully bombed it, these shortcomings in the navigation technology of the time, meant that on this occasion once again another city was the recipient of the bombs and the casualties were civilian.

As with the rest of the country the inter-war period saw a massive increase in aerial activity over the North-west and new airfields began to spring up across the region. With aviation seen as the transport medium of the future, many towns began planning their own airports. But the outbreak of WW2 was to change the face of the region as most of these airfields were taken over for the training of aircrews and for aircraft construction and maintenance. However, it was the region's major industrial and trade centres that were to attract the attention of the *Luftwaffe*, with the cities of Manchester and Liverpool becoming major targets of the Blitz and suffering particularly badly. As the conflict progressed, the American authorities also recognised the areas advantages and two airfields were taken over and turned into huge aircraft maintenance and repair depots serving the frontline bases to the south and further increasing the air traffic over the region. Therefore many of the wartime incidents we researched involved accidents during training or the ferrying and testing of aircraft. However, for the families of those who lost their lives, the memory of their sacrifice is no less important.

Aviation Archaeology may cover almost any form of research into, or collecting of, artefacts connected with the history of aviation. However it is most commonly associated with the research into, and more specifically the recovery of, artefacts from the crash sites of WW2 aircraft. Since the emergence of the hobby in the early 1960s Aviation Archaeology has always, it seems, caught the imagination of the public and also in our experience the media. Particularly following the release of the Battle of Britain film in 1969 there was an increased awareness of the events of 1940 amongst a new generation, too young to remember the events themselves. Unlike the rest of Europe there were no battlefields, with their abandoned tanks or weapons to find, or the vast network of fortifications built by the Third Reich to explore. Yet they discovered that with a little perseverance, relics of this great aerial battle still littered the countryside and as the first crude metal detectors became available, enthusiasts could be found most weekends searching for these lost aircraft. Initially such activities were mainly concerned with crash sites of aircraft that took part in the Battle of Britain over the southern counties of England. But following media coverage and the publication of a small number of books on the subject, the hobby gained increasing popularity and enthusiasts in various parts of the country began to explore their own areas, looking for sites to excavate. As with much of the UK, most wartime sites in the North-west have already been investigated over the years. Though all too often little research was done, often confined to merely ascertaining the basic details in order to obtain the required MoD permit to dig and in some cases sites were even incorrectly identified!

The Lancashire Aircraft Investigation Team (LAIT) formed in 1998 from a small group of experienced enthusiasts who were primarily concerned with detailed research into local incidents dating from WW1 through to the Cold War, regardless of the likelihood of artefacts still being present.

The author is a founder member of this team and one of our main aims has always been to try to trace eyewitnesses to these events whilst they are still available to be interviewed. However, first hand witnesses to wartime incidents are sadly becoming increasingly difficult to find and those who were excavating sites 30 years ago are now becoming important sources of information in their own right! This has led us to realise that in the past many sites were only partially excavated or in some cases even discounted altogether, as the crude metal detectors of the time failed to indicate that wreckage was in fact present. Additionally, those groups that were more successful often consigned less desirable artefacts back to the hole, as it was back-filled, due to a shortage of storage space brought about by the number of aircraft they had already excavated!

In theory this has left us with many potential sites for excavation, but it is also becoming apparent with the passage of time, that the light alloys used in aircraft construction are degrading at an alarming rate. However, although we remain one of the few active groups operating in Britain and continue to carry out regular excavations, this is not a hobby that can be rushed and any items we recover often require many hours of cleaning and conservation, which can be quite daunting when a major dig may yield some three tons of mangled aircraft!

Finds from all our excavations are displayed at the RAF Millom Museum, Haverigg in Cumbria, an organisation that was generous in giving us a building on their site to house our collection. By combining our research with recovered artefacts in this way, we believe that this allows the public to interpret more accurately the often fragmentary aircraft remains and gain an understanding of the events that they represent.

Please note that in the UK the remains of all aircraft that have crashed whilst in military service (whether on land or sea) are protected by The Protection of Military Remains Act 1986. Removal or excavation of such remains is illegal without a permit from the Ministry of Defence and may lead to prosecution. All LAIT projects are carried out with the consent of the Landowner concerned, as well as within the terms of this Act and in accordance with the *Notes for guidance of Recovery Groups* published by the Ministry of Defence and the British Aviation Archaeological Council's Code of Conduct.

CHAPTER ONE

THERE'S SOMETHING WRONG WITH OUR AIRCRAFT!

The loss of a popular test pilot was not only a major blow to morale on one of the biggest US air bases in England, but it was the second such loss in less than a month due to a design flaw in the P-51D aircraft. This had massive potential implications for US Fighter Squadrons being re-equipped with the new P-51D at this critical stage of the war. However, behind this incident was also a tragic personal story of a young English bride who only that very morning had given her husband the happy news that their first child was due.

The P-51 D with its distinctive bubble canopy is perhaps the best-known version of the famous Mustang fighter and was also the most widely used variant, with a grand total of 8102 machines of this type being built. Its development came about as a result of problems encountered with the Merlin-powered P-51B/C, particularly the poor view from the cockpit towards the rear. The RAF had designed and fitted the one-piece sliding, bulbous, Perspex 'Malcolm hood' canopy as an attempt to correct this deficiency. However, a more lasting solution was sought and in January 1943, Col. Mark Bradley had been sent to England to assess the problem and whilst there he saw the newly designed 'bubble' or 'teardrop' canopies that gave Spitfire and Typhoon pilots an unobstructed 360-degree view and he returned, convinced this was the answer for the Mustang. Another shortcoming of the P-51B/C was its limited firepower: only four 0.5-inch Browning machine guns, two in each wing. Additionally, these guns were mounted at an angle, requiring a kink in the ammunition belt-feeds and resulting in frequent gun jams. North American Aviation took the opportunity afforded by the development of the new Mustang to redesign the gun installation and the result was three 0.5-inch machine guns in each wing, mounted upright, in an enlarged gun-bay with the inboard guns having 400 rounds per gun and the others 270 rounds per gun.

Large numbers of the new P-51Ds began arriving in Europe from March 1944 and the huge Base Air Depot 2 at Warton (BAD2) became the centre for their final preparation before being flown out to front-line units. However, problems with the new design had already been identified, notably the lack of directional stability which was traced to the new cut-down rear fuselage. The fitting of a fillet at the base of the dorsal tail fin cured this and many of the newly delivered aircraft required such modification at the base. However, far worse was to come and the first incident occurred on 12 June 1944 when, during a routine test flight, P-51D Serial No. 44-13403 embedded itself in the Ribble mud close to BAD2 at Warton, killing it's pilot, Second Lieutenant W.T. Clearwater. Many personnel on the base, alerted by a dramatic change in the note of the aircraft's engine, witnessed the horrific final moments of Lt. Clearwater, when the starboard wing detached from the aircraft in flight and was seen fluttering down, as the fuselage with the pilot trapped inside dived into the marshes just the other side of the river from the base. Detailed examination of the recovered wreckage showed that there had been catastrophic structural failure of the wing assembly, but no definite cause could be ascertained.

It was some two weeks later that another BAD2 test pilot, 2nd Lt. Burtie Orth, was making a similar test flight in P-51D Serial No. 44-15393 on the Tuesday morning of 27 June 1944 over the nearby town of Preston. Weather conditions were not ideal with frequent thunder showers and 7/10 cloud cover at 1400 feet, but there were clear areas and the pilot may well have flown inland in order to carry out his testing schedule in just such an area. Although the aircraft's movements were not observed prior to the crash, it is believed that Burtie would have adhered strictly to the limitations on aerobatics flying which had been placed following the crash two weeks earlier. Exactly what happened next will never be known, but as in the case of the previous crash, the first indication of something wrong to those on the ground was the scream of the engine running out of control. At approximately 9.00 am morning assembly was taking place in the main hall at Fulwood and Cadley School, Preston, when the children's attention

Burtie Orth taken in 1943.
(*Pat Holt*).

16

was diverted by the noise and many ran to the windows – just in time to glimpse the last moments of the aircraft, a memory that was to stay with them for the rest of their lives. It appeared to those watching that the pilot somehow had some partial control over the direction of the aircraft's descent as it seemed to veer away from the school and houses below. The stricken plane exploded on impact, partly embedded in the ground in a hay meadow at Ingol Head Farm in the Cadley area of the town. Occupants of the farmhouse at the time recalled something striking the roof of the farmhouse immediately prior to impact and daylight being blotted out by the thick black smoke rising only a few yards from the front of the house. Workers from the farm were first on the scene, but quickly realised that they could do nothing for the unfortunate pilot, who they could see trapped in the cockpit, though they tried to reach him, they were beaten back by the flames. Several locals soon joined them and an RAF Warrant Officer named Bradley from the nearby Headquarters of No.9 Group, Fighter Command, at Barton Hall, managed to drag the unfortunate pilot clear and together with other personnel from Barton Hall they took charge of the body and arranged for an RAF ambulance to convey Burtie Orth to the mortuary there.

At the time of the accident it was suggested that although there was a recognised weakness in the wing of the new P-51D, the actual failure of the structure could have been triggered by the starboard main undercarriage leg inadvertently lowering into the slipstream at cruising speed and placing immense pressure on the wing spar. This was thought to be due to the omission of the additional mechanical locking system that was no longer fitted on the new P-51D, presumably as a weight saving measure. However, examination of the official crash reports for both incidents clearly places the blame on a weakness in the front wing-spar assembly and associated stressed skin structure between 'Rib stations 75 to 91.5', i.e. the enlarged gun-bay area. The report on Orth's aircraft does go on to suggest that failure of the retracting /locking system could be a contributory factor, but merely recommends further investigation.

By mid 1944, P-51D Mustangs fitted with drop-tanks were accompanying the B-17 Flying Fortress and B-24 Liberator bombers on their 1000+ mile round trips to their targets. The ability of escort fighters to accompany bomber formations all the way to their targets and still effectively counter intercepting *Luftwaffe* fighters led to a dramatic drop in bomber losses and added considerable impetus to the American daylight bombing offensive. At such a critical stage in the

17

conflict, the new Mustang had become an invaluable part of the war effort and, in light of the two losses at Warton, modifications were soon being made to P-51Ds on the production line to strengthen the gun-bay area. However, many aircraft had already reached their designated units and rumours of this weakness continued, with several pilots being lost in similar circumstances, including Hubert 'Hub' Zemke, Commanding Officer of the 56th Fighter Group, who fortunately regained consciousness in time to deploy his parachute after his P-51 D lost its starboard wing and disintegrated around him.

For many years local enthusiasts believed that both these incidents occurred close to the site of BAD2 at Warton, no doubt due to published BAD2 veteran's recollections of witnessing both crashes from the airfield itself. One group actually went so far as to identify the crash site of an American fighter on the marshes at Freckleton as being that of 44-15393 and partially excavated the site! (Now known to be the crash site of P-47 42-8621.) However, our brief examination of the known details soon showed that this deduction was flawed. Inspection of local papers close to the date of the accident revealed little, though a small note about local school children sending flowers for the funeral of an American pilot gave us our first clue and put us on the right track. Following information appeals in the local press we soon had several witnesses to interview – mainly former pupils at the local school which the aircraft had narrowly missed. Pinpointing the exact site proved a little harder – it had been well guarded and few of those interviewed had got near, though not for want of trying! Also, photographs of the crash site obtained from the BAD2 Veterans Association and the official crash report clearly showed a substantial farm building in the background – which we failed to locate. Fortunately, when interviewed, the present owner of the former farmhouse recalled demolishing the aforementioned building many years before and we had our match. However, aviation archaeology is a complex hobby and it was some time before we could start systematically searching the area with a metal detector. The field in question now belonged to the Commission for New Towns North and as it was not due for immediate development, it had been let to a tenant farmer. Several letters later we had permission to survey the field and soon began finding small aluminium fragments close to the hedge where the out-building had once stood. Each of these was marked with a peg and a pattern soon began to emerge that indicated a definite concentration of detector signals – so we brought in a more sophisticated detector, an ex-MoD Forster Bomb Locator, in order to

The aftermath of the crash of P-51D 44-13593 in 1944 (*George Gosney*)

pinpoint any substantial buried remains. This machine did indeed indicate that something larger lay below the surface, which we obviously wished to excavate, but there were problems! In addition to the landowners consent, the required MoD permit and the approval of the tenant, this site was to prove especially complicated as many of the underground services for the future development of the area were already in place and consultation with all the various service providers was also required, including North West Water, Transco and Norweb – our correspondence file for this project was becoming one of the thickest ever!

Finally our excavation of the site was scheduled to take place, coincidentally, on 27 June 1998 (27 June 1944 being the date the aircraft crashed) and in the meantime we had continued our research and this had led to our making contact with the family of Burtie Orth.

We already knew that the daughter of the pilot still lived in the North-west from a letter that had appeared in *Flypast* magazine in the mid 1980s, appealing for information on the crash. However, I was surprised to learn that not only did she still live in the area, but also worked for the same Library authority as myself and stranger still, had actually applied for and was the successful applicant for my own post when I gained leave of absence to attend university! Burtie 'Bud' Orth came from of a family of

Excavation of the crash site of 44-13593 gets underway in 1998

thirteen children from Richfield, Kansas, with eight sisters and four brothers. All four brothers were also engaged in the war effort: one, as a fighter pilot, had already shot down his first enemy aircraft, the

19

second and third in the Navy and the fourth working for Boeing. At 24 years of age Burtie was the second youngest of the Orth boys and his cheerful and friendly nature made him popular, both at home and at the BAD2 base where he had arrived in October 1943. Many of the servicemen from the base spent their recreation time in the nearby Lytham and Blackpool seaside resorts – indeed their graffiti can still be found carved into trees on a popular shaded path in the former town, where they would take local girls for Sunday afternoon walks. In the case of Burtie, romance blossomed with a local girl from Marton area of Blackpool and they were married in April 1944. With the war expected to be over soon and Burtie's position as a Test Pilot being relatively 'safe', their happiness must have seemed complete when three months later she found that she was expecting their first child, though it seems that Burtie must have still had some foreboding, as he made his wife promise him that if anything happened to him, she should take their baby back to his home in Kansas, where the family would take care of them both in his absence.

Although we knew from the start that very little was likely to be left of 44-15393, our trusty Forster Locator was giving a good signal, this was interpreted from experience as indicating that a medium sized object was quite near to the surface! Accordingly, excavation was to be conducted by hand so as not to miss anything, and we even had two trained archaeologists unofficially join the team! Considering the importance placed at the time on discovering the cause of these two tragic accidents and the suspicion cast on the possible failure of the undercarriage locking mechanism, we were most surprised to discover that the large ferrous item picked up by our equipment was, in fact, the top section of the starboard undercarriage leg, only feet below the surface. This comprised the complete pivot casting from the top of the leg encased in the corroded remains of the magnesium pivot block,

Pieces of Orth's Mustang begin to emerge from just below the surface.

mounted on a section of the front wing-spar and including the undercarriage lock-down mechanism. The position of the casting in the block clearly showed that the leg had in fact been in the fully retracted position at the time the remainder of the leg had been torn off. The force of the wing breaking away, with the wheel presumably held fast in the wheel well, had exerted immense pulling pressure on the four bolts holding the leg into the pivot casting collar and these had sheared allowing the wing to break completely away and the heavy undercarriage leg to fall free. According to one witness interviewed the latter item fell in nearby Mill Lane. Reports at the time had mentioned that the brake lines to the main-wheel had been found twisted and wrapped around the oleo strut – indicating that the leg had rotated and from this it seems that the leg had lowered in flight and been torn off. Our find appeared to indicate that it was not just the leg that had rotated, but the entire wing as it was torn off! Other smaller finds included: the remains of three instruments, including the main hydraulic pressure gauge, the push-button radio tuner control panel,

Left: **The LAIT team pose with the scant recovered remains of Burtie's Mustang, having reinstated the site. (*Stuart A. Clewlow*)**

Below: **Left to Right – Instrument mechanism, drop-tank release handle, hydraulic pressure gauge and the push-button radio tuner control face plate.**

spare lamp-bulb locker cover, drop-tank release handle, an electric motor and many very small fragments. A careful sort through these items revealed a small chrome plated object – a locking cone from the pilot's parachute pack, this was a sad reminder that Burtie had remained with his aircraft. As predicted the finds petered out at less than 1 metre in depth and the rest of the day was spent carefully checking through the spoil for missed items and reinstating the site just as we found it.

Burtie Orth was a popular figure at BAD2, Warton and his death was a severe blow to morale, especially in light of the fact that he had recently been married and doubly so as his wife had apparently given him the good news that she was expecting their child on the morning of the very day he died. He is buried in the American Military Cemetery, Madingley Road, Coton, Cambridgeshire, Plot Ref. F. Row No. 1 grave 95. He is still remembered fondly by those who knew him and the family still have many mementoes, including: his training logbook, flight checklist notebook, letters, his silver wings and the folded Stars and Stripes which covered his coffin at his funeral. Many of these items were loaned to be displayed alongside the parts excavated, for a special display at the Harris Central Library in Preston during October 1998, which was seen by many of the local people who had followed our quest to unearth both the remains of the plane and the story of this brave young pilot, as it had been reported at various stages in the local newspapers. This local press coverage also came to the attention of the head of the school governors and the head

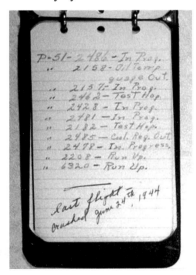

Burtie Orth's flight checklist notebook is among the mementoes still kept by the family.

teacher at the Fulwood and Cadley County Primary School and it was decided that Burtie's actions should be commemorated in a suitable way at the school. A brass plaque was funded by the British Aerospace North West Heritage Group and a dedication ceremony was held at the school on 25 June 1999, where the plaque was presented and later placed in the main entrance corridor of the school, together with a framed photograph of Burtie Orth, where it will be seen by everyone entering the main building. The ceremony took place in the same hall where the pupils at the time of the crash witnessed the dramatic events in 1944 during that morning assembly and was attended by most of those former pupils that were there that day, who we had managed to track down. Also present was Burtie's widow and their daughter Pat. The Lancashire Aircraft Investigation Team assisted throughout the planning of this memorial and also represented was the BAD2 Veterans association, the local RAFA & the local British Legion. More than 100 school children were present and several participated in the ceremony and all had been told of the events of that day in 1944, which has now become part of the history of their school.

Pat Holt, Burtie Orth's daughter beside his grave at the American Military Cemetery at Madingley, Cambridge. (*Pat Holt*).

CHAPTER TWO

WEEKEND FLYER

Although as a group, our activities are largely taken up with research, we do like to get out now and again and get our hands dirty on a 'dig'! With this in mind half a dozen like-minded individuals gathered on a bleak, wind (and occasionally rain) swept marsh near Freckleton, Lancashire in November 1996 for our group's inaugural dig. All were hoping that the readings from the borrowed Fisher two-box detector did indeed indicate that substantial remains of Spitfire RN 210 lay beneath our feet, although the sceptics among us cited a previous group's fruitless investigations of this site. Even with today's more sophisticated deep-seeking detectors, the hobby of Aviation Archaeology can still be something of a hit or miss affair. Every crash site is different and various sized pieces of aircraft at differing depths and with unknown soil conditions, can all affect the signals these machines give out. On some sites where an engine has been severely broken up, but recovered, residual and minute ground-up metal fragments can still give ghost signals; or a smashed undercarriage leg thrown back into the crater after the original recovery, and therefore near the surface, can appear to be far more substantial wreckage more deeply buried. In this Freckleton case it was known that at least two abortive digs had been carried out on the site – so at least we could discount any such shallow wreckage being the source of the readings!

Built by Vickers Armstrong at Keevil, Spitfire Mk F XIV RN 210 was accepted by the RAF at 39 MU on 22 February 1945 and initially was allocated to No. 41 Squadron in March, which was carrying out daily armed reconnaissance sorties based at Eindhoven in the Netherlands. The aircraft's combat career with this Squadron was somewhat brief: on the 25 April, RN 210 was involved in an incident whilst on operational flying which resulted in it being classified category AC. This resulted in the aircraft being returned to 409 Repair and Servicing Unit, from where, at the end of May 1945, it went on to Air Service Training duties. On the 23 August 1947 RN 210 was allocated to 611 West Lancashire Squadron, which had been re-formed in May 1946 as an auxiliary unit and was now based at RAF Woodvale, Lancs.

On Saturday 8 May 1948, 27 year old Flying Officer Robert Hugh Price Griffiths reported to RAF Woodvale for flying duties with 611

Squadron, as he did most weekends. Griffiths, from Crosby, Liverpool had originally volunteered for service with the RAF on 18 September 1939, beginning his RAF career as an Air Gunner with 26 Squadron in 1940. On the 27 June 1940 he received minor injuries when Lysander P1745 ran out fuel and overshot into a hedge whilst landing at West Malling at dusk after having become lost whilst on patrol and unable to relocate the airfield. He went on to Air Gunner duties with Nos. 239 and 151 Squadrons, before being selected for pilot training in 1942 in Canada and the United States. However, all did not quite go according to plan for him. On completion of his training he was allocated to instructional duties rather than the front-line squadron he had hoped for.

Griffiths resigned his commission as Pilot Officer in the RAF in late 1943 and early in 1944 he took up a commission as Sub/Lieutenant in the Air Branch of the RNVR where he joined No. 804 Squadron, which re-formed at Wingfield, Cape Town, on 1 September 1944, flying Hellcats. He embarked on the Assault Escort Carrier HMS *Ameer* in January 1945 to provide cover during Operation Matador, the Allied landings on Ramree Island. On the 26th she provided air cover for Operation Sankey, Allied landings on Cheduba Island. This was

F/O R.H.P. Griffiths and his brother, F/O W.P. Griffiths AFC taken circa 1943. (*Bill Laycock*).

followed by spotting, fighter cover, bombing, and tactical reconnaissance missions over Malaya and Sumatra and on 1 March 804's Hellcats shot down three Japanese aircraft. In April the squadron embarked on HMS *Empress* and HMS *Shah* for attacks on the Andaman Islands and the Burmese coast before returning to HMS *Ameer* in June for bombing attacks on Sumatra airfields and also operations off Phuket Island.

July saw *Ameer*, in company with HMS *Emperor* taking part in Operation Livery commencing on the 24th, conducting air strikes on Northern Malaya and providing air cover for minesweeping operations. Over a three day period, Hellcats from both carriers flew over 150 sorties and destroyed more than 30 Japanese aircraft on the ground, together with trains and road transport. On 26 July HMS *Ameer* was attacked by the only Kamikaze to strike at a British carrier in the Indian Ocean. Whilst in the Bay of Bengal a single Mitsubishi Ki.51 'Sonia' attempted to dive onto *Ameer*, but was hit and successfully deflected by fire from the ships defensive armament, splashing harmlessly into the sea some 500 yds away. All in all it seems Sub/Lieutenant R.H.P. Griffiths certainly saw his fair share of the 'action' he craved. However a quick check in Ray Sturtivant's invaluable Fleet Air Arm Aircraft 1939 – 1945 reveals that he was involved in the loss of Wildcat JV501 at Abbotsinch on 30 May.1945, so perhaps it did not all go his way?

Following the war Griffiths apparently found civilian life somewhat lacking in excitement, despite a powerful motorcycle and occasionally flying a small passenger aircraft for his employers at ICI. In November 1947 he applied to join 611 Auxiliary Squadron and was accepted in December and granted a commission as Flying Officer. It was just before 3.00 pm on a grey Saturday afternoon in 1948 that two Spitfires took off from Woodvale on a practice high-altitude climb. F/O Griffiths' wingman for this exercise was Sergeant John James (Doc) Morgan and some 35 minutes later the two aircraft were at 21,000 feet above the Ribble estuary. At this point Sgt. Morgan asked F/O Griffiths over the radio whether he intended to climb higher and Griffiths replied that he was checking his oxygen equipment, but did not indicate that there was a problem. A few minutes later Sgt. Morgan observed that F/O Griffiths' aircraft was rolling from side to side, but further attempts at radio communication could raise no reply. Shortly after this RN 210 went into a spin and began a steep dive. Sgt. Morgan attempted to follow, still vainly trying to establish radio contact, but he was forced to pull out before his own altitude became dangerously low and through the low cloud he observed F/O Griffiths' aircraft crash into a field near Freckleton and explode. Those who rushed to the crash site on the ground, realised immediately that the unfortunate pilot was beyond their help and servicemen from nearby Warton airfield were soon on the scene and sealed off the area. It was later reported in the local newspaper that Flying Officer Griffiths' remains were recovered during a strenuous 24 hour recovery operation involving up to thirty servicemen. Following formal identification he was buried with full military honours at St. Peter's church, Formby, close to Woodvale airfield. His home was at Clayton Avenue, Culceth near Warrington and he left a widow and young daughter.

As the excavation of RN210 got underway on another grey Saturday morning nearly 50 years later, it rapidly became apparent why such a large number of servicemen were required during the initial recovery attempt. The first trial trench, dug by hand, across the identified crater, hit running sand within 3 feet and not the 6 to 10 feet depth predicted by local farmers! Following a quick consultation it was decided to continue using a JCB and forgo the usual initial hand dig, whilst

Below: **Excavation of the crash site of RN210 underway, as a mainwheel tyre is retrieved.**

Left: **Guest on the excavation, David Ivins (son of Wg Cr. D.V. Ivins, KIA 18.05.1943) contemplates the shattered Rolls Royce Griffon engine.**

hoping that our trust in the Fisher would be vindicated. Fortunately, a relative of the landowner possessed such a machine and was itching to get involved, he was at the site within an hour. Progress was rapid and though there were relatively few finds in the initial few feet, the main engine driven generator had been recovered together with a shredded and burnt main-wheel tyre. We now had a pit some 10 feet square and 5 to 6 feet deep, with the main mass of wreckage lying in the bottom under some 18 inches of running sand and water. Following the removal of the second main wheel tyre, this time basically intact, it was decided that the hole was becoming too dangerous to enter. Consultation with the JCB driver resulted in an agreement that he would systematically 'trawl' the excavation, scoop the wreckage out and deposit it well clear of the hole for sorting. This method proved less haphazard than it sounds and the quantity and range of artifacts recovered proves its success: all five propeller blade hubs, both accumulator bottles, both main undercarriage legs and two oxygen bottles. During the day a number of interested locals visited the excavation to view the progress and some shared their recollections of the crash. One such individual had a most interesting story to tell us. Mr Hugh Dollin had been in the RAF and stationed at Warton at the time and took part in the recovery operation – in fact he was photographed in the crater by a local reporter and the picture appeared in the local paper report on the incident. He had later returned to the area to marry a local girl he met whilst serving there and settled in Freckleton. He recalled the atrocious conditions digging by hand in the liquid sand and how the only thing stopping the men sinking was the fact that they were stood on the buried engine! Because of the condition of the excavated crater by this stage of the dig, a 'Then and Now' style comparison photograph was clearly impossible – though Mr Dollin showed no inclination to re-enact the events of 50 years before in any case!

Most items were recovered from the area as predicted by the Fisher, but at mid-afternoon we were surprised to recover a fairly intact Hispano 20mm cannon and a 0.5-inch calibre Browning machine gun whilst digging a drainage sump to one side of the main excavation. Naturally we immediately switched the JCB to the opposite side of the crater but no such luck! The guns were slotted vertically into the ground, graphically demonstrating the angle and force of impact following RN 210's final dive. Finally at approximately 10 feet depth the JCB shuddered as a large object was encountered – the Rolls Royce Griffon 65 engine, we hoped! But as the driver struggled to get a purchase, the object began to sink! Luck was with us again as the JCB

Hispano 20mm cannon and 0.50 calibre Browning from the starboard wing of RN210 – Note: white, hand painted inscription "Star 210" on the breech of the 20mm!

had an 'extradig' telescopic arm and at approximately 15 feet depth we finally seemed to be winning as the shattered remains of the engine were lifted from the liquid sand 'soup' now filling the seemingly enormous crater. Barely recognisable at first, the mighty Griffon had split in two, with the forward three cylinders having been destroyed on both banks. The cylinder heads had fared slightly better, but virtually the whole crank case had shattered and disappeared and all the ancillaries had broken away. It would be several weekends of cleaning and careful reassembly before this twisted mass of cylinders and crankshaft would once again bear some semblance of an aero engine.

The following day was spent 'finger-tip' searching the spoil heaps prior to back-filling the hole – with the assistance of several very enthusiastic (and muddy) local youths who worked on the local farms. Thanks to their patience and diligence a wealth of smaller items, otherwise invisible in the liquid mud, were found. The finds included: the blind flying panel, several instruments, throttle quadrant, control column, rudder pedals, compass, ki-gas primer and many smaller components. The recovery of two oxygen bottles came as a surprise, considering that some form of investigation into the cause of the accident must have taken place, though the oxygen regulator was notably absent. Once cleaned, the two bottles revealed manufacture dates that would have made them between 7 and 10 years old at the time of the crash, apparently beyond the operational life of such items. We also later discovered that Griffiths had flown the same aircraft the week before the crash at an altitude requiring oxygen and had complained of 'spotting' in his oxygen mask from moisture in the system. If the cause of this had not been traced, could this moisture have frozen at the higher altitudes reached on the day of the crash and led to the failure of the system?

With the field reinstated and some three tons of wreckage removed for safe keeping, so began the mammoth task of sorting and cleaning familiar to all those involved in our hobby! Many components were in amazing condition, such as the tail wheel and oleo assembly which was retrieved intact and pressurised with a fully inflated tyre and which rotated freely on it's bearings. But many parts were affected by the intense fire that followed the impact and exhibited varying levels of corrosion, the worst naturally being on those items found closest to the surface and included the engine bearers and the few surviving sections of airframe, such as the radio compartment access door.

Sad reminders of the tragic fate of F/O Griffiths also came to light, including an intact silk parachute canopy, its pack with both seat and back pads. Saddest of all was his wallet containing a driving licence,

RN210's Griffon 65 engine reassembled and on display at the Millom museum.

personal papers and a lock of child's hair preserved inside his Cricket Club membership card – his daughter had been only three - years - old when he was killed. These latter items were carefully cleaned and conserved before being sent back to the RAF, who, after experiencing difficulty in tracing the pilot's next of kin, gave our group permission to attempt to contact the family regarding these items. An appeal on Channel 4's 'Service Pals' teletext pages brought us into contact with a former school friend of the pilot and his brother – all three had joined the RAF together at the outbreak of the war. He recalled Griffiths' widow returning to her hometown in Scotland following the accident. Several weeks after placing letters in a number of newspapers in that locality and contacting local family history societies we had almost given up, when late one evening the lady herself made a telephone call after having one of the letters brought to her attention by a friend. Though it obviously brought back some very sad memories, she was happy to talk about her late husband, and during several phone conversations the story of his brief but full life was related. She also kindly arranged for a copy of his RAF service record for our files and we arranged for his personal effects to be returned. However, these were then presented to us so that the story of both the pilot and the aircraft should be included in a display of the aircraft remains, in

31

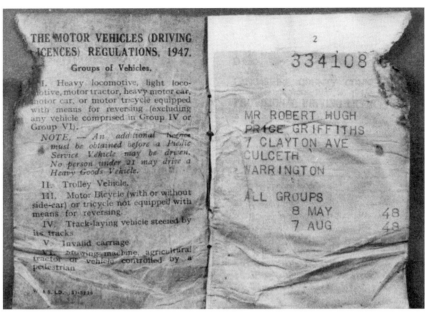

F/O R.H.P. Griffiths motor vehicle driving licence (provisional!) was among the personal effects recovered on the dig.

The saddest find of the dig was this cricket club membership card, which still contains a lock of his young daughter's hair.

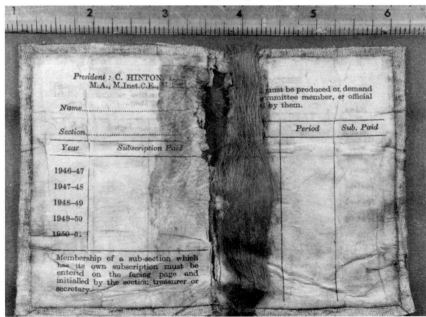

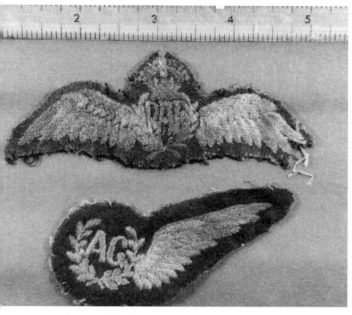

Still attached to a fragment of torn fabric were Griffiths' pilot's wings and surprisingly below them he also wore his Air Gunner's insignia.

accordance with the wishes of his family.

As with many such investigations, the research into this pilot and his aircraft is never really complete and often leads to other avenues for investigation. In this case the fate of F/O R.H.P. Griffiths' brother F/O William Price Griffiths AFC who served with No.148 Squadron as a Wireless operator/air gunner in Wellingtons, flying from Malta, until he was wounded and sent back to Britain to recover. He went on to join No.24 Squadron based at Northolt, a communications flight unit, which specialised in the transport of V.I.P.s. He was to lose his life on 5 December 1944 in Dakota FL588 on a flight from Northolt to Marseilles on the first leg of a flight to India carrying Glider Pilot Regiment officers and their equipment. The plane came down in atrocious weather conditions near Usson in the Massif Central, killing all the crew and all but five of the twenty passengers. Of the survivors, one succumbed to wounds and the cold before rescue and another died a few days later in hospital. All those killed are buried in Mazagues War Cemetery, Marseilles – F/O W. P. Griffiths in Plot 3, Row E. grave 58. The crash occurred at a critical period in operations and was to have serious repercussions for the setting up of glider-borne operations in the Far-East – but that's another story…

CHAPTER THREE

THROWN OUT!

No 308 'City of Krakow' Polish Fighter Squadron became operational on the 1 December 1940 at Bagington and arrived at RAF Woodvale from RAF Northolt with their Spitfires on 12 December 1941. Having been in action in the south of England for many months, they had scored fifty-two confirmed kills, ten probables, and thirteen damaged, making 308 Squadron the highest-scoring unit in Fighter Command in 1941 – it was now time to rest and train replacements. However, this did not prevent them looking for trouble because on the 11 February 1942 they damaged a Ju88 over Lancaster and were recorded as chasing another on the 21 February 1942. Most of their operational sorties whilst at Woodvale were routine convoy patrols protecting shipping in the Mersey Estuary and Irish Sea. Additionally much of the Squadron's time was taken up training new recruits, especially in defensive night flying over Liverpool.

Spitfire Mk Vb serial No. BL585 was built by Vickers Armstrong (Castle Bromwich) Ltd and would have been delivered between November 1941 and May 1942. Throughout 1941 No. 308 Squadron mainly flew older Mk I and Mk II Spitfires, and in late 1941, they began converting to the newer Mk Vb. Clearly BL585 was one of these new replacement aircraft and it is likely that it had only very recently arrived at the squadron.

On the morning of Friday 13 February 1942, BL585 was being flown by Flying Officer Boleslaw Paley P-0347 (Palej – correct Polish spelling), of No 308 Squadron based at RAF Woodvale near Southport. F/O Paley was conducting mock dog-fighting exercises with Sergeant Majchrzyk, when it seems Paley baled out of his aircraft! At the subsequent inquiry, he later admitted that there was no failure in the aircraft, but that he blacked out and only came to when he found himself no longer at the controls of his aircraft, but falling through the air with his parachute unopened. It seems that, fortunately for Paley, in his unconscious state, his training took over and he successfully baled out, the rush of cold air then bringing him round.

The loss of this 308 Squadron Spitfire from the RAF Woodvale airfield near Southport, had for many years posed something of a mystery to Aviation Archaeology enthusiasts in the North-west. Excavating a wartime Spitfire crash site has always carried a certain cachet amongst the various groups involved in this hobby and though the loss of this machine was clearly recorded in the squadron's Operations Record Book (ORB), no location was given and there was no Form 1180 available that might give further information. In fact the mysterious loss from the records of almost all the Form 1180s relating to incidents involving Spitfire V aircraft in the North-west, has for many years made research more than a little difficult. However, the ORB entry was quite detailed, noting that the pilot 'baled out' during a practice dogfight and as much of this activity from Woodvale was known to have been carried out over the sea, many enthusiasts simply concluded that this is where BL585 had ended up.

However, never being one to write off completely any lead without some form of proof, the details of BL585 joined the list at the back of my notebook in the hope that sometime in the future further information may come to light. It was several years later whilst researching the loss of a B-24 Liberator 42-7467 from Burtonwood, which crashed at Aspull near Wigan that one of those amazing chances of fate occurred, that not only filled in the missing piece of the BL585 puzzle but proved that there was a very good chance that the remains of this aircraft still lay where it had crashed and that it was only a few fields away from the B-24!

Through experience we have found that older locals are often a mine

317 Squadron pilots in a relaxed pose at Chailey in May 1944 - Flying Officer Boleslaw Palej is seated astride the Spitfire's propeller! (*Wilhelm Ratuszynski*)

of information when we are researching any incident. Sadly, though, as the years pass it is becoming harder and harder to find first-hand witnesses and consequently we always make a point of talking to as many people who recall a crash as possible. They often end up recounting other wartime reminiscences, which we try to record as well. Occasionally we hit a real gold-mine of information, such as the ex-policeman who it turned out knew nothing of the crash in question, but had been placed on guard at several others – were we still interested? In this case we were directed to a Mr Eric Turner, living in Hindley, near Wigan, who as a teenager had spent much of his spare time monitoring the wartime air traffic over the area. He had certainly seen the B-24 and knew of the crash, though he had not actually witnessed it, but would we like to see his logbook? This unassuming little hand-written diary contained meticulous notes of every aircraft to pass over the area – dates, types, numbers involved, regular mail flights, air-raid warnings – everything we could wish for! He immediately drew our attention to the 13 February the year before the B-24 crash: one Manchester, one Oxford, three 'Mails' (DH86Bs) and an underlined note in the margin next to a sighting of four Spitfires, it read: '& 1 Parachutist'!

A quick check through my notes on returning home came up with only one candidate – BL585 – but where had the plane actually come down? Our witness recalled seeing the airman deploy his parachute with a crack and a cloud of [chalk?] dust over Hindley, and he was seen to be drifting towards the Platt Bridge area by some of the residents of Aspull, though none seemed to recall the actual crash. The pilot landed safely in the yard of a colliery at Golborne, where upon his arrival he was nearly set upon by miners coming off shift, because, being Polish he was at first mistaken for a German! A check of the County Control Centre message books found references on this date to: a parachutist being seen at Hindley, a Polish Airman being found at Abram and an aircraft crashed at Aspull; the times of the reports recorded being between 11.05 am and 11.35 am. This gave us confirmation of the events, but no real further clues as to the precise location of the crash.

Our next break came as we had now made contact via email with another former local, Mr Hugh Heyes, now living in the United States. Mr Heyes had witnessed the aftermath of the B-24 crash, but also had actually seen the crash-site of the Spitfire – albeit from a distance, as it was apparently well guarded. Though with the passing of some 60 years he felt his memory was not quite as accurate as he hoped, he drew and sent us a fairly detailed map, indicating the approximate area and pinpointing two possible impact points. However the Aspull area has seen over a century of intensive mining activity and our witness's vantage point had in fact been the top of a large colliery tip – now even larger and completely overgrown and the map did not seem to fit the modern day features – had the crash site disappeared beneath thousands of tons of mine waste? Comparison of 1945 and modern aerial survey photographs allayed our fears and also revealed that some field boundary hedges had been removed, explaining a discrepancy with the witness's sketch map that we had been studying.

It was now time to contact the landowner and arrange for a metal detector survey of the area. However, delays were caused by ground conditions, the Foot and Mouth crisis and crops, but we finally mustered five detector users for a systematic search. After several hours of picking up old pennies, scraps of lead and assorted fragments of iron farm implements, one of our members finally found a small scrap of crumpled aluminium, soon followed by another with a couple of rivet holes visible when the mud was scraped away. An intensive search of the surrounding area yielded only a further handful of shapeless aluminium fragments, an aircraft battery clamp wing-nut and a couple of .303 calibre tracer-bullet heads. Not a promising start, but we duly pegged out the finds and assembled our two deep-seeking detectors. Unfortunately, the Fisher proved troublesome to tune due to mineralisation: in Victorian time fields in the area were regularly covered in 'night-soil' from the nearby towns, which means they are heavily contaminated with ash from the local industries, which was reused in the Ash-closets of the time. However, with perseverance the Fisher registered a medium sized contact in the expected area. Our Forster machine had no problem with the ground conditions, but gave some rather confusing (at the time) readings, with two deeply buried contacts some 15 feet apart and a large contact in the same central area indicated by the Fisher, but apparently close to the surface. We concluded this was due to the Forster machine only picking up ferrous metals and the Fisher detecting all metals, indicating that the remaining wreckage was well broken up and, from the size of the readings, clearly the Rolls Royce Merlin engine was no longer present.

Though the Landowner was somewhat less than impressed with our meagre finds and obviously not altogether convinced that the remains of a WW2 fighter lay beneath his field, he was kind enough to give his consent for an excavation of the site. Fortunately, in the absence of any official records indicating where BL585 had actually crashed, the MoD accepted our evidence and a permit was issued. With all the formalities dealt with, we finally arranged for the excavation to take place in September 2005 (some five years since that first clue came to light), however this was on the condition that the dig was to be conducted without a mechanical excavator. Initially this did not concern us as several members of the team armed with spades and trowels gathered on the Saturday morning. By lunchtime though, the heavy, compacted clay soil was taking its toll and we had barely reached some 4 feet in depth, with only a few small finds and what was to prove to be a 12 foot long iron bar protruding across the centre of the former crater we were excavating. Once this was removed, the area was re-scanned with the deep-seeking detectors and we were relieved to find the signals still distinctly discernable, and the Fisher was now giving much stronger readings. A consultation with the farmer's wife who had a keen interest in more modern aviation and a pilot's licence, elicited permission to bring in a small mini-digger. This was booked for the following day and we tidied the site up and arranged for an early start the next morning.

Sunday brought a fine day, but we had a somewhat depleted team of diggers and no sign of the promised machine. However, a few phone calls later (I think we may have woken someone!), we were assured it was on its way and sure enough half-an-hour later a 3-ton Volvo mini-digger was on site and with one of our members being a skilled plant operator, it was soon put to work. The first few feet that we had laboriously dug through the day before were cleared in minutes, though we were kept busy checking through the spoil as it was removed for smaller components. As digging progressed, an area of soft grey clay with small pockets of wreckage and a distinct smell of fuel and oil was soon apparent in the centre of the excavation, distinct from the surrounding natural red clay soil. The removal of the large iron bar, made more accurate use of the Forster detector possible and concentrating on the signal furthest from the centre of the crater we uncovered the back of the breech of a .303 Browning machine gun only some 2 feet below the surface. This was carefully excavated by hand and as the remaining two Forster contacts were now within the limits of the excavation, it was decided to concentrate on the centre to determine the depth that the aircraft had penetrated. At around 8 feet down we began to encounter larger fragments of BL585 and an almost intact compressed air accumulator bottle was recovered together with larger pieces of airframe structure, many showing signs of fire damage. As the hole got deeper, we soon found the limitations of using such a small machine and had to 'ramp-in' the digger to reach the bottom of the hole and at around 10 feet deep we hit another cache of wreckage and three volunteers descended to remove these parts by hand. These included the throttle quadrant and radio tuner push-button

The throttle quadrant from BL585 recovered from a depth of around 14 feet below the surface.

controller from the cockpit and an amazingly well preserved pilot's access door, with full locking mechanism to the inside and intact paint to the outer surface with the top bar of the letter Z clearly visible. The squadron code letters were "ZF" (Polish nickname "Zefiry"). Finally at approximately 12 feet we recovered two Merlin exhaust stubs impacted into the hard clean clay at the bottom of the hole indicating this was as far as the aircraft had reached.

However apart from the two exhaust stubs and the air bottle, there were no more ferrous finds and the Forster was still indicating two strong signals, one at each side of the now 12 feet deep excavation. We had expected that perhaps the main undercarriage legs had been forced into the ground by the engine or thrown back in by the recovery crew, but there was no sign of these. The answer came as I climbed out of the hole having scanned the bottom to make sure nothing lay deeper. A sharp pain to the sole of my foot indicated I had stood on something pointed, protruding from the natural red clay side of the hole. A trowel was called for and after two minutes scraping I recognised the oil buffer from the rear of a 20mm Hispano Cannon, attached to something very solid. As the clay was cleared by hand, revealing more of the weapon's breech, the digger began to clear the natural clay to the

The oil buffer fitted to the rear of the breach of a 20mm Hispano cannon emerges at a depth of nine feet below the surface.
***Inset:* The fruits of our labour! Following several hours struggle it all seemed worthwhile as a particularly fine pair of 20mm Hispano cannon once again see the light of day! (*Mark Sheldon*)**

same depth at the other side of the hole, where the second contact was still indicated. Several minutes more spadework revealed a second oil buffer, again attached to the breech and leading straight down. The two weapons had speared straight into the ground on impact, leaving the wings and presumably the ammunition on the surface, hence they were embedded in clean natural red clay with no other wreckage around them – or indeed any indication that they were there. The problem for us was that the back of one gun was 9 feet down, the other at 10 feet and these weapons were over 8

Portrait of F/O Palej drawn by a fellow POW whilst in Stalag Luft III "Sagan". (*L. Domanski*).

feet long! We dug carefully around the breech of each gun as far as we could with the digger, removing the final layers of clay by hand and attached nylon lifting straps close to the gun's protruding trunnions. The digger then attempted to pull each gun free vertically, as everyone kept well back (if the strain was too much then the straps would snap and could whip through the air). Progress was painfully slow and everyone found themselves willing the guns to rise from their 63 year entombment. Slowly and almost imperceptibly at first, the clay released its grip and then without warning the 8.5 feet long cannon hung in the air, the barrel perfectly straight and still looking menacing as its black finish showed through the clay. Though slightly deeper the second gun proved easier to remove because the clay surrounding it was much softer and although we thought the barrel appeared to be bent when in the ground, it proved to be almost as straight as the first, and both still had their distinctive muzzle brakes intact.

As we had lost all track of time, we now realised that it would soon be dark and fortified with refreshments kindly supplied by the farmer's wife, we set to work filling in the excavation and reinstating the site. Fortunately, the mini-digger was fitted with work lights and the owner had already visited the site and cleared it for us to keep the machine until we had finished, in fact he proved another convert to our hobby and was so fascinated by our finds that, he waived his normal fee and only charged us for the fuel used. The following weekend, suitably rested, members of the team reassembled to clean and sort the finds, uncovering several smaller plates and artefacts amongst the half-ton of shattered metal fragments, including the Rolls Royce engine maker's plate, the compass needle, remains of the cockpit clock, gun camera film indicator, brake guage and a plate bearing the aircraft's serial No. BL585. The finds were then boxed to await final preparation for display and the weapons were reported to the local police before the Hispano 20mm cannon were sent to be deactivated and certified in accordance with the Firearms Act, though the .303 Browning was inspected and deemed so badly damaged and corroded as to be outside the terms of the act and no longer a weapon.

Prior to our excavation we had already begun further research into the life and wartime career of Palej and had contacted a number of people who knew him, including: a fellow Polish Airforce cadet, a former commanding officer and a fellow PoW, as well as obtaining his service records. Boleslaw Henryk Palej was born on the 14 September 1915 at Bitkow in the district of Nadworna and later lived in Stanislawow, which is now part of the Ukraine. He studied mathematics and sciences at college before joining the Polish Airforce on the 27 September 1937 at the Polish Air Force Officers School in Deblin, No. 13 entry. Upon completion he was commissioned with the rank of Pilot Officer on the 1 September 1939. With the beginning of the war all pilots in his year were evacuated to Romania and then by train to France via Italy and after arriving at Lyon on the 8 January 1940 he became ill. Later he was posted to Chateauroux airfield, arriving on the 1 March 1940 and from there he was then evacuated to England, by ship, probably the *Arandorra Star* which arrived at Liverpool in late June 1940.

Upon arrival in England he first went to RAF Blackpool on the 26 June and was then sent to an operational training unit on the 1 March 1941, before being posted to No. 245 squadron in May 1941, based at Aldergrove in Northern Ireland, carrying out defensive duties. In July 1941 he moved to No. 303 Squadron who had moved from Northolt to Speke on 15th of that month for the defence of Merseyside. From there he moved to No. 308 Squadron in September 1941, whilst they were still at Northolt undertaking bomber escort missions over France. Following their time at Woodvale, 308 Squadron moved to Exeter on 1 April 1942 and resumed offensive operations, which meant long distances to and from sorties over northern Europe and on Bomber escort duties. Also they were on standby in case of local raids and their night flying training came in useful with the first of the Baedeker raids, which was launched against the cathedral city on 23 April. They moved again on 7 May 1942 to Hutton Cranswick near Driffield in Yorkshire, again carrying out shipping protection duties as at Woodvale, as well as patrolling over the sea to prevent German night-fighters infiltrating and attacking the Allied bomber streams returning to their Yorkshire bases from long distance raids. They moved again on 30 July 1942 to Heston on the outskirts of London, flying mainly Bomber escort duties, but were relocated back to Northolt on 29 October 1942 to provide defensive cover when German night attacks on London resumed, as well as flying offensive sorties against northern France, before returning to Yorkshire on 29 April 1943 to Church Fenton.

Palej then went on to No. 317 squadron in May 1943 based at Heston, again flying offensive sweeps over northern France as the Allies stepped up their efforts to defeat the *Luftwaffe* and gain air superiority. On the 7 June 1943 317 Squadron moved to Perranporth (Cornwall) for lighter duties, flying convoy patrols and escort duties over northern France and then to Fairlop, Essex on the 3 August 1943, before moving back to Northolt on 15 September 1943, where 317 was to re-equip with the Spitfire Mk IX and in December along with Nos. 308 and 302 Squadrons, 317 became part of the new 131 Polish Wing, as part of the Second Tactical Air Force in preparation for the forthcoming invasion of Europe.

At this point Palej was posted to an unknown unit at Croydon on the 15 December 1943, but in May 1944 he was reassigned to No 317 squadron, now based at an RAF Advanced Landing Ground (ALG) at Chailey in East Sussex and promoted to Flying Officer. From Chailey, 317 continued to fly offensive sorties over France and Belgium, escorting bombers and also attacking ground targets, including V1 launching-sites, which were well defended and very difficult to hit. With the invasion approaching the pace increased and such flights became more frequent, with the entire wing, including 317 Squadron, engaged in four full-strength patrols over the Normandy beaches on D-Day itself from 05:20 until their final return at 21:00.

The following day, 7 June, the squadron was sent to cover the 'Omaha' beach where the American forces were in a critical position. The Germans were still in possession of the remnants of their defences overlooking the beach and still able to direct harassing artillery fire on any part of the landing area. Weather conditions were poor with low cloud and poor visibility and the squadron was forced to fly very low and slow over the German fortifications, as it was otherwise impossible to locate the gun positions. Palej was forced to abandon his aircraft, Spitfire IX MJ310 following an engine failure, which he believed to have been caused by ground fire. He left his aircraft over Isigny-sur-Mer, and after baling out he landed between the Allied and

German lines, with soldiers of both sides rushing to get to him first but, the Germans were faster and he became a prisoner of war, ending up in Stalag Luft III 'Sagan' until the 7 May 1945 when he returned to RAF Blackpool and took up staff duties at the Polish Airforce HQ with the rank of Flight Lieutenant on the 21 May 1945.

Boleslaw Palej had married and had a daughter in 1943, he could speak Russian and German as well as English and had been an electrical engineer in civilian life. He apparently found the return to civilian life difficult and regularly attended Polish Air Force Reunions. He died in London on the 8 May 1996 after a long illness.

CHAPTER FOUR

'UNAUTHORISED AEROBATICS'

Throughout WW2 it seems that the temptation for pilots to divert from their allotted flight paths to fly over relatives or girlfriends homes, often indulging in some unofficial aerobatics at the same time, seems to have been irresistible. Perhaps in light of the realities of wartime, where the future must have seemed uncertain and pilots were already risking their lives on a daily basis, any additional danger posed by such antics did not worry them unduly and we should not view such high jinks too harshly. However, all too often they ended in tragedy and surely the most tragic of accidents must be those which occurred within sight of the families of the pilots concerned.

Over the years we have researched several such incidents – all equally tragic for the families concerned – but that involving Sgt. Pilot Robert (Roy) Short Timewell proved particularly moving. Twenty four-year-old Roy Timewell was well known in the small town of Burscough

Bridge, his parents owned a large Public House, 'The Royal Hotel' (now 'The Coach House') in the town and he was a keen Rugby player with Ormskirk RUFC. He had joined the Territorial Army before the war and at its outbreak, he had served in France initially and was evacuated at Dunkirk. He then volunteered for duty with the Commandos, but transferred to the RAF in 1941. In October 1942 he was flying with the newly formed No. 539 Squadron based at Acklington in Northumberland and equipped with Boston IIIs, and Hurricane II C aircraft. The Squadron was one of a number

Sgt.-Pilot Robert (Roy) Short Timewell.

formed in September 1942, when the various Turbinlite flights around the country were upgraded to squadron status, with No. 1460 Flight becoming No. 539 Squadron. Originally equipped with Havoc Is and

IIs, the Tubinlite flight aircraft were modified to carry a Helmore 2700-million candlepower searchlight (Turbinlite) in the nose and equipped with A1 radar. These used their radar to locate enemy aircraft, which were then illuminated with the searchlight, enabling accompanying fighters to attack the hostile aircraft. With the upgrading to squadron status, Hurricane fighters flown by pilots trained for night-fighting duties became an integral part of the unit, rather than operating with fighters from other squadrons. Obviously it was hoped that by combining the two elements of this form of night fighter defence, the, up to now, poor results gained could be improved. However, improvements in radar technology, particularly when fitted in aircraft such as the Mosquito, where it could be fitted without impairing the aircrafts firepower, soon led to the Turbinlite concept becoming redundant, resulting in the eventual disbandment of the squadrons.

Hurricane IIC BN205 was built by the Gloster Aircraft Co. Ltd and delivered to No. 29 Maintenance Unit (MU) on 17 December 1941. From there it was allocated to No. 1 Squadron based at Tangmere in Sussex, a unit selected for conversion to night-fighter duties. However, on 6 December 1942 BN205 was due to be shipped to Takoradi in West Africa (now Ghana) from Liverpool on board the SS *Nevada II*, a 5693 ton merchant vessel, built in 1915 and from 1940 used as a Ministry of War Transport managed by P. Henderson & Co. Unfortunately, she became stranded in fog off the Scottish coast and became a total loss, so it seems that the movement order was cancelled. On 8 July 1942 No. 1 Squadron moved to Acklington and re-equipped with Typhoon IBs. Its Hurricanes, including BN205 and several of its pilots being transferred to No. 539 Squadron on its formation in September 1942.

At approximately 10.00am on the morning of the 4 October 1942, Sergeant Pilot R.S. Timewell took off from No. 539 Squadron's base at Acklington, Northumberland in Hurricane IIC Serial No. BN205, in order to carry out 'Authorised Aerobatics' presumably in the vicinity of the airfield. Apparently several days before, Roy Timewell had mentioned in a letter to his parents that they should let everyone know that he would be flying over Burscough the following Sunday. Being something of a local celebrity, it seems, many residents turned out to watch and began to line the main street of the small town shortly before 11.00am and were rewarded when a short time later he appeared overhead – some 135 miles from his authorised location, according to the subsequent RAF report. He gave an impressive low-level aerobatic display for several minutes before flying off in a north-westerly direction. His parents apparently did not join the crowd and chose the more secluded vantage point of a nearby hump-backed bridge over the canal on School Lane to watch the show. Witnesses interviewed recalled that nobody suspected that anything had gone wrong and began to return to their homes as the display had clearly finished. However, one or two who continued to watch the aircraft, did note that the plane seemed to be losing height. What followed, though, deeply shocked everyone. It seems that as the plane disappeared from the view of those on the main street, behind the buildings, it lost height rapidly and it may well have been possible that Timewell was heading for open ground to attempt a forced landing. As the plane passed over the football field off Orrell Lane it clipped an 8 feet high corrugated iron screen that surrounded the pitch at the time and struck the ground some 50-80 yards beyond this in a farmers field. It seems that the aircraft began to burn almost immediately and as would-be rescuers began to approach the wreck, the fuel tanks ignited and it was completely engulfed. The pilot had apparently been thrown clear of the cockpit and lay on the ground a short distance from the aircraft with his clothing on fire. Those who reached him first managed to drag him to a safer distance from the burning plane, despite what they thought was ammunition exploding above their heads and although attempts

Crash site of BN205 was centre foreground – The fence struck by the aircraft is long gone and floodlights now surround the football ground.

were made to douse his smouldering clothing, it was obvious that he had died instantly in the crash.

The area surrounding the aircraft was quickly sealed off by the police and the unfortunate pilot was taken to a nearby council yard, out of sight of the gathering onlookers, and then on to the local mortuary. The burnt-out frame of the aircraft was still visible in the field after the fire had been extinguished, but sightseers were kept at a distance and the following day a 'Queen Mary' recovery trailer arrived to take it away. Such was the local feeling about the pilot and his family that extraordinary precautions were taken to prevent the usual schoolyard trading of fragments of the aircraft that might upset relatives. To this end a number of soldiers stationed locally were apparently employed for a week literally sieving the soil in the field to make sure nothing remained and local schoolboys were denied their usual souveniers! Sgt. Pilot Timewell was buried with full military honours at St. John the Baptist Church Burscough the following week and comments in the local paper referring to the 'painful sensation created in Burscough' and the 'sympathetic gathering' of residents, further reflect

local feelings. He was noted as being the fifth playing member of the Ormskirk RUFC to have lost his life in the Services in the previous twelve months. As usual no details of the incident were published due to wartime censorship and as the site was so quickly and thoroughly cleared, there were few clues as to the manner of this airman's tragic death. His grave was later marked by an impressive, privately erected, large grey granite memorial cross bearing the RAF badge and wings.

Roy Timewell's grave at Burscough, inscribed with a finely carved RAF insignia.

The Operational Record Book for No. 539 Squadron for 4 October reads:

Weather was rather unsettled and no night flying took place. The Hurricanes did low flying and practice. This was a black day for the squadron, as two Hurricanes crashed with fatal results to the pilots, Sgt. R. S. Timewell in Hurricane 2C BN.205 and F/Sgt. Williams, B. C. in Hurricane 2C BN.382 who took off at 1525 hrs to do practice acrobatics. Williams crashed at Gilsland and was reported missing believed killed and later confirmed killed.

It seems that F/Sgt. Williams took off that same afternoon, undoubtedly unaware of Timewell's fate, and was also directed to carry out practice aerobatics, which would normally take place in the vicinity of the airfield at Acklington. However, his aircraft was later seen to dive out of low cloud into the ground 3 miles NE of Gilsland, in Cumbria; as with Timewell's crash, located on the opposite side of the country. Though, with the 27 year old Williams originating from Auckland in New Zealand, it seems more likely that he had become lost rather than had deliberately flown off-course. His remains were discovered still in the cockpit of his aircraft in 1977!

Sgt.-Pilot R. S. Timewell, was by the time of his accident an experienced pilot and having logged some 164 out of his total of 358 solo flying hours on Hurricanes, he should therefore have been quite familiar with his aircraft, so it seems possible that whatever caused his crash could well have been the result of some mechanical failure but no details have been recorded. The final comment from the investigating officer on the RAF Form 1180 reads: 'State of flying discipline in squadron requires close investigation'. The squadron was disbanded in January 1943.

Some 57 years later, our investigation of this incident relied heavily on recording the recollections of local residents – though care had to be taken not to upset any family members who may still live in the area – so we decided that there should be no local press involvement. The crash site was soon identified, one of the witnesses interviewed living barely 100 yards away, his house overlooking the field concerned. Little had changed over the years, other than the corrugated iron screen that hid the football ground from view at the time had long since been removed and new floodlights now surrounded the pitch. We were soon informed, however, that there would be nothing to find as soldiers from the local home guard unit had spent a full week raking and sieving the soil after the wreck was removed. Indeed they had made a good job of it too, as two full weekends searching with a team of three experienced metal detectorists only managed to find a handful of small fragments of the aircraft. Though this was all we found, we were not really disappointed, as often such a project is not really about what there is to recover. All the parts found came from a relatively small area, at least pinpointing and confirming that we had identified beyond doubt the actual crash site.

The scant handful of fragments recovered after many hours detecting. Top centre is the gimbal lock lever from the master compass and to its left a headphone jack-plug.

CHAPTER FIVE

FALLEN EAGLE

Lancashire was temporary home to many servicemen, far from their own countries during the Second World War, with the Polish Air Force Headquarters at Blackpool and the huge American Base Air Depot Two (BAD2) at Warton being prime examples. Tragic reminders of their stay are still evident too, including the Polish Military Plot and memorial at Layton cemetery, Blackpool and, of course, the scattered fragments of their lost aircraft on the county's high ground, only occasionally seen by walkers and perhaps pondered upon for a moment before moving on.

One such lonely 'memorial' lies on the moors above the town of Darwen, where a water-filled hollow, with several jagged sections of alloy protruding, lies close to one of the numerous footpaths leading to and from the famous tower. Unnoticed by most passers by, this was the spot where a young Polish airman lost his life. It was July 1945 and the war in Europe was over – Many RAF pilots originating from Eastern European countries were no doubt wondering about their future, when a lone Pilot of No. 316 Squadron slammed into the high ground above the Lancashire mill town of Darwen at cruising speed and was killed instantly. At the time it was just another tragic accident that received little local attention and was very soon forgotten – local people wanted to put the war behind them and were concentrating on rebuilding their lives. Yet the contribution of the Poles (and others) is often overlooked and 316 Squadron was often in the thick of the action – indeed their last mission was as escort for the bombing of Hitler's retreat at Berchtesgaden – a mission in which this aircraft and pilot almost certainly took part.

Built as a P51-C in 1942, SR 411 began its wartime service with the United States Army Air force (USAAF) in 1943 under the serial number 43-12427 with the 8th Air Force Service Command. As part of an agreed Lend/Lease arrangement to supply Mustang fighters to the RAF, it was handed over to No. 22 Maintenance Unit (MU), RAF on 17 March 1944 before going on to Rootes Securities Aircraft factory at Speke, in May of that year, presumably for modification. Some 274 P-51Bs and 636 P-51Cs were supplied and re-designated Mustang IIIs by the RAF. The aircraft delivered to England still featured the hinged side-opening cockpit canopy used on earlier versions of the P-51 and it was considered that this gave too restricted a view for European operations. The RAF redesigned this arrangement, resulting in a fairly major modification in which the original framed canopy was replaced by a bulged perspex frameless canopy that slid to the rear on rails. This gave the pilot much more room and the 'goldfish bowl' effect resulted in a good view almost straight down or directly to the rear. Originally manufactured and fitted by the British company R. Malcolm & Co., this modification came to be known as the Malcolm Hood and was fitted to most RAF Mustang IIIs, and many USAAF Eighth and Ninth Air Force P-51B/C fighters received this modification as well. Other modifications that would have been required before allocation to an RAF Squadron would have included changes to the oxygen system to allow the use of the RAF oxygen masks and, of course, repainting in RAF camouflage. When ready SR 411 was sent to No. 20 MU to await allocation on 17 June 1944 and was taken on the strength of No. 65 Squadron at Andrews Field, Essex in November, where the Squadron was assigned to act as fighter escorts for Bomber Command's daylight raids. It would appear that SR 411 remained at Andrews Field when No. 65 Squadron moved to Peterhead in January 1945 and the aircraft was taken over by No. 316 (Polish) Squadron, possibly as a replacement aircraft.

No. 316 'City of Warsaw' Squadron was formed at Pembrey, South Wales on 15 February 1941 and had an active and varied career up to 1944 when in April of that year it was re-equipped with Mustang IIIs just before moving to its new base at Coltishall, Norfolk. From here the squadron was assigned to bomber escort and fighter-bomber duties under control of No. 2 Group. By mid July the Squadron moved to Friston, Sussex for Diver operations against the new threat - the V-1 Doodlebug. This proved to be a very demanding and risky business due to the high speed of the V-1 rockets (typically the V-1 flew at 370 mph) and the tendency for the warhead to explode when the missile was fired upon, often damaging the pursuing aircraft. The pilots of 316 Squadron proved to be particularly adept at this task and became the highest scoring Mustang Squadron with 75 Flying Bombs destroyed during the hectic two-months of the Doodlebug menace. From the end of August No. 316 was back at Coltishall and became part of the 12th Fighter Group, taking part in low level 'Rhubarb' sorties against shipping and ground targets over northern Europe. In October the Squadron moved to Andrews Field where several Mustang Squadrons were to be based to form No. 133 Polish Fighter Wing and provide a centre for long-range, daylight bomber escort operations, a task to which the Mustang was ideally suited. No. 316's main customers were the B-17s and B-24s of the 8th USAAF as well as the RAF Bomber Command's Halifaxs and Lancasters. This activity reached its peak in the Spring of 1945 and notable raids involving the squadron included; 10 August 1944, low level attack on enemy barracks at Poitiers. 31 October 1944 low level raid on Gestapo HQ at Aarhus, Jutland, escorting Mosquitos. Also notable was the escorting of transport aircraft involved in the ill-fated Arnhem airborne landings, where the squadron's efforts in keeping off the marauding enemy fighters was praised. Other duties included: Circus ops – fighter sweeps over enemy territory, particularly airfields to draw the fighters into battle, 'Rodeos' – general fighter sweeps over occupied territory and 'Roadstead' ops – Anti-shipping strikes by fighters. No. 316's last operation was Ramrod 1554 – with some 240 Mustangs escorting 359 Lancasters (including No.300 Polish Bomber Squadron) on 25 April 1945 for the raid which destroyed Hitler's retreat at Berchtesgaden. Five Polish Fighters squadrons took part in the mission: Nos. 303, 316 from No. 3 (Polish) Fighter Wing, and Nos. 306, 309 and 315 from No. 133 (Polish) Fighter Wing and it was to be the last mission in WWII for units of the Polish Air Force. With the war over, but No. 316's Polish pilots unable to return home, the Squadron continued as part of a Polish Mustang wing until December 1946 when the Squadron was disbanded at Hethel on the 11th.

At approx 3.30pm on 29 July 1945, SR 411 was flying over central Lancashire in poor visibility caused by the misty conditions combining with the industrial haze that was still a prevalent feature over northern mill towns of the time. It was being flown by 24 year old Herbert Noga, who, despite his age was a highly experienced pilot with over 1200 hours solo flying time to his credit, including 115 hours on Mustangs. He had taken off from No. 316 Squadrons base at Coltishall some two hours before. The flight was listed as ferrying duties and though no destination was given, it was noted that he was still on his allotted course. However, it seems that the pilot was unaware that he was rapidly approaching an area of high ground because he failed to maintain a safe height to clear such terrain and at 15.45 hours the aircraft hit the rising ground at cruising speed, some 1317 feet above sea level near Bull Hill, between Darwen and Bolton. The Mustang disintegrated on impact, embedding itself in the soft peat and killing the unfortunate Pilot

The only image traced of 24 year old Plt. Herbert Noga, enlarged from a group photograph.
(Sikorski Institute).

The crater caused by impact of SR411 is still discernable on the moors above Darwen, surrounded by a gradually diminishing collection of twisted fragments of the Mustang.

instantly. Locals who heard the plane flying low over the moors and the subsequent impact in the mist, alerted the police and a search was initiated. The wreck was soon located, but the sight of the pilot's body still strapped in the remains of the cockpit as water began to fill the crater proved that their efforts were in vain. Later that day an RAF recovery crew arrived and soon recovered Noga's remains. The removal of the larger sections of the aircraft took a little longer, but the incident seems to have been quickly forgotten as most people's minds were focused on the end of the war and getting back to normality.

The comments of the officers investigating this incident are brief to say the least, merely stating that the pilot failed to maintain a safe altitude over high ground in poor visibility. However, there is also a note that Noga failed to clear his flight properly with flight control and did not take a pre-flight briefing – yet this was a highly experienced pilot: he had served as a Ferry Pilot with No. 3 FPP (Ferry Pilots Pool), a pilot with No. 7 AGS (Air Gunners School) and had spent much of the war as an instructor with No. 16 Service Flying Training School.

Though his behaviour on that fateful day appears out of character, perhaps in light of events concerning the Poles at this time, it may be understandable how such lapses of concentration may have occurred.

Certainly by August 1945 the implications of the Yalta conference, held in February, for the future of Poland, must have been of immense concern and damaging to the morale of Poles serving in the UK. Additionally in June, the arrest and infamous show trial in Moscow of senior Polish politicians of the Underground Polish State deprived the new post-war Poland of many of its most likely leaders, leaving the way clear for the setting up of a new soviet controlled puppet government. There is little question of the sense of betrayal that the Poles who had fought alongside the Allies must have felt and the final insult came on 7 June 1946, with the omission of the Polish forces from the Victory Parade in London – an event that Herbert Noga was perhaps fortunate not to witness.

The post-crash recovery of the remains of SR 411 was haphazard to say the least – perhaps those allocated the task also had their priorities elsewhere as the war came to a close? The aircraft had impacted on the moor at a relatively shallow angle imbedding itself in a layer of soft black peat some 8 feet thick over a harder coarse gravel layer below. Witnesses described how the plane's Packard built Merlin engine had penetrated this peat layer, becoming detached from the airframe, before striking the harder layer below causing it to bounce back and reappear some 30 yards in front of the crater where the rest of the wreck lay. Unfortunately perhaps for later Aviation Archaeologists, such an easily accessible, major part of the aircraft was fairly straightforward to recover, though once this had been removed the recovery team seems to have become less diligent. Larger sections of the airframe, including the wings were also dragged off the moor via a disused quarry track that ran to within a few hundred yards of the crash site, but the rest was simply covered over and quickly forgotten.

It was to be some 30 years before interest was once again taken in the remains, with the recovery of the Mustang's large, mainly copper, radiator for its scrap value. The removal of this item led to much of the remaining wreckage becoming exposed and it wasn't long before local aviation enthusiasts, who were now taking interest in wartime wrecks, got to hear of the site. Over the next 10 years various individual enthusiasts and groups visited the site and at least one major excavation was carried out, probably believing that the engine was still present. Though few seem to have researched the circumstances surrounding the aircraft's loss and one group even identifying the remains as that of a Seafire!

It was the mid 1980s when I first heard about the site and, together with a friend, we spent the summer recovering many of the more recognisable parts that lay abandoned and scattered around the crater

55

from previous amateur recovery attempts. These included both remarkably complete main undercarriage legs, the entire starboard side of the cockpit – complete with circuit breaker panels, the winding handle for the Malcolm canopy and emergency canopy jettison lever – in the engaged position. Also the seat support frame with the armoured headrest attached, a tail-plane and some three feet of the tail end of the fuselage. Smaller finds included a superbly preserved propeller constant speed unit from the front of the Packard Merlin. It was found some 30 yards in front of the crater, just where the witnesses interviewed had said the engine resurfaced! Also we found the radio, though this had been dragged from the crater, only to be left at the mercy of the elements and being steel frame had corroded rapidly. We also had a chance find in a pond where we cleaned some of the parts – the top from the control column. As we became more familiar with the site and more experienced with our metal detector techniques we widened the area of our search and began to try to interpret what had happened. This led to the finding of a propeller blade tip embedded in a partly demolished dry-stone wall some 200 yards from the crater, indicating that this was the first point of contact for SR 411 and the Mustang had obviously staggered back into the air momentarily before plunging to the ground – had Noga engaged the canopy jettison lever in those final moments? A grid pattern search to the far side of the crater uncovered a filled-in pit crammed with components, obviously buried by the recovery crew and this cache included a gun-access panel from the wing, with intact paint to one side and the aircraft's serial number SR 411 stencilled to the inner surface.

Although we had successfully recovered almost all the accessible parts alone, it was becoming obvious that this hobby was not really suited to individual enthusiasts – there was no way we could excavate the actual crater ourselves and just what were we going to do with the artefacts that we had recovered so far? So it was to this end that SR 411 was the first crash site that I initiated an excavation of, by the no longer existent Pennine Aviation Museum (P.A.M.). With some ten willing volunteers and access to a 4X4 to bring equipment up to the site, the crater was soon drained and the excavation began to uncover numerous superbly preserved artefacts. Most of the parts from the crater itself came out of the ground seemingly as good as the day they went in: a hydraulic accumulator bottle, with intact paintwork and gleaming brass plates, then the rudder mass balance weight with a section of the doped fabric rudder covering still attached. Several sections of thick perspex from the distinctive bulged Malcolm canopy emerged, as well as the frame of the smaller glazed sections over the radio compartment and an intact radio mast. The heavy-duty cast alloy engine mounts, still with twisted and snapped bolts through them showed how the engine had torn itself free and only a small section of cam shaft and a solitary engine valve proved that the Merlin must have been almost intact. Finally, some 6 feet down we hit the hard shale-like gravel, but not before an almost intact propeller blade was revealed in the side of the hole. This again was in excellent condition with intact paint and stencilled manufacturers details on the de-icing boot at its base, though the tip was badly damaged where it had struck the dry-stone wall. Following the excavation we decided to donate all our finds to date to group's museum.

Some weeks after the excavation and being at a loose end my friend and I decided to return to the site for an afternoon's detecting and after our customary check with the farmer we made our way up to the moor. After a couple of hours with only a few stainless steel 'Wittek' clips to show for it, my friend decided to try his luck along the footpath that runs a couple of hundred yards beyond the crater - perhaps at least the odd coin dropped by passers-by could be found? Only a few minutes later an exited shout alerted me that he had indeed found something, but I was not prepared for what it turned out to be. Buried in the ditch running alongside the path and only a few inches below the surface was a complete, though severely corroded 0.5-inch calibre Browning machine gun, and alongside it lay the detached breech cover and the gun's electrical firing solenoid. Though obviously from the aircraft – the solenoid bore a USAAF plate dated 1942 – there was no way it

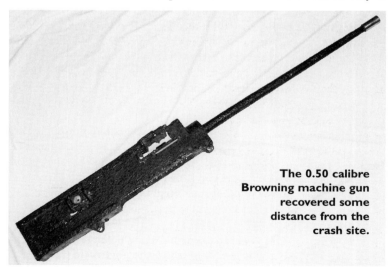

The 0.50 calibre Browning machine gun recovered some distance from the crash site.

could have been thrown so far and to add further mystery; how had the components become detached without damaging them and ended up buried alongside the gun?

It was to be some years later that the amazing story of how this gun came to be buried in such a way came to light. Following the winding up of the P.A.M museum, I had reclaimed the parts that we had recovered several years before and as no one else appeared to want them, I ended up with the remains recovered during their excavation of the site as well. With the setting up of the Lancashire Aircraft Investigation Team, we arranged various displays around the county at local libraries and museums and one of these took place at Darwen Library with the subject fittingly being SR 411 and Herbert Noga. The exhibition was very well received and following local press coverage, I began to get phone calls from interested locals, which soon resulted in the donation of another propeller blade from the plane, picked up on the site in the 1960s. However, on collecting the relic, I was amazed to see that it had lost its tip and was almost undoubtedly the same blade whose tip we had found embedded in the wall some 10 years before – though of course sadly this was now also lost.

The next call was even more intriguing and although the caller was at first a little hesitant about giving the details, it soon became clear exactly how our Browning machine gun had come to be buried. It seems that the caller and a friend had been teenagers at the time and had attempted to visit

The donated propeller blade belonging to SR411. Note: severe damage to the edges and missing tip from striking the dry-stone wall, before becoming embedded in the relatively soft peat.

the wreck site soon after the crash, but finding it guarded had been turned away. So the following evening they waited while the servicemen engaged in the recovery had departed – it seems no guard was left overnight – and they returned to see what they could find. Their primary goal seems to have been ammunition that they could recover the cordite from to fill their own cartridges for a spot of unofficial game hunting. However, on reaching the wreck they were at first disappointed as there was no ammunition to be found, but on examining one of the severed wings of the aircraft they discovered that the guns were still inside and formulated a plan to remove one for their own purposes. They returned the following night with some tools and having removed the gun decided it was too risky to try to make their way back to the road with their prize, so selected a suitable spot and buried it. The caller described, without prompting, the exact spot and told how they had to remove the solenoid to withdraw the gun – everything fitted perfectly! However, these two young tearaways had already caught the eye of the local bobby for some of their other antics, about which he did not go into detail, and after his friend received a stern warning over an incident with a shotgun on the moors, they were far too frightened ever to go back and recover their prize!

Smaller artefacts from SR411 including carburettor plates, a radiator repair plate, face from the hydraulic accumulator gauge and centre, the top from the control column.

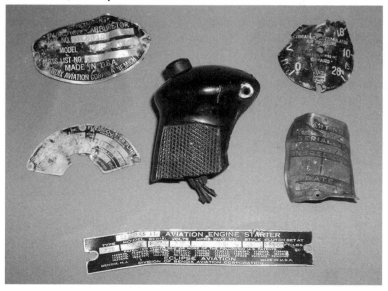

CHAPTER SIX

ONE OF OUR AIRCRAFT
IS MISSING

Most people would probably associate missing aircraft and their pilots with the remoter areas of the Scottish Highlands and few appreciate just how bleak and remote the high ground of Lancashire can be, even in Summer! The following two incidents clearly demonstrate, as most experienced walkers well know, just how quickly picturesque moorland can turn into a harsh, alien and deadly environment.

Both the aircraft involved coincidentally were Spitfire Mk. Vs with Polish pilots, both flying from RAF Woodvale and both lost within 5 months of each other. The research into these two incidents was initially hampered by the already mentioned loss of most Spitfire Mk V record cards for incidents in the North-west, as this proved to be the case for both of these aircraft as well.

In the case of the first incident, the loss of this vital piece of information was compounded by administrative errors, during the war, in the recording of the loss of Spitfire V W3628, due to which the pilot, Sgt. T. Nawrocki of 315 Squadron was recorded by the Sikorski Institute as having lost his life at Lunecliffe, near Lancaster. This sadly led to the pilot's daughter being misdirected, when visiting the UK several years ago and visiting the latter site in error. Following discussion with our associate member Mr. R. Danilo (former 307 Squadron Pilot) who knew Nawrocki, we decided to investigate further and inquiries at Lunecliffe soon traced an eyewitness to the crash – of a Hurricane! We quickly identified the site as being that of Hurricane IIb BM 955, which crashed on a ferry flight on 09 December 1941, resulting in the death of its pilot Second Officer A.E. Green A.T.A. However, tracing the true crash site of W3628 was further complicated by an error in the entry in 315 Squadron's ORB in which the dead pilot and his aircraft are reported as having finally been found at Mossop Ridge, Lancashire, a place name which does not exist, even in local usage. Finally, a further document came to light via the MoD Air Historical Branch, giving the location as Dunsop Bridge, complete with a grid reference, albeit using the wartime Cassini system.

Sgt. Tadeusz Nawrocki escaped from France on the last evacuation ship the *Arandora Star* on 24 June 1940. Carrying some 5000 men it reached Liverpool on the 27th. An accomplished pilot, he had already

60

trained as an instructor. He began operational flying with No. 306 'Torunski' Squadron on 11 October 1941, flying Spitfire IIs, shortly after the squadron had moved from Northolt to Speke for the defence of Merseyside. On 27 November he moved to No. 315 'Deblinski' Squadron based at Northolt and flying Spitfire Vs, carrying out fighter sweeps and bomber escort duties over northern France. This year had been a busy time for the pilots of 315 Squadron, with total claims of thirty-three enemy aircraft destroyed, twelve probable and seven damaged, in return they had lost some fourteen pilots killed, three captured and two wounded, with a loss of some eighteen aircraft.

By the beginning of April 1942, they were due for a rest and the squadron moved to RAF Woodvale, with most flying being training and lighter operational duties including flying defensive patrols and protecting the convoys coming into and leaving Liverpool, as well as occasional scrambles to intercept enemy aircraft. One pilot managed to damage a Ju88 in May, which barely made it back to France on one engine.

Sgt T. Nawrocki vanished on a routine test flight of a recently overhauled Spitfire in unseasonably deteriorating weather conditions. He took off from Woodvale on the morning of Thursday 16 July 1942 in

Right: **Sgt Tadeusz Nawrocki.**
(Wilhelm Ratuszynski)

Below: Spitfire V W3628 Code PK-W undergoing major overhaul work at Woodvale, prior to its loss.
(Wilhelm Ratuszynski)

Spitfire V serial No. W3628, which had recently undergone a major 240-hour check and though the weather was described as 'uncertain', other flying activities took place, including formation flying and low level photo attacks. The squadron's operations record book (ORB) frequently comments on the weather at Woodvale and notes that there was a tendency towards mist in the morning in the area around the airfield and that the Lancashire weather was very unreliable, being more like April than July, with changeable conditions and frequent rain and mist.

When Nawrocki failed to return from the flight, it was at first thought that he had encountered some technical problem and landed at another airfield, however, after two hours and still no word they began to fear the worst. Despite deteriorating weather conditions, two pilots took off to conduct a search, but with the hills in the area that Nawrocki was thought most likely to have come down on, obscured by the low cloud and rain, it was called off. The following morning was once again misty with intermittent rain and the ORB notes that the feeling of gloom was not confined to the weather. Further search flights were sent out along his assumed flight path during the day but again without success. The following day, the 18th, the weather improved slightly and evidence suggested that Nawrocki's aircraft had come down to the east of Preston, with a local police receiver having picked up a message on the 16th, saying that he was running out of fuel. Further search patrols were sent out, concentrating on the area between Pendle Hill and Mossop Ridge [Dunsop Bridge], but by the afternoon nothing had been found. Then on the evening of the 18th a report came through that a wrecked aircraft had been spotted by a farmer tending to sheep on high ground above the tiny village of Tarnbrook. However, when a rescue party reached the aircraft, they found the cockpit empty. The aircraft had impacted close to the summit of the 1730-foot Wolfhole Crag, gouging a furrow in the sloping hillside as it broke up. Both wings had broken off, as well as the tail and the engine had broken free and lay some 150 feet in front of the rest of the wreckage. However, the fuselage with the cockpit was largely intact, but there were traces of blood indicating that Nawrocki must be injured. Evidence suggested that he had climbed from the cockpit and lain his parachute opened on the ground next to the aircraft, presumably to aid any aerial search; he had also attempted to light a fire using flares, but there was no sign of him in the vicinity and with darkness closing in, there was little they could do but wait until the following day to conduct a search.

The weather on the morning of Sunday 19th was at least fine as some 180 Army, locals, home-guard and personnel from Woodvale began a systematic sweep of the moorland. Even with the help of a tracker dog it was to be late afternoon before local home-guard member Bill Worswick, spotted an unusual shape amongst the heather, after climbing a small mound to get a better view. It seems that Nawrocki's RAF uniform blended too well with the heather bloom, effectively camouflaging him from view. Sadly on reaching the airman it was obvious that he had succumbed to his injuries some time before, apparently having set off in the direction of the nearest habitation, possibly after having spotted a chink of light at night? He had in fact only covered some 900 yards from the wreck of his Spitfire, having suffered a serious head wound and lacerations to his legs in the crash. He lies in St Mary's Churchyard, Formby, Grave No. 16, Row 1, Section G.A. His headstone bears the date on which his body was found – 19 July 1942.

Nothing remains of W3628 today on the bleak moor above Tarnbrook, the whole area was heavily burned by moorland fires during the 1960s and a few fragments apparently spotted several years ago by beaters on this private shooting estate had long since vanished by the time of our visit. During our research, we were fortunate enough to trace two witnesses to the search for Sgt. T. Nawrocki, following an appeal in the local press, both of whom gave remarkably clear accounts of their role in the operation and their recollections of the crash site. Having gained permission to enter the moor, we used this evidence to locate the area, but unsurprisingly no evidence of the tragedy 57 years before could be found.

Looking downhill towards the crash site of W3628, which came to rest approximately centre of picture, just beyond the heather.

Whilst visiting the area we took the opportunity to record any remaining wreckage of Anson N4919, which came to grief on the same summit on the 9 February 1944. This aircraft encountered adverse weather conditions during a cross-country navigational exercise flying with No. 2 (Observer) Advanced Flying Unit based at Millom in Cumbria. Although the pilot knew he was still some 6 miles from the estimated position where it was safe to descend, he was forced to lose altitude due to icing up of his aircraft. Despite a severe lack of visibility he was fortunate in managing to effect a forced landing on the moors and of the five crew on board three including the pilot were injured in the crash, the remaining two escaping unscathed, surely a tribute to the skill of the pilot and the surprising strength of the flimsy looking Anson. Today the site can be somewhat tricky to find – the few larger panels remaining appear to have been collected up and hidden amongst nearby rocks, perhaps to deter curious walkers from leaving the paths and heading out across the private grouse moors on which the remains lie. Much has been removed, mainly by the now defunct Pennine Aviation Museum, including the largest piece, a main undercarriage leg assembly, the fate of which is unknown.

The second incident involved Flying Officer Wladyslaw Pucek serving with No. 317 'Wilenski' Squadron, which had moved from Northolt to Woodvale on the 5 September 1942, taking over from No. 315 Squadron, which now returned south. As with their predecessors, flying duties at Woodvale were intended to be a rest period and training

Flying Officer Wladyslaw Pucek.
(*Wilhelm Ratuszynski*)

replacement pilots. No. 317 had also had a busy time, before moving to Woodvale: carrying offensive operations over northern France and defensive patrols against German aircraft attempting to infiltrate at low level. This year had also been a busy time for the pilots of 315 Squadron, with total claims of eighteen enemy aircraft destroyed, five probable and five damaged. However in return they had lost some seven pilots killed, four wounded, with a loss of some sixteen aircraft. No.317 soon got used to the routine of defensive patrols and shipping protection operations, as well as training flights and the occasional scramble to intercept enemy aircraft. The Squadron also inherited some of 315 Squadron's aircraft, as they were upgrading to the Spitfire Mk. IX, including a Spitfire Mk Vb serial No. AD230. Formerly PK-M it now became JH-M of No. 317 Squadron. This aircraft was a presentation Spitfire and bore the inscription 'Palembang Oeloe IV' named after an island in south-eastern Sumatra and part of the Dutch East Indies (N.E.I.) at the time. AD230 had also seen it share of action and, on 8 December 1941, was the mount of F/L Czaykowski Zbigniew of No. 315 Squadron when he had claimed a BF109F destroyed.

Pucek was a graduate of the Polish Air Force cadet officers' school in Deblin, becoming a Second Lieutenant Pilot on 1 September 1939. Following the 'Polish September Campaign' he escaped to France and was then one of the first Polish airmen evacuated to Britain, arriving in December 1939. At first he was attached to No. 271 squadron, which was re-formed at Doncaster on the 28 March 1940 and, equipped with obsolete Harrow bombers to perform transport duties for No.12 Group of Fighter Command. But as of the 27 April they were transferred to Bomber Command, though still performing the same basic task of moving squadrons from one base to another. The squadron did however prove particularly valuable immediately prior to the Dunkirk evacuations, in transporting RAF personal and equipment back to Britain. He attended a training course for operational flying with Fighter Command's No. 55 Operational Training Unit based at Usworth in County Durham. From there Pucek joined No.317 Squadron at Exeter on 1 October 1941.

Once again the Squadron's ORB frequently comments on the poor weather conditions over Lancashire, though at least now they were perhaps more in keeping with the season. On the morning of Monday 28 December there was a significant improvement in the weather and the squadron certainly made the most of it with some twenty-six gun-camera sorties being made, as well as formation and low flying practise flights taking place. In the afternoon five Spitfires of 'A' flight took off on one of these flights heading for the area of high ground to the north of Blackburn known as the Trough of Bowland. During the flight the weather conditions began to deteriorate, with low cloud over the hills and the pilots were forced to rely on their instruments. All five aircraft entered one such area of cloud together, but on emerging only four planes were present – F/O Pucek flying Spitfire AD 230 had simply vanished and neither the flight nor operations could contact him by radio or trace him and at approximately 1600 he was reported missing.

Shortly after the flight landed back at Woodvale, two pilots took off to continue looking, but despite an extensive search, nothing was found and no further news of the missing pilot was received from any source. The search flights continued, weather conditions permitting, for several days, but nothing was found or heard and eventually it was assumed that he must have become disorientated and ended up flying out beyond the coast and eventually crashed into the sea. The Squadron left Woodvale on 13 February 1943 for Kirton-in-Lindsey in Lincolnshire and it was some two weeks later, on the 28th, that a report was received that wreckage had been spotted amongst the thawing snow drifts on the Lancashire moors.

Pucek's plane had impacted on bleak, open moorland at an altitude of approximately 1800 feet, some 7 miles from the nearest road and 4 miles from the nearest track. His body was soon recovered and buried with full military honours in the Polish Memorial plot at Layton cemetery, Blackpool, Grave No. BB494.

The salvage of AD230 was allocated to No. 75 M.U. based at Wilmslow and they began work on what was to prove a mammoth recovery effort on the 2 March. Billeted in farm buildings as close to the site as they could get, it was still a three-hour climb for the M.U. personnel to reach the crash site, until they managed to secure the loan of a jeep which reduced the walking time to one hour each way. Two tractors were also borrowed from RAF Weeton, near Blackpool – one to pull the other out when they got stuck in the by now very boggy thawing ground – these were used to tow a wooden sledge to which the dismantled Spitfire was secured piece by piece. The recovery took until the 26th of the month hampered by prevailing very high winds and the unusually heavy rainfall of early 1943. Needless to say, despite many rumours, nothing has ever been found by enthusiasts to indicate the precise site of Wladyslaw Pucek's unfortunate demise, though considering the weather conditions and hardships faced by the recovery team this may seem odd, it is less surprising when you are familiar with the nature of Lancashire's high ground areas.

CHAPTER SEVEN

'MILK RUN'

With the two largest US Air Bases in England located in the North-west, there was perhaps more air traffic over this region than most areas of the country and the combination of war-weary aircraft, tired crews, deteriorating weather and high ground, all to often proved fatal.

One such combat veteran was B-24 J Liberator serial No. 42-50668, assigned to 854th Bombardment Squadron – Heavy of the US 8th Air Force, 491st Bomb Group, based at North Pickenham. The 491st had the distinction of having flown more operations than any other B-24 group and the aircraft (Code 6X M-) was a veteran of some twenty-six missions by February 1945 and although it had been recently overhauled and fitted with two new engines it was now scheduled to be returned to Base Air Depot 1 at Burtonwood, presumably for replacement with a new lighter B-24-L.

The 491st Bomb Group was one of fourteen B-24 Liberator Groups of the 2nd Air Division, 8th Air Force, that took part in the Air Offensive against Nazi Germany in 1944 and 1945. Comprising the 852nd, 853rd, 854th and 855th Bombardment Squadrons, it arrived in England on 1 January 1944 and flew its first operational mission on the 2 June, followed by almost daily missions against airfields, bridges, and coastal defences both preceding and during the invasion of Normandy. Missions were then concentrated on strategic objectives in Germany, such as communications centres, oil refineries, storage depots, industrial areas and shipyards. Whilst participating in a mission to bomb the oil refinery at Misburg near Hannover on 26 Nov 1944, the group was attacked by enemy fighters en masse and although

Veteran of some 26 operational missions, B-24 Liberator 42-50668, Coded 6X M- . (Kevin Mount).

67

approximately half of its planes were destroyed, they still managed to bomb the target. The group was also called upon to support the D-Day landings, their target being Coutances, an important communications centre for access to the Cotentin peninsular. They also flew in support of ground forces at St Lo in July 1944, bombed V-weapon sites and communications lines in France during the offensives following D-Day. They dropped supplies to airborne troops on 18 Sept 1944 during Operation Market Garden and bombed German supply lines and fortifications during the Battle of the Bulge in the winter of 1944/5.

Missions flown by B-24 J Liberator serial No. 42-50668:

Date:	Target:	Pilot:
27.08.1944	Oranienburg (Hienkel Factory)	Capt. William M.Long
05.09.1944	Karlsruhe (Marshalling Yards)	Capt. William M.Long
08.09.1944	Karlsruhe (Marshalling Yards)	1st Lt. Dee.W. McKenzie
11.09.1944	Hannover (Marshalling Yards)	Capt. Green R. Davis
12.09.1944	Misburg (Oil Refinery)	1st Lt. Dean B. Strain (KIA 17.01.1945)
22.09.1944	Kassel (Ordnance Works)	1st Lt. Dean B. Strain
02.10.1944	Hamm (Marshalling Yards)	Capt. William M.Long
09.10.1944	Koblenz (Marshalling Yards)	Capt. William M.Long
15.10.1944	Cologne (Marshalling Yards)	1st Lt. Lindell E. Hendrix
19.10.1944	Mainz (Ordnance Works)	Capt. James C. McKeown
22.10.1944	Hamm (Marshalling Yards)	Capt. William M.Long
25.10.1944	Neumunster (Airfield)	1st Lt. Charles N. Haney
26.10.1944	Minden (Canal Locks)	2nd Lt. Donald E. Woodward
06.11.1944	Minden (Aqueduct)	2nd Lt. Donald E. Woodward
08.11.1944	Rheine (Marshalling Yards)	2nd Lt. Donald E. Woodward

29.11.1944	Altenbeken (Viaduct)	Capt. Harold W. Burdekin
11.12.1944	Hanau (Airfield)	1st Lt. Charles N. Haney
12.12.1944	Hanau (Airfield)	Capt. William M.Long
23.12.1944	Ahrweiler (Railway Junction)	Capt. Charles N. Haney (Promoted)
24.12.1944	Wittlich (Bridge)	Capt. Harold W. Burdekin
31.12.1944	Neuwied (Railway Bridge)	Capt. Charles N. Haney
02.01.1945	Engers (Railway Bridge)	Capt. Charles N. Haney
14.01.1945	Hemmingstedt (Oil Refinery)	Capt. Harold W. Burdekin
17.01.1945	Harburg (Oil Refinery)	1st Lt. Edward L. Sunder
29.01.1945	Munster (Marshalling Yards)	Capt. William M.Long
06.02.1945	Magdeburg (Marshalling Yards)	Capt. Harold W. Burdekin

The pilot selected for the 'milk-run' ferry flight to Burtonwood in 42-50668, was First Lieutenant Charles Goeking who had just arrived back at the Squadron's North Pickenham base following leave, but too late to take part in a forthcoming raid on the Seigan marshalling yards in Germany. Four other members of his crew joined him, including T. Sgt. Howard E. Denham Jr. who apparently volunteered in place of a sick colleague. The aircraft took off on the afternoon of Monday the 19 February with six passengers on board for the 150 mile trip, into what turned out to be deteriorating weather conditions as they made their way northwards. By the time they reached their estimated destination the ground was completely obscured by low cloud, rain and fog. On observing a break in the cloud cover, Goeking attempted to descend through it, in order to confirm their location and glimpsed a built up area that he

1st Lt. Charles A. Goeking.
(Goeking family)

assumed to be Liverpool, not realising that he was in fact looking at the towns of Accrington and Burnley. His mistaken assumption as to their position now apparently confirmed, he then began to climb again and flew a new heading of 90 degrees towards the area he assumed the Burtonwood base would lie.

A resident of the town below – Edward Rawlinson, a junior photographer for the local newspaper and keen aircraft spotter – was startled by the sudden noise and commented later: "During the war with very little traffic noise around, a piston engined aircraft of that size makes a tremendous noise when flying low in dense cloud."

In fact 42-50668 was in the midst of Lancashire's hill country and as the aircraft re-entered the cloud, the base of which was now at about 900 feet, Goeking had no way of knowing that he had in fact set a course for Black Hameldon, which at 1571 feet is one of the largest hills surrounding the mill town of Burnley. Shortly, he became aware of the dark shadow of the hill now confronting him and pulled back on the control column as hard as he could in order to try and lift the heavy aircraft over, but it proved to be a futile gesture and at 16.25 the B-24 slammed into the bleak moorland hillside, tail-first and under full power. The impact ripped the fuselage in two, the tail section breaking away, killing those members of the crew stationed within instantly. The remainder of the aircraft ploughed on some 100 yards up the slope, catching fire as it disintegrated, fortunately throwing Lt. Goeking through the armoured windscreen, to land beyond the flames and exploding ammunition. Only the characteristic twin stabilisers of the B-24s tail remained recognisable amongst the twisted and smouldering wreckage.

At Cant Clough Reservoir on the lower slopes of Black Hameldon, a Corporation

Aftermath of the crash, which left only the distinctive twin stabilisers of the B-24's tail remaining recognisable amongst the tangle of wreckage. (Kevin Mount)

Water Department work party were preparing to make their way back to Burnley, having spent the day working on the inlet to the reservoir on the edge of the bleak moor. They were just awaiting the arrival of the wagon that was to be their transport home, when their attention was drawn to an irregular knocking sound coming from the mist enshrouded moor. Leaving one man to inform their superintendent on his arrival, the other four set off to investigate and before long came upon the burning tail section of the B-24, with the knocking sound now clearly ammunition 'cooking-off' in the fire. The fire brigade and ambulance service were soon summoned and with the help of the workers they were directed to the crash site, together with a passing doctor, who was flagged down by the superintendent. Lying amidst the wreckage six seriously injured crew members, (five having been killed instantly in the crash), awaited rescue for what must have seemed like hours in the fading light of a cold February evening. In fact help arrived amazingly quickly, with some fifty further men and two more doctors summoned to the scene as the extent of the tragedy became clear, though conditions were such that it was 7.45pm before the first survivor could be brought down from the crash site and rushed to the town's Victoria Hospital. In fact the survivors had been lucky: if the accident had happened just 10 minutes later the workers would have been on their way home, with little chance that anyone would have spotted the wreckage until the following morning at least, by which time there would have been little hope for them.

Edward Rawlinson continues:

On the Monday we had no idea at the Burnley Express, our weekly newspaper, that the aircraft had come down and not until the Wednesday did it start to filter through about the crash. During the war everything was top secret and the emergency services were governed by strict security rules, our information came via Burnley's Victoria Hospital. It was then that the chief reporter and the rest of the staff remembered a low flying aircraft being in the vicinity.

On the Saturday following the crash I travelled to Cant Clough Reservoir and followed the crowd on to the moors to visit the site. The flow of people was like an army of ants moving towards the aircraft and everyone seemed to be coming back with a wartime trophy from this tragic accident. On guard was an American serviceman ensconced within a tent and with a local girl sitting inside it. He was carrying a revolver which was a great attraction to the local kids and he allowed them to climb all over the wings where the fuel tanks still contained aviation fuel, it was a very dangerous situation. His interests, it seemed were elsewhere! The aircraft's guns were lying about and live shells were scattered all around and being picked up as trophies. I spotted part of a radio receiver and asked the American guard if I could have it as a memento, he told me that it was no use then went back inside the tent. It looked good to me, a going-on 16 year old, with its dials and knobs. The Saturday was a crisp Winter's day far different from the previous Monday and I cursed myself for not taking a camera, but with the war-time restrictions I never thought I could get near enough the site to take photographs. The aircraft hadn't been completely demolished by fire and I remember the engines and propellers being quite intact although not together and the wings still either side of the cockpit.

Over the next few days three more of the crew succumbed to their wounds and it would be some two years before the most seriously injured, 1st Lt. Goeking, finally left hospital, though he would show the scars of his ordeal and walk with a limp for the rest of his life (Sadly he died in 1989).

Fates of those on board 42-50668 on 19th February 1945:

Name:	Position:	Status:
1st Lt. Charles A. Goeking	Pilot	Major Injury
1st Lt. George H. Smith Jr.	Co-pilot	Died of Injuries
T. Sgt. Howard E. Denham Jr.	Engineer	Died of Injuries
T. Sgt. Leslie E. Johnson	Radio operator	Major Injury
1st Lt. Frank E. Bock	Navigator	Died of Injuries
Sgt. Robert E. Hyett	Passenger	Major Injury
2nd Lt. Joseph B. Walker III	Passenger	Killed
F/O David A. Robinson Jr.	Passenger	Killed
F/O Gerald Procita	Passenger	Killed
2nd Lt. Elmer R. Brater	Passenger	Killed
Sgt. Randolph R. Mohlenrich Jr.	Passenger	Killed

Much of the wreck of 42-50668 was left on the moor and became a magnet for local schoolboys after the war and many souvenirs from the aircraft probably still lie forgotten at the bottom of draws in Burnley! Sometime in the 1950s much wreckage was removed, apparently by an enterprising local scrap merchant, though the heavier items such as the remains of the engines and huge undercarriage forgings were left *in situ*, forming an unofficial memorial at the crash site. Well known in

Crew photo belonging to T. Sgt. Howard E. Denham Jr. (standing 3rd from left). From the legible signatures: T. Sgt. Leslie E. Johnson is standing 1st left. 1st Lt. George H. Smith Jr. is seated 2nd from left and 1st Lt. Charles A. Goeking seated 3rd from left. *(Denham family)*

the area and frequently mentioned in subsequent years in the local press, it was one of the first crash sites I ever visited.

Much research on the aircraft and those on board was initially conducted by local enthusiast Kevin Mount, a time-consuming and difficult task in those pre-internet days! He had first visited the wreck as one of those local schoolboys looking for souvenirs, but the need to know more took hold, as it does with many enthusiasts, giving rise to the hobby of Aviation Archaeology. He arranged trips to the site for the pilot, Charles A. Goeking and his wife in 1972 and later for George Gosney, a former serviceman from BAD2 at Warton who had been assigned to the original recovery team. It was Kevin who first gave me the location of the crash site and suggested a visit and as I made my way up the moorland slope of the hill, ordnance survey map in hand, marked with a grid reference he had provided, I had little idea what, if anything, I would find. At that time three of the engines were still visible lying on a large area devoid of vegetation, together with both huge main undercarriage legs and occasional live rounds of 0.5-inch calibre ammunition and smaller parts of the aircraft scattered around. Lying on the surface I found part of a maker's plate bearing the partial

73

inscription Consolidated Aircraft San Diego which was one of the few artefacts that I picked up and later sent to Charles Goeking's relatives in the USA. It was visits to this and several other sites suggested by Kevin that made up my mind that this was the hobby for me; sadly he died from cancer several years ago.

Today, however, no engines are visible at the crash site, having been removed by unknown individuals, though one has now found its way to the Newark Air Museum, where it has been placed on loan by a private individual and is exhibited in their 'Engine Hall'. The huge undercarriage legs do still remain and the odd small fragment can still be found poking out of the bare peat, particularly after heavy rain. The footpath to the crash site is now heavily rutted by 'dirt-bike' enthusiasts that seem to plague the moors, without regard for the wildlife or others who wish to visit the area. Though on the crash site itself, unknown individuals, obviously aware of the significance of the site, have erected a loose-stone memorial cairn, topped by the broken lower section of one of the undercarriage legs.

Parts from 42-50668 do occasionally reappear and recently a number of artefacts, recovered by a local enthusiast from the site in the 1970s, were donated to the LAIT collection, the largest being the front turret armour, still with the chalk inscription, made by George Gosney on his return to the crash site in 1974 just about visible. Also a four-foot section of tail fin structure and a complete reduction gear assembly were included together with a box of smaller items. These fragments of the B-24 finally completed their journey to Burtonwood, when they were displayed at the Heritage centre there.

Crash site of 42-50668 today, marked by the massive main undercarriage legs from the B-24 and more recently a dry-stone memorial cairn.

74

CHAPTER EIGHT

HOLLOW VICTORY

Apart from London, Liverpool was probably the most heavily-bombed British city and together with the surrounding towns of Bootle, Wallasey and Birkenhead, Merseyside was attacked mainly because of its huge port system, which provided the main link between Britain and the USA, and was a vital entry point for food, fuel, raw materials, aircraft, weapons and troops from across the Atlantic. Liverpool was also strategically important due to its factories, as they concentrated their production to the war effort: Rootes works at Speke turning out bomber aircraft and the Royal Ordnance Factories in Fazakerley and Kirkby producing guns and munitions being two of the most obvious examples.

The first attack on Merseyside came on the 9 August 1940 at Birkenhead, with Liverpool being first hit on the 17th. By the end of 1940 there had been over 300 air raids, with the casualty toll rising steeply after a number of tragic direct hits on crowded air raid shelters. The main raids on the City occurred on the 12 and 13 March, 7 and 26 April. The 12 March raid consisting a force of 316 bombers despatched against Merseyside by the *Luftwaffe* and dropping a total of 303 tons of high explosive on that one night. More was yet to come, with The May Blitz between the 1 to the 7 May 1941, involving some 681 *Luftwaffe* bombers which dropped 2315 high explosive bombs, 119 land mines and approximately 112,000 incendiaries. This was the most concentrated series of air attacks on any British city area outside London during the war and the result was that half the docks were put out of action, as well as 1741 people killed and 1154 people injured throughout Merseyside. The heaviest night of bombing came on the 3 May, which also saw the worst single incident of the Blitz when the SS *Malakand*, a cargo ship carrying around 1000 tons of bombs and shells, exploded in Huskisson Dock No. 2, devastating the surrounding docks and hurling debris up to 2 miles away. The final bombs to be dropped on Merseyside during the War exploded on the 10 January 1942, with the total casualties for the 16-month long aerial campaign against Merseyside coming to just under 4000 killed and 3500 seriously injured. Today one of the most vivid reminders of the Liverpool Blitz in the city is the burnt-out shell of St Lukes Church - destroyed by incendiary bombs on the 5 May 1941.

Throughout the Blitz on Merseyside, strict media censorship, though intended to boost morale and deny the enemy information, meant that few reports appeared describing the horrors that the people of Merseyside were suffering. Those that were printed often stated the location as simply 'a Northern Town' and the raids as 'incidents'. Even the actions of the night-fighters protecting the city were rarely reported, leaving the inhabitants feeling that Liverpool and their efforts were undervalued and that the city was not receiving the protection that it deserved. In fact, during the Blitz several night-fighter squadrons were allocated to the region as it was recognised that Liverpool and Manchester would become likely targets of the *Luftwaffe* and needed protection. RAF fighters, based at Liverpool's airport at Speke as well as airfields in Cheshire (Cranage), Shropshire (Tern Hill and High Ercall), North Wales (Llanbedr and Valley) and Blackpool (Squires Gate) were allocated the task of protecting the city. Initially No. 308 (Polish) Squadron equipped with Hurricanes was transferred to Speke from Blackpool Squire's Gate, though they were replaced in September 1940 by No. 312 (Czech) Squadron and it was one of No. 312's Hurricanes that recorded Speke's first kill, a Ju88 on 24 November 1940.

As the raids increased in intensity the organisation for the air defence of Merseyside developed. On the 18 December, 1940 No. 96 Squadron was formed specifically for the defence of Merseyside, initially being equipped with Hurricanes and based not at Speke but at Cranage, Cheshire, where conditions could best be described as basic. They soon converted to Defiants and flights from the squadron were despatched to Squires Gate and Tern Hill at various times, before the squadron eventually moved to RAF Wrexham in October 1941. The defence of the City was supplemented by two balloon Squadrons – Nos. 919 and 921 – with headquarters at R.A.F. Fazakerly. These units, working in co-operation with the Army anti-aircraft batteries, which had some seventy-six guns sited around Merseyside, provided defensive cover. However, despite blackout restrictions, the city proved relatively easy for enemy raiders to locate and in an attempt to overcome this, some fourteen decoy sites were set up, where oil fires were lit at night to draw the raiders away from the city. Finally in December 1941 a new fighter airfield for the defence of Merseyside was opened - RAF Woodvale near Southport.

In addition to No. 96 Squadron's Defiants, from 26 March 1941, further Defiants from No. 256 Squadron were based at Squires Gate and provided an important part of the cover for Merseyside as well as patrolling for German raiders heading for other west-coast ports.

On the night of Monday the 7 May 1941, several of No. 256 Squadron's Defiants were flying just such patrols, whilst the *Luftwaffe* were launching a major attack on the Glasgow and Clydeside ports involving nearly 500 bombers. The primary targets were Greenock, Dumbarton and Hillingdon, with Liverpool and Bristol also being targeted. In the event many bombers failed to reach their northerly objectives and instead turned south and added their payloads to the latter two targets or bombed targets of opportunity. One such enemy aircraft was Ju88 Werke No. 8138 of II *Gruppe*, *Kampfgeschwader* 54, based at St. Andre-de-L'Eure, which was one of 213, *Luftflotte* 3 bombers ordered to attack Greenock. Though No. 8138 apparently reached the target area, the crew were unable find their aiming point due to cloud and turned south towards Liverpool. At 23.45, they were spotted by Sgt. R.T Adams and his pilot Flight Lt. D.R. West in Defiant N3445 of 256 Squadron and following a brief but perfectly executed attack, the raider was shot down in flames over the Ribble estuary. Many locals both sides of the river witnessed its fiery demise and although three of the four-man crew escaped the burning bomber as it dived to earth, one was badly injured and another landed in the river and was lost, his body finally being recovered over a month later.

Meanwhile only a few miles away, another drama was taking place in the moonlight above the clouds over the Southport area.

Defiant N1694 had also taken off from Squires Gate, somewhat earlier than N3445 and was piloted by Flight Sgt. John Stenton, with his gunner Sgt. William Ross and they too had flown in the direction of Liverpool hoping to intercept raiders. However, during the patrol their aircraft suffered a major electrical equipment failure, resulting in complete loss of use of all wireless equipment and, being above the clouds with no visible landmarks to guide them, very soon they were completely lost. By 23.30 they were running low on fuel and risked descending, breaking through the cloud cover at 4000 feet, but they were still unable to determine their position and elected to abandon the aircraft. This decision could not have been taken lightly as the Defiant was never an easy aircraft to bale out of, especially for the gunner, who had to avoid hitting

Flight Sgt. J. Stenton, Pilot of Defiant N1694 on its final mission. (*Dilip Sarkar collection*)

the tail as he jumped clear and it seems that all did not go well on this occasion. The abandoned Defiant impacted on farmland close to Lowlands Farm off Plex Lane, Halsall near Southport at 23.45, bursting into flames and although the fire seems to have been brief, with little or no fuel left to sustain it, by the next morning, when curious locals came to view the by now well-guarded wreck, there was little recognisable left. Although Stenton made a safe descent, Sgt. Ross was reported as injured, with a broken leg on landing, and taken to Ormskirk Hospital. In fact the situation proved more serious, as another pilot from the squadron notes in his personal diary, 'Ross worse than we thought, broken leg and fractured skull. Not expected to live, relatives called for'. However, a couple of days later he notes that 'Ross will pull through after all' and the following week he went to visit him at Ormskirk where he was 'pulling through OK, but won't be flying for months'.

The celebrations at Squires Gates, on 256 squadron's First Kill must have been somewhat tempered by the news of the loss of N1694 and no doubt there was considerable anxiety whilst they awaited news of Stenton and Ross. Sadly it seems that luck wasn't with the squadron, as early the following morning Defiant N3424 lost height on take-off from Squires Gate and crashed, killing both its pilot Sgt. J.D.H Cunningham and air gunner Sgt. A.D. Wood.

Having researched the fate of N1694, we were obviously keen to locate the crash site, though as with many such sites in the North-west, as in other areas of the country, we knew that we were not the first to look for it. In fact we knew that at least two previous attempts had been made to find N1694 but that little had been found or was thought likely to be found. Today most of the local farms in the Halsall area are private residential developments and very few locals living there now know anything of the events of nearly 60 years before. It took perseverance to track down the few remaining locals who were actually living in the area at the time of the crash and even their recollections were somewhat vague. In fact, they had only seen the aftermath of the crash, the following morning; – though fortunately one remembered that the wreck lay close to a natural hollow that forms a pond in very wet weather. The field where the aircraft had come down was by now considerably enlarged, as old hedge boundaries had been removed, but for once the wet weather prevalent at the time was in our favour and such a pond had indeed formed, enabling us quickly to pinpoint the site! However, as is often the case with the hobby of Aviation Archaeology, we had to be patient and our excavation of the site had to wait some 12 months for the necessary permit to be obtained and for a window in the crops on the field that coincided with suitable weather for the dig. Our detecting equipment had indicated a relatively small contact area just below plough depth, so we were not expecting major components and a small team of four individuals gathered for a hand dig of the site.

With favourable weather conditions, the excavation of N1694 proved a pleasant day out, though despite the dry weather the week prior to the dig, the field still proved too soft to risk taking a Land Rover to the crash site itself. As the excavation progressed we found, as predicted, that the aircraft had only penetrated to a maximum depth of approximately 4 feet and that the engine had been recovered at the time, but had obviously completely shattered. Also there was evidence of a fire, though parts were scorched rather than melted, indicating this was probably brief, no doubt due to there being little fuel left on the aircraft to burn. However, there were still many smaller parts and careful sifting of the sandy soil soon rewarded us with some nice finds. The main engine maker's plate with the Rolls Royce name flanked by two lions proved the star find of the day and as well as the maker's engine serial number, it bore the all important Air Ministry engine serial number, which matched that recorded on the Form 1180 perfectly. Also the Rolls Royce maker's plate from the reduction gear casing, again bearing the makers engine serial number and the maker's

Just below the plough layer, the first parts of N1694 are revealed.

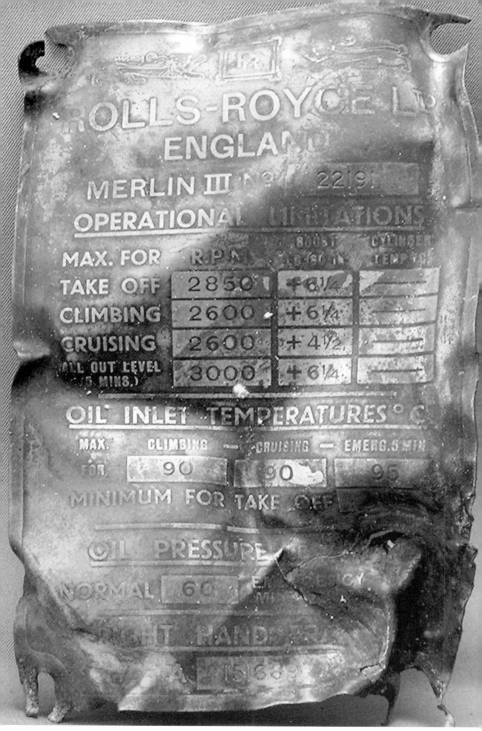

An early prize find during the excavation: The Intact maker's plate from the Rolls Royce Merlin III, matching the engine number given on the Form 1180.

plate from the turret gun sight were found. Other finds included: the hydraulic pump for the undercarriage, several shattered instruments, an amazingly intact Morse code key unit, remains of the Remote Contactor, direction finding device, the control unit from the de Havilland variable pitch airscrew, parts of the instrument panel, plus many fragments of switches, lamps, instruments, fuse boxes etc. Relatively few sections of the actual airframe structure of the aircraft came to light, but it was interesting to note that some parts were found clearly showing the black Night-Fighter finish of the Defiant. The bottom of the hole was saturated in oil, with chunks of crankcase and many smashed engine fragments, including crankcase bolts, engine valves and an exhaust stub. Finally, below this the three counterweights from the propeller hub were found embedded in the clay – showing we had reached the limit of penetration. All the parts were carefully bagged and carried to a waiting trailer and the hole carefully backfilled, whilst checking for any missed artefacts and then the site was reinstated as we had found it.

As usual the cleaning and conservation of the recovered parts would take far longer than the excavation itself and as is often the case yielded a few more surprises. First, whilst cleaning the unusually few rounds of .303 calibre ammunition we had recovered, several of them exploded, it was noticed that one broken, but unexploded, case had in fact been fired – perhaps the gunner had tested his guns during the flight? The next was a seemingly ordinary looking hydraulic

The Author's son examines the recovered remains of N1694 - not much to look at - but some superb smaller finds were recovered by careful checking.

The control unit and three balance weights from the Defiant's de Havilland variable-pitch propeller.

component that to date has not been positively identified. However, it bore a surprising inscription stamped into its aluminium casing – Made in Germany! Finally, and perhaps most remarkable of all, was discovered jammed inside the rear of the control unit from the de Havilland variable pitch airscrew. This unit would have mounted on the front of the propeller hub and we had already noted that unusually, it still retained most of it printed maker's label and instructions to the front plate, but the rear, where it had sheared from the hub was jammed with baked hard debris and as these were removed a circular disc of metal fell out, which on examination appeared to have some form of printed inscription. This obviously required very careful cleaning, as we knew from experience that printed rather than engraved lettering can all too easily be lost if any form of abrasive cleaning is used and even a careless rub with a thumb at the dig site can ruin an interesting artefact. In fact even when such items appear to have survived intact, the lettering can also simply curl up and peel off as the object dries out, if not treated with a suitable stabiliser, such as a solution containing microcrystalline wax. However, in this case we

A very rare find, the maker's badge from the propeller's spinner.

were fortunate as the printed surface appeared stable and well preserved and soon revealed that we had found perhaps the rarest of finds in Aviation Archaeology: the de Havilland spinner badge, from the extreme tip of the spinner. This fragile aluminium disc would have been the first point of contact as 8,470 lb (or over four tons) of Defiant N1694 impacted into the ground, making its survival little more than miraculous!

CHAPTER NINE

ALMOST MADE IT

Almost from the start of WW2 Liverpool's civilian airport at Speke became a hive of military activity and its proximity to this strategically important sea port resulted in it becoming a centre for an inevitable influx of aircraft flown into Speke, dismantled and shipped abroad, to such destinations as Rhodesia, South Africa and various points along the West African Coast. Additionally inbound from the U.S.A. came thousands of American aircraft, mostly shipped into the docks and then transported to the airport for assembly. Both the Douglas Aircraft Company and Lockheed Aircraft Corporation used the two main hangars at Speke to assemble Hudsons, Mustangs, Thunderbolts and Lightnings etc. Meanwhile, in the adjacent shadow aircraft factory, Rootes Securities began producing Bristol Blenheims and later Halifax bombers at a steady rate. Speke was often overcrowded, with up to 200 aircraft being evident at any one time, including new aircraft awaiting ferrying: those belonging to training units based there and, of course, fighters belonging to the various squadrons tasked with the air defence of Merseyside. Surprisingly, the airfield seems to have attracted little attention from the *Luftwaffe*, being attacked only twice: on the 17 September 1940, when an unsuccessful attack was made and on the 7 October 1940, when one aircraft was destroyed and one damaged.

Once assembled and tested, the aircraft destined for US units, were flown out from Speke, mainly by the 310th Ferry Squadron, which was stationed at Base Air Depot 2, Warton (BAD-2). Their destination initially being either BAD-2 or the other huge Base Air Depot 1 at Burtonwood (BAD-1), for further equipment fitting or modification prior to issue to an operational squadron. By 1944 the Merlin powered P-51Bs and Cs were very much in demand, not least due to its ability to provide long-range fighter escorts for the daylight bombing missions deep into enemy territory, that were regularly being undertaken by US bombers. By this time the 310th were delivering some 1200 aircraft a month, but February was to prove a black month for the Squadron with thirteen crashes resulting in the deaths of four of its pilots. One of these tragic final missions involved what should have been a routine flight of a new P-51B, collected from Speke on the morning of 16 February by 26-year-old Flight Officer Eugene Stanley Rybaczek.

P-51B Mustang 43-6635 was built by North American Aviation at its Inglewood, California plant. It was accepted on 30 October 1943 and departed the US on the 11 January 1944, arriving at Speke on 18 January 1944. On Wednesday 16 February, Rybaczek took off from Speke, probably at around 11.30am, for the short ferry flight heading for BAD-2 in the newly reassembled 43-6635. However, after only being airborne for a short while, the aircraft apparently developed a fault, resulting in a fuel or glycol leak, that rapidly filled the cockpit with fumes and left the aircraft streaming a vapour trail that was seen by witnesses on the ground. Clearly Rybaczek was in trouble and it must have seemed a stroke of fortune, when he spotted an obvious runway set in the wooded parkland below. What he had seen was in fact an RAF airfield known as No. 49 Satellite Landing Ground, set in the Earl of Derby's estate at Knowsley Park and used by No. 48 Maintenance Unit for the dispersal of newly built Handley Page Halifaxes, also from Speke. However, Rybaczek's attempts to save his aircraft were to have tragic consequences. He was observed by personnel on the airfield at about 11:50am as he approached the landing strip with the obvious intention of landing. But in order for him to have landed on the runway he would have had to have made a right turn, but for reasons unknown, a slow left turn was attempted and the aircraft stalled and spun in from an altitude of about 150 feet, impacting about 50 feet from the western end of the runway killing Flight Officer Rybaczek instantly. The aircraft hit the ground nose first, rolled over, then exploded and disintegrated across the threshold of the runway and the wreckage was engulfed in flames. RAF personnel from the airfield immediately ran to assist, but with only hand-held fire extinguishers available, they could do little and it was immediately obvious that nothing could be done for the pilot, who lay amid the wreckage, clearly dead. The airfield's fire tender and further RAF personnel were quickly on the scene and soon extinguished the flames.

Flight Officer Eugene Stanley Rybaczek (T-190748) wearing his USAAF uniform and in the cockpit of a P-51B (*Rybaczek family*)

Eyewitness accounts all stated that a vapour or smoke trail was clearly seen coming from the tail of the aircraft prior to the crash and it was assumed that this was either coolant (glycol) or fuel leaking into

Crash site of P-51B 43-6635, 16 February 1944.

the fuselage due to some form of mechanical fault. It was concluded that if this was the case, then it was entirely possible that Flight Officer Rybaczek was totally or partially blinded or rendered completely or semi-unconscious from whatever the nature of the failure was.

One such witness was Leading Aircraftsman (L.A.C.) R. Grace:

During my course of duty on Wednesday, 16 February 1944 at approximately 12:00 hours, a Mustang aircraft of the USAAF flew across the runway at approximately 100 feet. As it approached the west end of the runway vapour appeared to be pouring from its tail. The aircraft went into a left bank and approached as if he were going to 'shoot up' the runway. When about 50 feet from the runway its nose went down and he dived into the ground. The aircraft exploded and burst into flames, disintegrating over the runway.

Mr T Rothwell on the estate also witnessed the accident:

I was standing about 500 yards away from where the machine hit. The machine passed over my head, travelling in a north-east direction. It appeared as through black smoke was coming from the tail of the machine. The machine made a left-hand turn, as he did so he rolled over and a half turn of a spin. The machine burst immediately into flames upon striking the ground. When I first saw the machine it was 200 feet high.

Eugene Stanley Rybaczek was born in Terryville, a village of the Town of Plymouth, Connecticut on the 25 May 1918 to parents of Polish decent. He graduated from Terryville High School in 1937 and went to university. Whilst working as a machinist in the aircraft industry in Texas, he voluntarily enlisted in the Polish Forces under British Command at the Polish Army Recruiting Centre at Windsor, Canada on the 9 July 1941 and was given the service No. P794675. His basic training was undertaken at the Tadeusz Kosciuszko Polish Army Training Camp in Owen Sound, Ontario, Canada and he was then sent to the UK on the 17 October 1941 and Posted to RAF Padgate near Warrington, HQ of No. 20 (Training) Group, presumably for his RAF basic training. Following training at No. 25 Polish Elementary Flying

Training School at RAF Hucknall and No. 16 Polish Secondary Flying Training School at RAF Newton, he was awarded the permanent war rank of Sergeant and also received his pilot's title and wings on 2 December 1942. Rybaczek was initially posted to the Polish Airforce Depot at RAF Blackpool and then on to No. 6 Anti-Aircraft Co-operation Unit (AACU) at RAF Cark on 22 December 1942. During late January 1943 he was posted to No. 6 AACU unit detachment at RAF Belfast, Northern Ireland, where on the 8 February he was involved in an accident to an Oxford aircraft serial No. R6273. Whilst taxiing, the undercarriage of the aircraft collapsed but he was uninjured. There was no evidence of technical failure and it is considered that Eugene selected the undercarriage lever up in error when the warning horn sounded.

After a spell with various RAF Flights on target tug duties, Rybaczek was honourably discharged from the Polish Forces under British Command on the 25 May 1943, where his conduct had been considered to be very good. He transferred to the USAAF were he was given his pilot's rating of Flight Officer on the 26 May 1943, at some point after this he was posted to the 310th Ferry Squadron stationed at BAD-2. Eugene was involved in another minor accident at Speke airport on the 29 November 1943 whilst he was taxiing P-51B serial No. 43-6365 prior to a delivery flight. After signing all the paperwork and collecting the aircraft, he was taxiing along the perimeter track at 15:15 to get to the take-off position for a ferry flight to Warton, when his right wing scraped a lorry parked on the outer grass verge, close to the perimeter track. The collision resulted in the wing-tip being torn off and the outboard end of the starboard aileron being damaged. The windscreen of the lorry was also smashed and the aircraft was subsequently repaired on site by Lockheed.

At the time of his death Eugene was engaged to be married to a girl from the Nottingham area and they were saving for their wedding which was to have been in June 1944. He was initially buried on the 22 February 1944 at Brookwood Cemetery, London and later repatriated to the United States, arriving home on the 26 July 1948, to be buried in St Mary's Cemetery, Terryville, with full military honours on the 29 July 1948. The Rybaczek family were devastated by the loss and his father bought a plot of Land, off Ashton Drive in Terryville, near to Eugene's former home and named it Eugene Park in his son's honour. In the park were a merry-go-round, pond and a hall there and many Polish celebrations took place there. His brother Joseph was even married in the park.

Some of Eugene's friends, contacted during our research, recently recalled that he was a very popular person in his home town and that he liked Ford cars which he drove fast, ending up with a brush with the law on at least one occasion. He was also a close friend of actor Ted Knight (born Tadeusz Wladyslaw Konopka) who also came from Terryville and was perhaps best known for his role as the newscaster, Ted Baxter, on the Mary Tyler Moore TV show. Knight also saw service in Europe during World War II, in the 296th Combat Engineer Battalion. Eugene's nickname according to the 1937 Terryville High School year book was 'Ryba' and he was known as Best Dancer, Biggest Bluffer and he was never expected to be seen without money. Though a fascinating insight on this pilot's character, reading such documents is always tinged with sadness, knowing that this popular and promising young man's life had but a few short years left before he became caught up in the turmoil of the Second World War.

The hobby of Aviation Archaeology certainly takes us to some unusual places and searching for the remains of a WW2 fighter amid the exotic wildlife of a safari park was certainly an experience. The Earl of Derby's Estate at Knowsley Park is now a well known tourist attraction and following some lengthy negotiations, in 2002 a small group of members of the Lancashire Aircraft Investigation Team visited the Knowsley estate to attempt to locate the crash site of 43-6635, under the watchful (and extremely helpful) eye of the Head Forester. Having spent the morning viewing some of the scant remains of airfield buildings and dispersals etc. we turned our attention to calculating the approximate area of the threshold at the western end of

Examining derelict WW2 RAF buildings at Knowsley Park, used by No 48 Maintenance Unit as a satellite landing ground.

the runway, where the aircraft was known to have dived into the ground. Fortunately, the area we wished to examine lay outside the enclosures for the Park's wildlife, though we noted a rather large and obviously somewhat territorial ostrich was taking an interest in our activities, so we ensured that we kept well clear of the fence!

Nearly 60 years on, identifying the boundaries of the actual runway proved more difficult than we had anticipated, though fortunately two copses of trees proved to be in the same position, enabling us to make comparisons with the original photographs from the crash report. Having identified the approximate area we began a systematic metal-detector grid search, starting off with relatively wide lanes, due to the area of ground we had to cover. Three quarters of an hour later we found our first fragment: an aluminium hydraulic pipe with a US made brass connector. Readjusting the search pattern to narrower lanes in the vicinity of this piece, soon brought to light several more fragments including a headphone earpiece from a flying helmet and the face of the airspeed indicator, all showing signs of impact damage. One larger

Just below the surface, small fragments of 43-6635 begin to be revealed.
The face from the air speed indicator gauge found at crash site in May 2002.

signal proved to be a small cache of remains just below the surface indicating the actual impact point. Only a few inches down, there were still traces of oil and scorched earth, as well as a WW2 vintage asbestos fire blanket bearing testimony to the events of 56 years before. A final scan with our deep-seeking detecting equipment registered no further contacts, but our goal had been achieved and the handful of fragments recovered would be carefully cleaned, to be displayed with the story of this young American pilot.

The largest finds proved to not be from the aircraft! – Two RAF asbestos fire blankets used to douse the flames 60 years before, which had to be taken away for safe disposal.

The remainder of the fragments of 43-6635 found at crash site in May 2002.
(Mark Gaskell)

CHAPTER TEN

WHEN LUCK RUNS OUT

By the summer of 1943 the North African campaign was over and the various heavy Bombardment Groups of the Eighth Air Force that had been assigned to support the campaign there, returned to England. One such group was the 93rd Bombardment Group (Heavy), known as Ted's Travelling Circus and comprising the 328th, 329th, 330th and 409th Bomb squadrons, which was now based at Hardwick, Norfolk. Here, the surviving veterans who had completed their tours of duty, were sent home, their places being taken by replacement crews now arriving from the United States and the battle-weary B-24Ds also began to be replaced, by brand-new B-24H and J-model Liberators. Also, as the 'Mighty Eighth' continued to build up strength, new units were being flown in from the United States and the daylight deep-penetration raids into enemy territory began, targeting aircraft, ball bearing and oil production centres. However, enemy defences were also being reinforced and tactics improved, resulting in steadily increasing losses, which would by the end of the year prove unsustainable and lead to a change in strategy.

Supporting the combat groups of the 8th Air Force was a network of Air Depots at Warton in Lancashire, Langford Lodge in Northern Ireland and the huge Burtonwood base near Warrington in Cheshire. The purpose of the depots was the preparation, assembly, overhaul and repair of USAAF aircraft and their systems, including those which were damaged in battle. The depots also supplied spare parts to the squadrons and field modification kits to update aircraft. In fact Burtonwood was probably the largest military base in Europe during World War II, processing over 11,500 aircraft between 1943 and 1945 and with over 35,000 men under the direct control of Burtonwood and 18,500 servicemen on the base itself by the end of the war. As the air offensive against Germany stepped up, so did the work required of the Air Depots and Burtonwood became a hive of activity with aircraft arriving and departing almost constantly, so it is perhaps hardly surprising that the base suffered its share of mishaps. But to lose two new, consecutively serial numbered B-24s within three days of each other must certainly have raised some questions. Though in both cases, the complete destruction of the aircraft by the post-impact fire was such that no definite conclusions as to the cause could be reached.

The first incident occurred during a routine test flight of a recently delivered aircraft on Friday 27 August 1943. B-24H 42-7467 took off from Burtonwood at 19.00, crewed by 1st Lt. Richard L Hester – Pilot, 2nd Lt. William H Campbell – Co-Pilot, and 2nd Lt. Bernard H Froelich. The aircraft circled the airfield twice and climbed to 8000 feet, then headed in a northerly direction. A few minutes into the flight, the Co-pilot noticed that No.3 propeller was running faster than the others and trying to adjust the speed he found there was no response from the propeller control. The pilot, Lt. Hester also tried the propeller control with no result and discovered that in fact all four propeller controls were inoperative. After about two minutes the propellers started to run away and the aircraft began to lose altitude and became violently unstable despite all the efforts of the crew, so at about 4000 feet, Lt. Hester called for parachutes and headed the aircraft towards the sea, as having a large amount of aviation fuel onboard he did not want the aircraft to fall on a populated area. At about 1000 feet the pilot regained enough control to attempt a crash landing. Lt. Campbell came to assist in preparing for a crash and preparing to cut the switches as the aircraft settled onto the ground. On touching the ground, the aircraft bounced back into the air, breaking apart as it went and when the shattered bomber finally came to rest Lt. Hester was thrown through his windscreen, Lt. Campbell went through his and Lt. Froelich was found lying unconscious some 20 feet from the aircraft. Aviation fuel was seen to be pouring from the port wing and a small fire, which broke out, soon totally engulfed the aircraft. The B-24 had crashed at 19.20 at Aspull near Wigan and although the pilot and co-pilot would recover from their injuries, sadly Lt. Froelich did not regain consciousness and died in the ambulance en route to the hospital. The subsequent investigation was severely hampered by the lack of examinable evidence and it was assumed that it was a complete failure of the propeller controls, which had caused the accident.

B-24H Liberators serial numbers 42-7467 and 42-7468 were built by the Ford Motor Company at their huge Willow Run factory at Ypsilanti, about 30 miles west of Detroit, Michigan and they both arrived in the UK on 15 August, probably via Prestwick. By the 30 August 1943 B-24H Liberator 42-7468 had been prepared for service and was ready to be delivered to the 392nd Bombardment Group (Heavy), airfield at Wendling, Norfolk. This unit comprised the 576th, 577th, 578th and 579th Bomb squadrons and had sailed from New York on the 25 July 1943, arriving in England on the 30 July 1943. They arrived at the yet to be completed Norfolk airfield on the 1 August and although most of the accommodation had been built, there was mud from the construction everywhere and their aircraft were yet to arrive. The B-24s began to be ferried in over the next few weeks and the group flew its first mission on the 9 September 1943, when twenty bombers took off from Wendling for Abbeville in France.

It was just three days later, following a satisfactory final short test-flight, that 42-7468 was given clearance for the ferry flight to Wendling at approximately 16.05 on the 30th and the senior flying control officer at Burtonwood briefed the crew for the trip. It seems that the crew were keen to get going and as word of the opportunity of an evening flight to the Norfolk base got around, others were also, with Captain Maurice A. Lofgren obtaining clearance to board the flight only five minutes before take-off. The aircraft departed Burtonwood at 17.00, making a good take off in excellent weather conditions, described later as being 'CAVU' (Ceiling And Visibility Unlimited). The landing gear was seen to be retracted when the aircraft was at an altitude of approximately 100 feet and the aircraft continued on a straight course from the west end of the East/west runway, gaining height all the time. When it was about 1 mile from the airfield it was observed to make a right turn of ninety degrees out of the traffic pattern. This immediately brought the aircraft to the attention of the Flight Control Office as it was noticed that the aircraft had turned to the right, when in fact a left-hand turn pattern was the rule at the station and it was concluded that there must be a problem on the aircraft and that it was attempting to return to the base. After making the right turn it continued on a straight course, then began another turn, this time steeply to the right, whilst executing this manoeuvre the nose of the aircraft started to drop towards the ground and as it lost altitude, the aircraft disappeared out of sight of the control office, whilst approximately 1.5 miles North-west of the airfield. This was immediately followed by an explosion and flames were seen rising at least 200 feet into the air. Ambulances and fire crews were despatched to the scene immediately and shortly after the crash it was brought to the attention of the Flight Control Office that two further men, T/Sgt. Hyman Schwartz and T/Sgt. Walter F Murphy had in fact boarded the aircraft immediately prior to take-off, without being declared on the clearance form.

The B-24 had struck a small earthwork, known locally as 'Battery Cob', standing some 32 feet high in the middle of otherwise level farmland, belonging to Northfield Farm, Clock Face, Bold. The Cob had been built by the 2nd Lancashire Engineer Volunteers in 1871 and was some 30 yards long by 15 yards wide, triangular in section with an 8 feet wide flat top, it was used by local volunteers as the stop butts for a rifle range during the Boer War and 1st World Wars. When the B-24 hit the cob, the aircraft was approximately in a 30 degree right turn, striking the ground first with the right wing-tip about three feet above the base of the Cob. The force of the impact threw the major part of the aircraft over the top of the mound and scattered remains for about 200 yards beyond. Several locals witnessed the accident.

Off duty police constable Edward Longland was in the yard of Northfield Farm when the aircraft flew overhead:

> *I heard the sound of an aircraft approaching from the Burtonwood direction. The plane then came into view and I saw that it was travelling in a north-westerly direction at a very low altitude. At this time it would not be more than half a mile away from me and I had a broadside view.*

He noted that the engines appeared to be running normally and did not falter, but that it was losing height.

> *The right bank became more acute, so acute that I could see the outline and upper surface of both wings. To me the plane appeared to be turning around the Cob as if it was returning to the aerodrome when suddenly there was a loud explosion and the plane burst into flames and crashed into the field adjoining Northfield Farm about 300 yards from where I was standing.*

He immediately ran to the scene and upon arrival saw that the aircraft was a mass of flames and had broken into two parts with wreckage strewn over a large area. He then noticed a body lying on the ground near the front of the fuselage which was burning furiously and shielding his face with a sack that he had been carrying, he managed

Left: In the aftermath of the crash, little remained of B-24H 42-7467 by the time the fire crews arrived. (USAF Historical Division)

Right: The force of the impact threw the bulk of the B-24 over Battery Cob, leaving only the charred frame of the tail section recognisable. (USAF Historical Division)

Nothing remains to mark the crash site today - "Battery Cob" stood in the top right hand corner of this field.

to drag the crewman clear, but unfortunately he was already dead. Other locals were by now on the scene and he was assisted by Civil Defence Warden Robert Wilson and Special Constable Redhead, as they made repeated attempts to recover other members of the crew from the wreckage. However, although they could see other bodies apparently lying dead amongst the burning wreckage, they were unable to recover them owing to the intense heat and smoke. As further rescue efforts proved impossible and there were numerous minor explosions amongst the wreckage, they instead concentrated their efforts on keeping the immediate area clear of sightseers who were now beginning to gather.

Charlie Morley, now in his 70s, was a 12-year-old eyewitness to the incident. His recollection of the Battery Cob crash is still vivid in his mind:

> *I was blackberry picking nearby with a couple of friends, when we heard the explosion as the aircraft crashed and saw the flames and smoke in the distance. We ran to the site and by the time we got there, the N.F.S.* [National Fire Service] *was already there, but the fire engine had run into the ditch at the side of the track up to Battery Cob and was lying over on its side.*

Mr James Rearden, a colliery overman aged 44, was cycling

towards Clock Face, Bold, when he noticed the low flying B-24:

> *The machine was flying low but not dangerously low and the engines sounded very healthy. I then noticed the plane banking to the right and appeared to be losing height, but the engines were still running normal. Just before the machine reached Battery Cob I definitely heard the engines rev up as if the pilot suddenly noticed the Cob and was trying to clear it. The next thing I saw was that the plane appeared to collide with the top of the Cob and simultaneously there was a terrific explosion and the plane was blown to pieces.*

Firemen from St Helens and Whiston National Fire Service together with a fire-fighting unit from the Burtonwood Base were soon on the scene and proceeded to tackle the flames with chemical fire extinguishers and water pumped from a nearby pond through lengthy hoses that appear in many of the photos taken for the accident investigation report. Before long fires were brought under control and the bodies of a further four crewmen could be recovered. By this point further USAAF personnel arrived and took charge of the situation and the fire was finally completely extinguished by 19.00 and the remainder of the bodies could be recovered and taken to the Base mortuary. A guard was placed on the wreck overnight and the following day the remains were examined for any clues as to the cause of the accident. Though it was noted that the aircraft had reacted normally during the brief test flight, immediately prior to taking off for its final flight, the emphasis of the investigation seems to have been directed towards the propeller hubs. It was noted that the settings were found to be abnormal, but once again due to the level of destruction of the aircraft it was impossible to determine any definite cause and no recommendations could be made.

In February 1944 at Widnes Police Court a special ceremony was held, the occasion being the presentation of awards by The Society for the Protection of Life from Fire, the awards were handed out to Constable Longland who received a bronze medal along with a merit badge and a money grant, and a framed certificate together with three guineas each, to special constable Redhead and Warden Wilson. All those on board were initially buried in Brookwood cemetery, London. After the war most of the casualties were repatriated and the remainder moved to Cambridge American Cemetery, where 2nd Lt. Merle F Tompkins, F/O Virgil R Bell, 2nd Lt. Eugene V Maloney and T/Sgt. Walter F Murphy now lie.

Name	Serial	Unit	Location/Position	Status
2nd Lt. Merle F. Tompkins	0-740004	329th Bomb Sqn, 93rd Bomb Group	Pilot	K.
F/O Virgil R. Bell	T190735	330th Bomb Sqn, 93rd Bomb Group	Co-Pilot	K.
T/Sgt. Reed Armstrong	39827450	? Bomb Sqn, 93rd Bomb Group	Flight Engineer	K.
2nd Lt. Eugene V. Maloney	0-801485	578th Bomb Sqn, 392nd Bomb Group	Navigator	K.
T/Sgt. Leo E. Lovasik	33278427	329th Bomb Sqn, 93rd Bomb Group	Radio Operator	K.
T/Sgt. Hyman Schwartz	13045512	578th Bomb Sqn, 392nd Bomb Group	Crew Chief	K.
2nd Lt. William McKnight	0-801490	578th Bomb Sqn, 392nd Bomb Group	Passenger	K.
Capt. Maurice A. Lofgren	0-727895	? Bomb Sqn, 93rd Bomb Group	Passenger	K.
T/Sgt. Walter F. Murphy	11008976	579th Bomb Sqn, 392nd Bomb Group	Passenger	K.

During our research into this incident, we were fortunate in being able to make contact with relatives in the United States of some of those who lost their lives on board this aircraft and one particular individual, Technical Sergeant Leo E. Lovasik, it seems was a remarkable young man, though sadly recognition of this was to come posthumously. His strong religious beliefs and family background may seem alien to the youth of today, but in many ways he represents the younger generations that were caught up in the conflict, all too often with tragic results.

Leo was born on 13 November 1921, one of eight children from a Slovak family at Tarentum, Pennsylvania, a steel-town about 20 miles north-east of Pittsburgh. The family were devout Catholics and he seemed destined to follow his eldest brother by training to enter the priesthood, but after much soul searching decided this was not for him. However, he remained committed to his faith and as he began his basic training in July 1942 he took every opportunity to promote these principles amongst his fellow men, though sometimes this was not always welcomed. He must certainly have been quite a character, because, even though he was the only Catholic on the 11-man crew of his B-24, he persuaded them to name their aircraft *Valiant Virgin* in honour of the Virgin Mary. After he explained the protection he felt this would bring to them, the name was duly painted in large white letters on the nose, before their departure across the Atlantic! From his letters it seems that his conviction in this protection was confirmed when a potential emergency somewhere far from land during this trip passed without incident and they landed safely in England.

Leo had a strong sense of duty and an unerring conviction that the conflict he was entering was one of good versus evil, in which he was prepared to play an active part. Unfortunately, he never saw action, because, after he flew with his crew and their B-24 to England at the end of May 1943, there followed a period of intensive further training and his letters mention gunnery courses, cross-country navigation exercises and regular low-level mass formation flying, in

Technical Sergeant Leo E. Lovasik. (*Daughters of St. Paul*)

preparation for an unknown forthcoming operation! However, he was based on an operational airfield and seems to have been well aware of the realities of war, having ample opportunity to speak to fellow airmen already flying over enemy territory. Elements of the 329th Bomb Squadron did indeed take part in the infamous low-level Ploesti raid on 1 August, no doubt the reason for the low-level practice Leo mentions, but he makes no mention of this in his letters. However a letter on the 18 August was to upset Leo deeply as news reached him that a friend from his hometown, who had also joined up as an air-gunner, had been killed aged 21, apparently on his first raid over enemy territory. Following this news the tone of his letters changed, mentioning trips to London to see the sights, attending a mass in a Cathedral and quoting poetry including High Flight, by Pilot Officer John Gillespie Magee RCAF (Killed 11 December 1941).

Leo had in fact been assigned to communication duties from early August – ferrying B-24s around the country and just three days before his death he writes of this work, describing the long hours flying this has entailed and mentioning that he is expecting the call to operational duties at any moment. His final letter was to his mother, written on Monday 30 August, no doubt whilst awaiting the return of the B-24 they were about to ferry to Wendling, from it's final test flight. Leo had by now been at Burtonwood for three days, having been due to leave the previous morning. He had attended a mass conducted in the Base auditorium and although his letter was no doubt intended to comfort his family, a strong sense of foreboding clearly comes across that each flight could very well be his last. Following Leo's death, his elder brother, Rev. Lawrence G. Lovasik, wrote a booklet containing a collection of the prolific letters Leo had written home to his mother and sweetheart, titled 'Knight of Our Lady, Queen of the Skies'. Intended to be an inspiration to Catholics serving in the forces, this booklet was reprinted three times in 1943, and some 100,000 copies were distributed to US servicemen during World War II. The work was revised and enlarged after the war and such was the demand, a new hardback edition was published in 1960. Though this work focuses on his religious beliefs, it provides a unique insight into the short life of this young idealistic American aviator. Leo's death came as a severe blow to all those who knew him, including his sweetheart, who entered a convent in 1945. In 1947 his body was returned to the United States and now lies close to other members of his family in St. Clement Cemetery, Bakerstown Road, Tarentum, Pennsylvania.

CHAPTER ELEVEN

AN 'OLD WARRIOR'

The Boulton Paul Defiant was, perhaps unsurprisingly, designed in response to an Air Ministry issued specification (F.9/35) for a new fighter concept. Armed with a power-operated gun turret, it was envisioned that the aircraft would infiltrate unescorted bomber formations and bring its formidable fire-power rapidly to bear on the unsuspecting enemy. Boulton Paul were pioneers in the design of power operated, enclosed gun turrets and the resulting aircraft proved a modern looking low-wing cantilever monoplane two-seater fighter of stressed-skin all-metal construction, with retractable landing gear and similar in appearance at first glance to the Hurricane. It first flew in 1937, but due to various production delays it was to be December 1939 before the first operational squadrons were equipped with the new Defiants. Though the weight of the gun turret adversely affected performance, handling was good and with no other such aircraft in the skies, it took many *Luftwaffe* fighter pilots by surprise.

Despite some early successes over France in 1940, it rapidly became clear that the aircraft was outclassed as a day-fighter and once the enemy pilots learned to identify correctly the slower moving Defiants and discovered its lack of forward-firing armament, losses began to mount alarmingly. By the end of August 1940 it was withdrawn from daylight front-line operational use, though it was noted that the interception of unescorted German bombers had often proved successful – a factor that no doubt contributed to the Defiants newfound role as a night interception fighter.

The two squadrons equipped with Defiants became dedicated night-fighter units and their aircraft were painted all black and fitted with flame damping exhausts. Success came quickly, with the first night kill, a Heinkel HeIII, being claimed by No. 141 Squadron on 15 September 1940. Also that month No.151 Squadron received its first Defiants. The Squadron flew defensive patrols during the early months of the war and its Hurricanes provided cover for evacuation of Dunkirk and flew missions over northern France during May and June 1940. As the Battle of Britain came to a close, No. 151 moved to Digby in Lincolnshire for a rest period and to re-equip and commence training to become a night-fighter squadron. On the 28 November they moved to Bramcote in Warwickshire, primarily a training base, as part of an

Boulton Paul Defiant Mk.1 serial number N3328, during its time with No.151 Squadron, wearing its distinctive Shark's Mouth nose art. (*Bob Pearson*)

attempt to redeploy the RAF's over-stretched night-fighter resources more effectively. The base was considered well positioned to intercept enemy bombers heading for industrial targets in the Midlands and of course, nearby Coventry, which had been devastated in a raid on the 14th of that month, by a massed force of 552 enemy bombers. The squadron received further Defiants whilst at Bramcote, including Mk.1 serial number N3328, allocated on 12 December 1940 and given the code letters DZ-Z. Equipped as a night fighter and finished in the standard all black colour scheme, this aircraft was, unusually for a British fighter, soon given a striking piece of nose art in the form of an aggressive sharks mouth and eye.

On the 22 December, No. 151 Squadron was again on the move, this time to Wittering in Northamptonshire, where they flew mainly night patrols, as well as convoy protection patrols, with both Hurricane IICs and Defiants. Tasked with protecting the countries key industrial areas from attack, by intercepting the German raiders along the air corridors they used over the east of the country.

The Squadron's first success came on the night of the 15/16 January 1941, when Pilot Officer R. P. Stevens shot down two raiders in one night, a Dornier Do17 and a Heinkel HeIII, whilst flying a Hurricane. Their next victory went to a Defiant, during an attack on Derby, when Sergeants H.E. Bodien and D. E.C. Jonas shot down a further Dornier Do17. Then on the night of 8/9 April during yet another attack on Coventry, Pilot Officer R. P. Stevens excelled again, bringing down two raiders, both Heinkel HeIIIs and a further HeIII was shared by Flight Lieutenant D.F.W Darling and Pilot Officer J.S Davidson in a Defiant, together with anti-aircraft fire. The Squadron's Hurricanes and Defiants were busy again the following night as some 450 enemy bombers made for Birmingham and Coventry, with eight being shot down, including a Heinkel HeIII credited to Flight Lieutenant D.A.P. McMullen and Sergeant S.J. Fairweather in a Defiant. Pilot Officer R.

P. Stevens shot down his fourth raider within only three days, with a HeIII on the night of the 10/11th and increased his score again on the 19/20th with a further Heinkel. The squadrons Defiants brought down two further raiders, on 2/3 May and 3/4 May and Stevens another on the 7/8th.

By mid-1941 an improved version of the Defiant fitted with a Merlin XX engine featuring a two-speed supercharger was becoming available and No. 151 Squadron replaced its old Mk Is with the new Defiant Mk II and in August N3328 was returned to Reid and Sigrist at Desford, presumably for overhaul or repair. From the autumn of 1941, Airborne Interception (A.I.) Mk IV radar units began to be fitted to Defiants, with the display screen in the pilot's cockpit and this arrangement saw limited success. But by the beginning of 1942, it was obvious that the Defiant was now too slow to catch the latest German night intruders and the night fighter units began to re-equip in the period of April to September that year, as the new A.I. radar-equipped de Havilland Mosquito and Bristol Beaufighters took over the role. As the Defiants were withdrawn from front-line operations, some were re-assigned to Air-Sea Rescue (ASR) units and were modified to carry dinghy packs under each wing that could be dropped to ditched airmen. Other aircraft were modified for use as Target-Tugs, towing target banners for air gunnery practice, with their turrets removed and the space used for an observer's station with a small canopy. N3328 was spared the ignominy of this conversion and on the 8 April 1942 it was allocated to No.1 Air Armament School at Manby in Lincolnshire, to be used to train Air Gunners.

Later in 1942, N3328 was to be transferred to No.10 Air Gunners School (A.G.S.) at Walney Island near Barrow in Cumbria. On 23 October 1942 Flight Sergeant John Leslie Goulter from No.10 A.G.S. was flown to Manby via Grimsby, as a passenger in an aircraft flown by the Officer in Command of No.10 AGS, Squadron Leader Hubert Norman Gravenor. En route he was briefed regarding his duties concerning the collection of the

Flight Sergeant John Leslie Goulter (*Goulter family*)

aircraft from Manby, as he had not previously collected an aircraft from another unit and he was warned to check thoroughly over his charge before taking off. Also in light of the prevailing weather at the time, he was reminded that there was no urgency for the flight and he was to await suitable conditions before making his return flight. Goulter had trained initially at No.8 Elementary Flying Training School (E.F.T.S.) at Narrandera in New South Wales, Australia, gaining his flying badge on 27 July 1941. He was considered one of the most experienced pilots at No.10 A.G.S., with some 650 hours total flying time on aircraft such as the Tiger Moth, Harvard, Miles Master and Lysander, with over 180 hours of this being on Defiants and he was due to be selected for operational duties. Aged 22, he came from Glen Niven, Queensland, Australia and was the oldest of five children. His younger brother, Flight Sergeant Howard M. Goulter was already flying Wellingtons with No. 12 Squadron, based at RAF Binbrook and on the night of 1/2 of June 1942 was commended for his bravery and skill. He had been taking off for a night raid on Essen, carrying a single, large bomb, when at around 500 feet the Port engine failed. Jettisoning the bomb was out of the question and he managed to return to the airfield and land his Wellington safely, away from the other aircraft and the main flare-path. He had been one of the first aircraft to take-off and his skill in landing the aircraft cross wind and away from the other planes waiting to take off had averted a major disaster.

At 09.30 on the 24 October 1942 Flight Sgt, Goulter was completing the necessary paperwork for his flight; the aircraft had been inspected and the Form 700 (aircraft servicing record) signed, meaning that he had taken responsibility for the aircraft from the ground crew. The flight had been properly authorised and the weather conditions checked and found to be good at the time of take-off with visibility of 12 miles. The forecast did however note that thundery rain showers and thunderstorms were likely and that visibility would be reduced as he made his way west, but should improve. Finally after having checked his maps and giving the duty pilot at Manby an Estimated Time of Arrival (E.T.A.), at 10.40, Flight Sgt. Goulter took off for the approximately one-hour long flight. Although he had been briefed for a route via Doncaster, Selby and Harrogate, it was later found that he had in fact taken a more direct route. He was, however, still on course for his chosen route when he arrived over Barnoldswick during a severe hailstorm at approximately 11.30 and his plane was heard by witnesses, circling above the town in the low cloud. It was assumed that for some reason Sgt. Goulter had lost confidence in his position and was seeking to verify his location. However, he was almost certainly all too aware that he was likely to be in the proximity of high ground and knowing the danger would have been very reluctant to descend through the cloud. It seems likely that he lost control of the aircraft whilst flying on instruments in the cloud and the aircraft stalled into the ground, crashing on farmland between Barnoldswick and Gisburn at 11.45.

Eyewitnesses to the final moments of the flight heard the aircraft before they caught sight of it and observed it come out of the low cloud, variously estimated at about 600 – 1800 feet, though visibility, even below the cloud, was severely restricted, first by the hailstorm and then by the heavy rain which followed. Probably closest to the scene was 28-year-old farm worker, Edward R, Dean:

> *At about 11.50 am, I was cutting kale in Flass Field which adjoins the one belonging to Lower Clough Farm* [the crash site]. *I heard an aeroplane circling overhead and suddenly the noise of it became more intense. I could not see the aeroplane at first because of the low cloud, which was at about 600 feet high. The aeroplane suddenly came out of the cloud flying towards the ground at an angle of about 45 degrees. The engine was running full out, in a power dive. It was coming from a westerly direction. As far as I could see the plane was the right side up. It crashed into the ground with a loud explosion about 150 yards from me in the next field. I ran there and found that the main part of the plane was buried in the ground and parts of it were scattered over two fields. There was no sign of the pilot. At the time of the crash it was raining hard and just before there had been a very heavy hailstorm.*

A number of local people heard a loud explosion and those who ran to the scene found the bulk of the aircraft embedded deeply in the ground with fragments scattered about. No crew had been seen to bale out and no immediate sign of the pilot was evident from the wreck. Meanwhile at No.10 AGS at Barrow, there was some confusion: at 11.00 they had received word that Goulter was leaving Digby shortly for the flight to Barrow and at 11.45 they received confirmation that he had taken off from Manby at 10.40. Though Goulter's E.T.A. was given as 11.40, it seems that they believed he had landed at Digby and it was 13.30 before any action was taken and the aircraft reported overdue. Enquiries made with Manby, Digby and Doncaster all proved negative, with Digby confirming that no Defiant aircraft had landed or taken off from there during that day. It was not until 19.30 that information was received that an aircraft had crashed, but that there was no sign of the pilot. Obviously hoping that Goulter had managed to bale out and may be lying injured in a field or on open moorland close to the crash site, 10 AGS's Commanding Officer ordered preparations to be made for some 100 personnel to be conveyed to the area of the crash to conduct a thorough search. At 02.30 on the 25th it was reported that home guard personnel were still digging on the site and soon after this Barnoldswick Police contacted Barrow to inform them that evidence had been discovered at 03.00, that there was a body still in the aircraft and the proposed search party was called off.

The following morning personnel from No.10 AGS arrived at the crash site and they confirmed the identity of N3328 and began to remove parts of the aircraft from the crater, eventually they managed to recover Sgt. Goulter's body and removed it to RAF Barrow, where the medical officer made the formal identification. Also found was the pilot's personal satchel containing three maps, still folded and obviously not used on the flight. The investigation report noted that although Sgt. Goulter was an excellent pilot he was relatively inexperienced in cross-country navigation, and that this was his first such ferry flight, collecting an aircraft from an unfamiliar station. His apparent lack of use of the maps provided and deviation from the course given to him were noted as factors contributing to the accident. However, it was also stated that he was on course for his chosen, more direct route and no mention was made as to whether the intended route would have avoided the extreme weather conditions he encountered. Finally, one witness interviewed during our investigation clearly recalled seeing a large section of outer wing at the crash site immediately after the crash with the gap between the wing and its still attached flap being filled with frozen, impacted hailstones.

Flight Sergeant John Leslie Goulter, aged just 22, was buried at 16.00 on Wednesday the 28 October 1942 in Barrow-in-Furness cemetery, Sec. 5 (Nonconformist). Grave 2017. His brother had been informed of his death and was able to arrange to attend the funeral on what proved to be his own 21st birthday.

Our excavation of N3328 took place on Saturday 25 May 2002, using a 6-ton tracked excavator from the start because of the ground conditions and the fact that a previous excavation of the site was known to have been undertaken in the 1970s. As predicted, the first 3 feet or so of soil removed revealed very little trace of N3328, almost certainly due to this previous hand-dig, but once this material was removed a distinct dark shadow in the soil was revealed and our detecting equipment continued to register a major contact below.

As the day went on the weather improved, as did our spirits as the excavator began to reveal substantial remains of the Defiant. First the lower section of a main undercarriage leg, together with a shredded tyre, then an escape axe clearly marked with the Air Ministry crown and dated 1941, as well as instruments, switches and sections of wiring from the cockpit area. However, it soon became apparent that the artefacts were being uncovered in a haphazard order, rather than the expected usual stratification where the aircraft's components lie in the ground still in context to their original position on the aircraft.

Then the excavator shuddered on contact with a very solid object about 6 feet down and to prevent damaging any artefacts, three volunteers climbed down to uncover the object by hand and assess what we had found and how to best recover it. This proved to be the propeller with one full blade and three quarters of another still attached, as well as the reduction gear from the front of the Merlin engine. It took an hour of careful digging to reveal fully and recover the propeller using heavy-duty nylon lifting straps so as not to damage

The Defiant's propeller had apparently been returned to the crater to discourage any disturbance of the aircraft's remains and it certainly proved tricky to extract 60 years later!

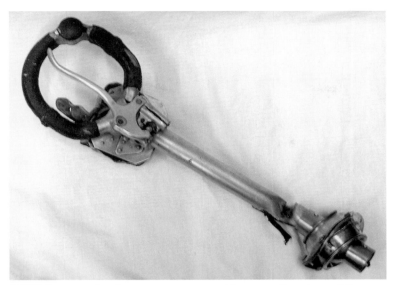

N3328's control column was recovered in exceptional condition, with a remarkably intact spade-grip – the broken off base section was found during meticulous cleaning and sorting of all of the recovered remains.

any still intact painted finish. Normally, the propeller hub would be expected to be the last and deepest object found. Once this had been removed a tangled mass of further wreckage was revealed below and immediately under the propeller a remarkably intact control column, complete with its spade-grip was a spectacular find.

Carefully pulling this mass of wreckage apart, again by hand, more instruments were found, including the altimeter, still registering 900 feet, the approximate height of the crash site above sea level. Also the turn and bank indicator, the signal flare rack, clock and the remains of two oxygen regulators, one from the cockpit and one from the turret. A few sad reminders of the unfortunate pilot also came to light, such as fragments of a Mae West life jacket, an eyepiece from a pair of flying goggles and then a small scrap of cloth, which proved to be the remains of a jacket pocket together with its contents. Clearly this last item was the personal property of the pilot and as such would have to be returned to the authorities. As we continued, evidence that the engine had completely shattered on impact came to light with the finding of three cylinder liners with pistons, the generator, oil, hydraulic and coolant pumps, starter motor, the shattered carburettor and many smaller

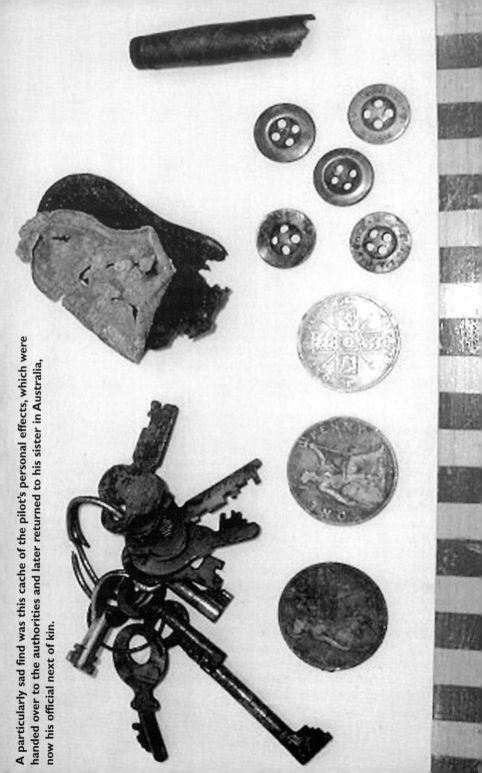

A particularly sad find was this cache of the pilot's personal effects, which were handed over to the authorities and later returned to his sister in Australia, now his official next of kin.

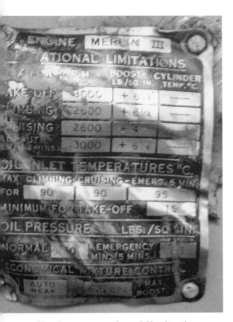

Engine operational limitations plate for the Defiant's Rolls Royce Merlin III engine.

engine components including exhaust and inlet valves, exhaust stubs etc.

Later whilst interviewing local witnesses it emerged that a small crane and several days digging were required to recover the engine just after the crash and as we started sorting the large pile of fragments recovered during our dig, evidence of this was soon found: a couple of large broken links of heavy duty chain, a pair of wire cutters and numerous empty food cans showed that it must have been quite a struggle! Though after all these efforts the investigation report merely states that the engine was too disintegrated for examination. As usual this process also revealed further interesting artefacts missed during the dig, including the large brass engine limitations plate from the cockpit, various modifications plates, the base of the control column and many smaller parts.

Contact was made with relatives of the pilot, including his sister, now his official next of kin and we were able to supply this information to the authorities when we sent them the recovered personal effects. Though only comprising a small bunch of keys with leather fob, a few coins and buttons and a shattered fountain pen, his relatives in Australia still proudly keep his memory alive and these artefacts were of course of immense value to them. Naturally we were only too pleased to be able to effect their return and additionally the lamp from the cockpit, that we had also recovered, was selected as a suitable memento from his aircraft and sent to the family. In return they kindly provided LAIT with copies of his Australian Archive file and the photograph of him in this book.

Defiant N3328's propeller, once again under darkening Northern skies. (*Russell Brown*).

CHAPTER TWELVE

ENTER THE JET AGE

Most enthusiasts would probably assume that by the 1950s aircraft recovery operations had reached the stage that little if anything would remain at a crash site, especially when the aircraft concerned was one of the latest jet fighters, rather than an obsolete wartime design. Although we had excavated one or two post-war crash sites in the past, these had generally been incidents involving a former wartime aircraft and some purists question excavating or even researching later types, but when does history officially begin? However, the subject of this investigation was the loss of a Supermarine Attacker which, as well as being Britain's first carrier-based jet fighter, had direct Spitfire ancestry; not to mention there only being one surviving example in the world.

The Attacker was originally developed as an interim measure for the RAF to fulfil an immediate need for a jet fighter, but was rejected, though the Admiralty showed an interest in it and in response Supermarine offered a navalised version of the Attacker for the consideration of the Fleet Air Arm (F.A.A.). The design was derived from the unsuccessful Supermarine Spiteful, a direct development of, and intended replacement for, the Spitfire, which used a new laminar flow wing, which was hoped to offer better high-speed performance. However, initial handling problems and marginal performance figures meant that it was not taken up by the RAF, which was now looking towards jet propulsion for its future fighters. The new jet aircraft had been designed alongside the Spiteful project and used the former aircrafts complete wing, housing four 20mm cannon and wide-tracked undercarriage and was initially referred to as the Jet Spiteful, the prototype first flying on the 27 July 1946. This meant that the Attacker retained the conventional propeller aircraft undercarriage layout using a tail wheel, rather than the more conventional nose wheel jet layout. The first navalised prototype flew on 17 June 1947 and the first production aircraft (the F1) flew in April 1950, becoming the first jet aircraft to enter F.A.A. front line service in August 1951. In 1952, in response to a need for ground-attack capability, the wing was strengthened and attachment points for bomb pylons were fitted to create the FB1 (fighter-bomber) version.

Researching the incident brought a number of surprises: the first

111

and most worrying, being that there appeared to be no record of the burial of the pilot, secondly and less surprising was that there was no accident card available – the records for all aircraft in F.A.A. service prior to 1952 were officially destroyed in 1956 and it seems that few records pre-1954 actually survive either. Further enquiries with the Fleet Air Arm Museum did elicit photocopies of the squadron diary entry relating to the crash, but we were informed that details of the Board of Inquiry were still held by the MoD and not available to the public. What at first sight had seemed a relatively straight-forward reasearch project was rapidly turning out to be far more complicated and frustrating than investigating a wartime loss! However, we had recently discovered that in addtion to the traditional Aviation Archeaologists source – the Form 1180, even in wartime, a number of accidents were more thoroughly investigated and copies of the Board of Inquiry reports for these incidents could be found at the Public Record Office (P.R.O.) at Kew. Furthermore, these reports were indexed online and whilst checking through the listings, one of our members spotted a familiar serial number, WA 535.

The report, when it arrived, was indeed detailed, though not complete, as it seems that the document deposited at Kew, was only a copy and not the original, so most of the attachements, including photographs and eye-witness statements taken by Lancashire Constabulary, were missing. However, as the list of attachments mentioned photos of the pilot's remains, this was perhaps for the best, though it did at least indicate that he had been recovered. One attachment that was still present was a map of the crash site, with the positions of all the identified parts found at the scene, together with key landmarks, meaning that for the first time on an excavation we had a document showing exactly where the aircraft would lie.

There was of course still the matter of ensuring that the pilot, Roy Collingwood, had indeed been recovered and this too was solved by a series of fortunate coincidences. Being a post 31 December 1947 casualty, we knew that the Commonwealth War Graves Commission (C.W.G.C.) database would not be able to help and we had already tried the Ministry of defence (MOD) without success. Our first clue came from local newspaper reports, which in addition to the name of the pilot, mentioned that he was from Thorpe Bay in Essex, so contact was made with local enthusiasts to see if his grave had been noted in the area. Initially this proved fruitless and contact was made with the Fleet Air Arm Association and we were fortunate in being able to track down, through them, a former collegue of the pilot: Arthur Stewart who attended No. 15 Rating Pilots Course with him. From information gained through this source, we discovered that he had been a Korean veteran and this piece of information was to prove to be the key. Another member of the association had been checking on unmaintained former servicemen's graves in the Essex area and he had noted that an unmarked grave of a Korean veteran lay at Holy Trinity Church, Southchurch, an area of Southend-on-Sea adjacent to Thorpe Bay. A quick check of the burial register and it proved this indeed was the grave of our pilot and it is now maintained by the Association.

Roy Edwin Collingwood was an only child born in Thorpe Bay, Essex circa 1930. He joined the Navy at HMS *Daedalus* (Royal Naval Air Station (RNAS) Lee-on-Solent), which, after the end of WW2, remained the headquarters of the Fleet Air Arm. He entered the service as a Probationary Pilot with No. 15 Rating Pilots Course in July/August 1948, being one of the successful twenty out of around eighty initial entrants, after aptitude tests and medical examinations. He went on to train at RAF Syerston in Nottinghamshire, which had been transferred to No.23 (Flying Training) Group on 7 January 1948, becoming No.22 Flying Training School after the 1 February, when No.22 Service Flying Training School (S.F.T.S.) arrived. This unit specialised in training pilots for the Fleet Air Arm using Tiger Moth and Harvard aircraft. On the 5 April 1950 he gained his flying wings/badge, one of only six of the original twenty to qualify, becoming a Pilot Fourth Class and paid 7/6d a day. He then moved on to complete Part 1 of the Operational Flying School Course (OFS 1) with No. 766 Squadron, Fleet Air Arm, flying Fireflies and Seafires at

Mr Roy Edwin Collingwood in the cockpit of a Sea Fury during the Korean War, during which he carried out over 100 operational sorties. (*Arthur Stewart*)

HMS *Fulmar* (RNAS Lossiemouth). For Part 2 of his Operational Flying School Course (OFS 2), he moved to HMS *Seahawk* (RNAS Culdrose), flying Seafire F.XVIIs and Sea Furies with No. 738 Squadron, part of the Naval Air Fighter School. Here he was trained for operational flying, including air-to-air and air-to-ground firing in preparation for allocation to his first squadron. He joined No. 807 Squadron, based at HMS *Gannet* (RNAS Eglinton in Northern Ireland), probably shortly before they embarked on the Light Fleet Carrier HMS *Theseus*, departing for Hong Kong. This had been the first Naval Air Squadron to be equipped with the Hawker Sea Fury, F Mk. Xs in August 1947 and had now been re-equipped with the new F.B. Mk. IIs and was on its way to play its part in the war in Korea, which had broken out on the 25 June 1950.

When *Theseus* sailed from Hong Kong on Monday 2 October, there had been some concern that the new Sea Furies would present identification problems with other friendly pilots and all aircraft were to be painted with additional recognition stripes to help avoid this. The period from the 9 to 11 of October saw the first air attacks directed against enemy defences and communications. Operations continued through October, hitting supply lines, bridges, and other targets of opportunity. Nineteen out of the twenty Sea Furies, and eleven or twelve out of twelve Fireflies, carried on *Theseus* being operational at any one time. In all *Theseus* completed ten operational patrols during her tour of duty, up to the 23 April 1951. In that time her aircraft flew 3446 operational sorties, mainly in the close-support role, in eighty-six operational flying days, for the loss of only three pilots killed and one taken prisoner.

By now using the official title 'Mr.' denoting commissioned status for a Naval Pilot, he returned to Britain with *Theseus* in May and following a refit, No. 807 Squadron remained with the carrier, to be based at Gibraltar and then in early 1952 at Malta. In October 1952, he moved to No. 767 Squadron, a second-line unit, based at HMS *Blackcap* (RNAS Stretton) in October 1952 and in December he went to Culdrose for a short Jet Conversion Course with No. 759 Naval Air Squadron, an element of the Naval Air Fighter School there, equipped with Meteor T.7 trainers and Sea Vampires. Following his return to Stretton, No. 767 Squadron received its first jet aircraft on the 16 January 1953 – Supermarine Attacker WA 535.

Supermarine Attacker WA535 was completed as an FB. Mk.1 variant and was built at Vickers-Supermarine's South Marston factory near Swindon. It was ready for collection on 21 March 1952 and was delivered initially to the Royal Navy Test Squadron, 'C'

Supermarine Attacker FB.1 WA535 at Supermarine's airfield at South Marston, Wiltshire, in August 1952 (*Author's collection*)

Squadron, at the Aeroplane & Armament Experimental Establishment, Boscombe Down on loan on 31 March 1952 for clearance trials of the fully sealed elevator. The aircraft was subsequently flown to the Vickers test airfield at Chilbolton, Hampshire on 9 May 1952 and then back to South Marston on 4 June. On the 9 October 1952 WA535 was finally delivered to the Royal Navy Aircraft Holding Unit at Abbotsinch (today Glasgow Airport) where it was prepared for service, before being allocated to No.767 Squadron. WA535 only flew for a total of forty-one hours and no code is known to have been allocated to the aircraft.

An experienced pilot, Lieutenant F.D. Bailey from No. 803 Squadron based at RNAS Ford, an operational Attacker Squadron, was loaned to Stretton to instruct the three pilots selected, including Mr. Collingwood, on the new type. Each pilot was required to carry out four formal familiarisation (Famil) flights under the guidance of Lieutenant Bailey, but due to other commitments, this officer was replaced and it seems that Roy only received briefings for his first two flights. On Thursday 5 February 1953 he took off from RNAS Stretton near Warrington in Supermarine Attacker FB.1, serial No. WA535 on what was to be his third Famil flight at 15:30 and at 15:32 he was given the signal 'Go' on Channel Baker. Shortly after, at 15:37, he was called up by Mr Lines, a commissioned Pilot, who was then flying a Meteor aircraft. In the course of a short conversation Mr Collingwood said he was flying at 17,000 feet and was climbing, presumably to the necessary height in order to carry out a high speed run which he was required to perform during this flight. Nothing further was heard from Mr Collingwood, but at 15:58 news was received at Stretton from

Manchester Zone Control at Ringway aerodrome that an unidentified aircraft had crashed near Burtonwood. Efforts were made to call up Mr Collingwood on all frequencies, an aircraft being diverted from ADDLS (Assisted Dummy Deck Landings) to call for him on Channel Baker, but there was no response. In the meantime, air traffic control at Stretton contacted Burtonwood by telephone for further details and were informed that a jet aircraft of unknown type had been seen to crash at 15:50, in a position 3 miles east of the base and that the USAF had sent out their crash services. The aircraft already diverted to call for the missing pilot was now vectored to a position east of Burtonwood to search for the crashed aircraft and at 16:16 the pilot reported that he was over the scene, but was unable to identify the crashed aircraft.

A party from Stretton was despatched to the scene of the crash at 16:30, including personnel from the station's crash services, the Duty Air Traffic Controller and the Inspection Officer, to identify formally the aircraft. On arrival, they found that all required action had already been taken by the USAF personnel, who had extinguished the fire and had posted guards. Additionally, the local police were also on the scene and arrangements were made for them to collect eyewitness statements. The aircraft had apparently entered the very soft and waterlogged ground at an approximately vertical attitude, with no evidence of an oblique entry. The resulting crater was approximately 10 feet in depth and filling with water. The main planes had sheared off and been reduced to small fragments in the impact, leaving linear impressions to each side of the main crater and debris had been spread over a wide area to a distance of 100 yards from the impact point, mainly in an easterly direction. Most of the parts of the aircraft, which remained on the surface, had been reduced to small, crumpled and unidentifiable fragments of metal. Only a few larger, recognisable components lay amongst the debris, such as the main wheel oleo struts, but one portion of wreckage was recovered which bore the aircraft's serial number, WA535. Over the next few days, all surface debris was removed, which included the remains of the pilot, whom it was concluded had initiated ejection in the last moments before impact – far too late to save himself. Attempts were also made to uncover the buried remains and the nozzle of the jet pipe was uncovered by digging to a depth of 6 feet, using two pumps working continuously, as the hole rapidly refilled with water as soon as pumping was suspended.

According to the Naval Board of Inquiry convened on the 10 February, the aircraft was embedded in unstable waterlogged soil to a depth of 20-25 feet and would probably require an operation using a drag-line excavator to recover. In light of the witness statements already taken and after consulting with a civil engineer, who found it difficult to produce a firm estimate, the board decided that nothing of value would be obtained by the salvage of the wreckage and its recovery was abandoned. Arrangements were then made with the farmer for the erection of a wire fence around the crater and for periodical visits to be made by Naval personnel to the site to ensure no unauthorised excavation had taken place. This fence stood for many years until the crater was filled in and all traces of the crash removed.

Although he had only been with the squadron since October 1952, Roy Collingwood, aged 22, had become an extremely popular squadron member and would have undoubtedly been much missed. He was buried in Holy Trinity Church, Southchurch, Southend-on-Sea on the 13 February 1953.

In the absence of material evidence, the witness statements put before the Board of Inquiry were crucial and the key witness proved to be Captain Van Horn, a USAF pilot, who was on the tarmac at Burtonwood when he saw an aircraft approach from a distance of 3 to 4 miles from the west, and kept it in view until he saw it enter the ground at a point to the north-east.

When I first saw the aircraft it was approaching slightly from the north-west at about 3000 feet, gradually loosing height and increasing in speed, but it appeared that the aircraft was under control. As the aircraft reached the centre of the airfield it went into a climb and proceeded in a vertical climb to a height of 8000 to 9000 feet. At the top of the climb the aircraft 'winged' over left and went into a vertical dive. It still appeared that the aircraft was under control and I expected it to pull out of the dive. But it continued diving to earth without, as far as I could see, any apparent effort to pull out and then I realised there was something wrong.

However, the board were unable to draw any definite conclusion as to the cause of the crash, though they did note that the unusual manoeuvres witnessed by Captain Van Horn, could be due to the pilots inexperience on the type. They were not satisfied that proper instruction had been given to Mr Collingwood and that he may not have been aware of the aircraft's tendency to nose down when approaching compressibility and therefore would have adjusted his elevator trim to nose up in order to counteract this. As the aircraft left the zones of compressibility the aircraft would have considerable nose-up trim causing the aircraft to go into a vertical climb at the top of

117

which the pilot loses control and dives to earth. The board also noted that Anoxia [a deficiency of oxygen] could equally have explained the unusual behaviour of the aircraft, as seen by the witness, but of course there was no equipment found to check. Finally, they considered the possibilities of unauthorised aerobatics and jamming of controls by loose equipment, but thought the latter two explanations unlikely.

A few days later, however, further evidence came to light after another witness came forward. A local man, Mr Hambling, had been waiting to catch a bus in Leach Lane, a few miles from the crash site towards Rainhill, when he saw the Attacker flying over the road in a very fast, inverted shallow dive. As he watched, he saw an object fall away from the aircraft as it climbed steeply into the clouds, which then crashed into the street and at the same time a distinct thud was also heard behind some nearby houses. A search was made and parts including the canopy rails and pilots helmet were found on near-by farmland about 2 miles from the crash site. Later still, the remains of the canopy itself were discovered in a dismantled state on a nearby farm, where the perspex had been removed to be used as domestic firelighters. The Board of Inquiry was reconvened and in light of the evidence, ruled that Anoxia was considered to be the most likely cause of the accident. The manoeuvres performed by the aircraft were noted as consistent with an aircraft flying itself with very little assistance from the pilot. The jettisoning of the canopy and a possible attempt at ejection at the moment of impact also pointed to a certain amount of returning consciousness to the pilot. They presumed that the pilot became Anoxic in the climbing attitude with nose-up trim set on the aircraft, which then stalled and went into a dive, from which, with increasing airspeed, it recovered and went into a climb due to the trim. From this climb the aircraft again stalled and repeated the manoeuvre, gradually loosing height. It would appear the pilot's helmet had been unfastened and when the canopy left the aircraft, the slipstream buffeting in the cockpit was sufficient to lift the helmet off the pilot's head and out of the cockpit.

Having satisfied ourselves and the MoD that the pilot's remains had indeed been recovered shortly after the accident, a permit was duly issued and we began our investigation of the actual crash site. Our initial attempt to pinpoint the site at an early stage in our research had proved far from promising, with only one or two small crumpled fragments being found. However, we had been relying solely on accounts from eyewitnesses who had been kept well clear of the impact point by the personnel guarding the site. With the documentary evidence we had now amassed, we were able to identify the correct field and using the map, walk straight to the site – in fact we then had to retrace our steps as it proved impossible to tune our detecting equipment due to being stood directly over the buried wreck! The contacts indicated by both our Fisher and Forster machines were indeed major, though with this being our first Jet impact-site and we are not quite sure what to expect. However, having come this far, we decided to attempt a recovery that, according to the records at the time of the crash, was thought to be impossible!

Following discussions with the Landowner, arrangements were made to hire a suitable excavator from a local firm and a date was set for the excavation to fit in with the farmer's crops. On the day of the dig, in September 2003, the weather was glorious and the water table, that had defeated the authorities 50 years before, was at the lowest in living memory. Though the Board of Inquiry report stated that some 75% of the aircraft remained unrecovered, we were still a little apprehensive as to how recognisable what was left would be. At first very little came to light, then at approximately 6 feet down in the very sandy subsoil we uncovered the end of the stainless steel jet-pipe – exactly where the recovery team reported it to be when they dug down to it in 1953. Digging carefully each side of this revealed a mass of compacted wreckage just below, thankfully not 25-30 feet below as the recovery team had estimated!

Soon we were finding recognisable pieces including the complete arrester hook, the Attacker's distinctive double-tail wheel assembly, oxygen bottles, armour plate etc. The engine proved to have shattered

Perfect weather as the excavation of WA535 progresses.

Above: **LAIT** members carefully recovering the dinghy and parachute pack.

Left: **A remarkable find considering the force of impact and destruction of so much of the aircraft, was this almost intact survival suit, carried in case of ditching in the sea.**

Right: **Also from the pilot's survival pack, this dinghy was complete with paddles, emergency repair kit, water-filter, ration packs and sea anchor.**

The intact turbine from the engine, amazingly heavy and still coated in oil.

but even the pieces proved awkward and very heavy, including a remarkably intact turbine disk and several flattened combustion chambers. By now we were at a depth of some 10 to 12 feet and digging was halted as a couple of volunteers descended to recover the emergency dinghy which had been revealed. This was soon followed by a complete, folded immersion suit and a parachute, still in its pack – sad reminders of the fate of the pilot.

The trail of wreckage petered out at approximately 15 feet in depth and amongst the last finds were the nose armour-plate bulkhead and a large compacted mass which proved to be the instrument panels, radio remains, batteries and the fixed nose balance weight – all welded together with the force of the impact. Careful sorting through the spoil as the hole was back-filled brought other smaller artefacts to light, including survival ration tins, an almost intact survival manual, throttle levers, remains of a few badly fragmented instruments and controls, as well as literally dozens of turbine stator blades. With the site reinstated and a bit of extra work replacing the field drain that crossed the crater, to ensure that it would not sink as the soil settled, we all agreed that this had been a most worthwhile excavation.

As usual a few further artefacts were discovered during the cleaning and sorting process, including the compass face, the Exhaust temperature gauge and a fragment of a book that proved to be the 'Pilot's Notes' booklet for the Supermarine Attacker! There were still a couple of surprises though over the next few weeks as more items were cleaned. One complete oxygen bottle had been recovered and on examining the inspection stamps we were amazed to see that it had been manufactured in 1944! A makers plate from the hydraulic actuator, showed that the component had been manufactured in Warrington, just down the road from the crash site and finally, whilst unfolding the remarkably intact dinghy, it was found that a small section had been torn out and was missing – on checking the list of identified parts recovered from the surface just after the crash, there was an entry for 'piece of dinghy fabric 8in x 8in' exactly matching the hole!

Only the rear section of the Rolls Royce Nene engine remained in one piece and is seen here on display at Millom.

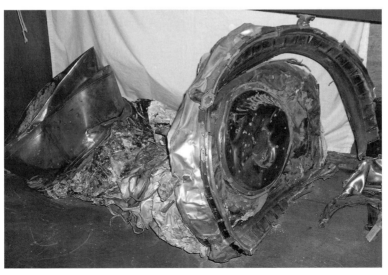

CHAPTER THIRTEEN

A LONG WAY FROM HOME

Many hill walkers still come across the scattered fragments of long lost aircraft whilst tramping across the moors and the regular emails our group's website receives from such fresh-air enthusiasts, asking for further information about such finds clearly vouches for their interest. One classic North-west high ground crash site, which for many years remained unidentified, is that of an RAF Mustang I and for a single engined fighter, a surprising amount of airframe lies exposed. It lies just off the beaten track in one of the most popular walking areas for visitors to the picturesque Forest of Bowland. Its Canadian pilot was a long way from home and was sadly killed when his aircraft struck the hillside in poor visibility.

Early in the Second World War, the British Government looked to the Dominions for the training of much needed Air Force personnel, as it had soon been realised that British airfields were already becoming over-crowded with wartime air traffic, not to mention their vulnerability to enemy attack. In December 1939 an agreement was signed, setting up the British Commonwealth Air Training Plan (BCATP), involving Britain, Canada, Australia, New Zealand, South Africa and Southern Rhodesia. The aim was to provide some 50,000 trained aircrew a year, for the duration of the conflict and each country was to provide a quota of trainees and take on a proportion of the costs. Canada was to be the most important location for the plan due to its wide-open spaces, suitable for navigation training, aircraft production industries and geographical location. Under the agreement, aircrews were to receive their elementary training in the various Commonwealth countries involved, before travelling to Canada for advanced instruction. Initially the participating countries understood that their recruits would be assigned to designated national squadrons within the RAF, but in practice they were often assigned to British units and this would be a source of tension between Britain and the other countries throughout the war. By the time the programme came to an end in March 1945 over half (72,835) of the 131,553 graduates were Canadians.

Flying Officer Sholto Paton Marlatt RCAF was one of these trainees; he came from Cranberry Lake, a suburb of Powell River, British Columbia, Canada, where he attended Brentwood College

School and was a graduate of the University of British Columbia. It seems he enjoyed his time at university and was a keen piano player and jazz enthusiast and was often to be found in the orchestra pit at the campus theatre during impromptu musical sessions with fellow musicians, sometimes, it was noted, to the neglect of his studies. Known as 'Hob' to his friends, he had a reputation as a stylish dresser and was also an active member of the university's dramatic society. On his graduation he had become an accountant, as well as assisting his long time friend Jim Spilsbury with his marine radio business, accompanying him on boat trips to isolated communities to install or repair equipment. Perhaps they also had a mutual interest in

Flying Officer Sholto Paton Marlatt RCAF, circa 1941. (Marlatt family)

aviation, as Spilsbury bought his first aircraft in 1943, eventually ending up with a fleet of thirty aircraft and Canada's third largest airline by 1955.

Hob enlisted with the RCAF at the Vancouver Recruiting Centre on 24 October 1940 and as he had recently married, his wife Vera travelled to be with him during his early training, as did many young Air Force wives at the time. He was posted overseas in July 1941, leaving his wife in Canada, expecting their first child. It is not known exactly when he arrived in the UK, but at the time of his accident he had some 574 solo flying hours to his credit, including 132 on Mustangs, in addition to 54 hours instructional flying time and 99 hours on the Link trainer. He is believed to have only served with No. 4 (RAF) Squadron, which, though not a designated Canadian squadron, did have other RCAF personnel already attached, including Flight Lieutenant W. S. Barton, who was awarded the DFC in July 1940.

No. 4 (RAF) Squadron was assigned to Army Co-operation duties, equipped with Lysanders, and in October 1939 they were based in France with the British Expeditionary Force. Because of their slow speed and ability to land and take-off from unprepared ground, the

Lysanders were considered suitable for these duties and were largely used for reconnaissance and photography. However, they were also very vulnerable to enemy fighters and anti-aircraft fire and of some 170 Lysanders sent to France, with Army Co-operation units, only fifty came back. As all attempts to halt the German advance failed and the retreat from Dunkirk began, No. 4 was the last RAF Squadron to leave France, with German motorcyclists literally appearing on the far side of their airfield, as the last truck carrying the Squadrons ground staff was leaving!

The Squadron returned home in May 1940, and switched to coastal patrol and air-sea rescue duties, patrolling the coastal areas of south and east England at dawn and dusk as an anti-invasion reconnaissance measure. It was planned that in the event of an invasion the Lysanders would bomb and machine-gun German troops on the beaches. On the 27 of August 1940 they arrived at RAF Clifton, near York. The base was still being developed into a full RAF Base. Originally intended to be York's airport, it was taken over in 1939 by the Air Ministry as a dispersal airfield for bombers from the nearby RAF station at Linton-on-Ouse. Here this squadron returned to its Army Co-operation role, still equipped with Westland Lysanders. With the continuing threat of invasion, it continued to be employed on coastal patrols and was also trained in dropping mustard gas should this have taken place. However, its usual duties included co-operating with the army on exercises, and even with the Home Guard at times.

No. 4 Squadron, was based at Clifton up until March 1943 and their Lysander aircraft remained in use until April 1942 when they were replaced by Curtiss Tomahawk Is. Though the Tomahawk II fighter saw operational use in North Africa with the RAF, a batch of Mk.I aircraft had also been received, but were considered unsuitable for combat use. These earlier aircraft had been intended for a French order, but were diverted to Britain when France was overrun in 1940. They were therefore fitted with French equipment and instruments, as well as lacking self-sealing fuel tanks and armour to protect their pilots. Consequently, these Tomahawk Mk.Is were relegated to reconnaissance duties, though by 1942, maintenance problems meant that their usefulness was further limited and their time with the squadron was shortlived.

However, by February 1942 the first of the new North American Mustang I fighter aircraft were reaching RAF squadrons and after initial trials, the RAF decided to use the Mustang in the Tactical Reconnaissance role with its Army Co-operation squadrons as a replacement for the Curtiss Tomahawk. During testing, their long range and excellent low-level performance were judged useful for ground-attack duties, but it had soon become evident that the Mustang's performance at higher altitudes was not up to the standard of other fighters in the European theatre at that stage. No. 26 Squadron at Gatwick, was the first to be equipped and by June 1942 most of the Squadrons, including No. 4 had been re-equipped with the new fighter. These Mustang Mk Is were armed with four 0.50-in machine guns and four 0.30-inch guns, with two of the 0.50-in guns mounted in the underside of the nose beside the engine crankcase and synchronized to fire through the propeller arc, with the rest of the guns being mounted in the wings. For their Reconnaissance role, they had an F-24 camera mounted immediately behind the pilot's head armour, looking obliquely out to the left and to the rear. Later, a second camera was installed vertically ahead in the rear fuselage for photography from higher altitudes.

Twenty-nine-year-old, Flying Officer Sholto Paton Marlatt took off in Mustang Mk I serial No. AP208 at approximately 10.20 on the morning of Sunday 29 November 1942 from No. 4 Squadron's airfield at RAF Clifton near York, having been detailed to undertake a non-operational photographic sortie. His aircraft had apparently not deviated from its assigned course when only some 20 minutes later it struck the bleak, mist shrouded, moorland above a natural crag known as Holdron Castle near Dunsop Bridge in the Forest of Bowland. It would appear that he was heading towards the relatively flat coastal area to the west, beyond the high ground that he was flying over and it is likely that he believed he had already cleared the hills and he started to descend through the low cloud. His route would have already taken him over the Pennines, probably skirting the lower edge of the Yorkshire Dales where several peaks rising over 2000 feet above sea level lay to the north and no doubt his pre-flight briefing and previous experience would have made him aware of this. Even the less substantial Bowland peaks still rise up to 1800 feet high and he had yet to clear the area's last major obstacle, a final ridge of high fells including Haythornthwaite Fell which, at just under 1600 feet, lay almost directly in his path. The aircraft ploughed into the gently sloping moor at approximately 1200 feet above sea level, still flying at cruising speed, breaking up on impact and killing the Canadian pilot instantly.

Parts of the shattered Mustang were strewn over a wide area and following the recovery of the body of the pilot, the maintenance unit assigned to clear the wreckage used the simple expedient of burying much of the aircraft where it lay. Hob Marlatt was laid to rest in

Above: **Small parts of AP208 lie scattered across the moor at the crash site today.**

Left: **Author's son with a large piece from the centre section of AP208 revealed following a recent moorland fire.**

Lytham St Annes (Park) Cemetery, Lancashire, Grave Reference No. 731. Back home in Canada, his relatives were devastated at the loss of this lively and talented young man. Hob's son, whom he never saw, was less than a year old and Hob's father had apparently owned a cine camera and sent some home movie footage of the baby to England. Sadly, Hob Marlatt was still trying to arrange the loan of a projector to view the film when he was killed.

Many of the parts of AP208 that still lie at the crash site today, have probably been uncovered, from where they were buried by the recovery crew, by enthusiasts in recent years. Indeed at least two groups are known to have carried out excavations on the site and many parts have been removed including a 0.50 calibre machine gun, propeller blade, oxygen bottles and smaller components such as instruments from the cockpit. Unfortunately, many such artefacts taken from high ground wreck-sites are often later discarded once the finder's curiosity subsides' and even the whereabouts of officially recovered items can often be impossible to ascertain.

Over the years the author has been able to at least view a few of the major finds from this site, though none are on public display at present. Additionally, several years ago a small box of artefacts from AP208 was donated to our collection including the oxygen regulator gauge, the remains of Hob's leather flying helmet (found lodged amongst the heather in the late 1960s), a fragment of the instrument panel and several components from the Allison-1710-F3R engine. Recently a small manufacturer's data plate from one of the Mustang's wing flaps and a representative piece of twisted airframe were collected together, to be sent to Canada with photographs of the crash site as a tangible memento for the relatives of Flying Officer Sholto Paton Marlatt. His two sisters are now in their nineties and his son, Alan, is now a grandfather. Sadly, his widow passed away recently. Today several sizeable pieces of AP208 lie at the site, forming an unofficial memorial to this Canadian pilot. The most recognisable items being sections of wing flaps and self-sealing fuel cells, lying amidst many scattered smaller fragments of aluminium aircraft structure. On a recent visit to the site these remains were found to have been further exposed by recent moorland fires that have burnt off much of the heather and a large section of wing root had been revealed, which amazingly for an artefact of this size, had not been visible on previous visits. No doubt the moorland vegetation will soon reclaim the site, but a few parts should remain visible to the observant walker to ponder upon before continuing on their way.

Oxygen regulator gauge picked up on the surface at the crash site several years ago.

CHAPTER FOURTEEN

BERLIN AIRLIFT

With the defeat of Germany at the end of the Second World War, the country was divided and occupied by the Allied powers, with Britain, France, the United States, and the Soviet Union each controlling a zone. As the capital of Germany, Berlin, fell inside the larger area, controlled by the Soviet Union, it too was divided into four sectors and a provisional government was set up, based in the city, to oversee the rebuilding of the country. However by 1948 cracks were beginning to appear in this policy of joint government of the occupied former enemy and tension was mounting over how the new Germany should be developed, particularly with regard to reunifying the country. As the policies of the other Allies put pressure the Soviets to compromise, they responded by becoming increasingly uncooperative and finally on 24 June 1948 by closing all access to traffic, by land or water, into or out of the western Allied-controlled sectors of Berlin. This left the only remaining access routes into the city via three 20 mile-wide air corridors across the eastern Soviet controlled zone of Germany. As diplomacy failed, the western Allies became even more determined to maintain their presence in the City and plans were drawn up to supply Berlin's inhabitants and the Occupying Force by air and on the 26 June, the United States began Operation Vittles, when thirty-two flights by United States Air Force (USAF) C-47s brought some 80 tons of food into Berlin. Two days later British Aircraft joined the effort and the French contributed also, in what was to become the Berlin Airlift – one of the greatest humanitarian endeavours and aviation feats of all time.

Initially at least, the airlift got off to a shaky start, with the USAF only having 102 C-47s available for the operation, which could deliver approximately 300 tons a day, while the British contribution was about 750 tons. This 1050 tons per day was nowhere near the estimated requirement of 4500 tons per day and the C-47 Skytrains, with their two to three ton load capacity, were phased out in favour of the 10 ton capacity of the C-54 Skymaster and this aircraft became the workhorse of the airlift. Soon pilots were flying using an extremely rigid system of traffic control which required each pilot to fly an exact route at predetermined speed and altitude, with aircraft flying at three levels along the corridors and allowing for landing at the rate of one plane every three minutes. In addition to the dangers of such intensive flying, pilots also faced regular Soviet harassment in the form of radio jamming, searchlights directed at aircraft at night, buzzing of cargo planes by Russian fighters and barrage balloons allowed to drift into the air corridors. However, the western Allies remained determined to maintain the airlift and aircraft and crews were required to fly longer hours than had previously thought possible and the USAF soon devised a system to keep their planes in the air the longest.

The first C-54 aircraft had arrived at the American Rhein-Main Air Force Base, near Frankfurt in Germany on 28 June 1948 to join the massive effort supplying Berlin during the harsh winter of the Russian blockade. The Skymasters, with their large cargo capacity and easier loading were sorely needed, as large quantities of coal were now required to be flown into the city in addition to the other essential supplies. By the beginning of July, the C-54s were slowly taking over airlift flights, and were operating 24 hours a day, with Rhein-Main Air Base now an exclusively C-54 base. By January 1949 they had been instrumental in increasing the tonnage from approximately 3000 to some 5500 tons of supplies a day flown into the city, though the toll on men and machines of this non-stop effort was beginning to show. Even though the USAF aircraft were inspected every 50 hours, they were required to be taken out of service for a more thorough check every 200 hours flying time, though this was still double the 100 hours for RAF operated aircraft.

Soon American servicing facilities at Oberpfaffenhofen, near Munich, were stretched to the limit. To cope with the workload, from November 1948, the huge wartime Base Air Depot 1 (BAD1) at Burtonwood was selected to undertake inspection and overhaul of some of the overworked aircraft taking part in the airlift. With over 300 of the aproximately 400 C- 54s in service, hauling supplies to the city at the height of the Berlin Airlift, the BAD1 Base came into its own as the main servicing and overhaul centre for all the US aircraft taking part in the operation. Once again Burtonwood became a hive of activity and was soon despatching five newly overhauled C-54s per day back to Rhine-Main.

As the airlift continued a further problem became apparent to the USAF personnel maintaining the C-54s as they found that the Pratt & Whitney R-2000 radial engines used on these aircraft suffered rapid and excessive wear as a result of the continual short-range operations. Although a dedicated maintenance facility was established at Rhein-Main Air Base to cope with the routine servicing and repair of these engines, there was soon a steady stream of R-2000s requiring return to the United States, for more major overhaul and full rebuilds, before being quickly returned to Europe for fitting to aircraft continuing the airlift. As with the airlift itself, no flight was to be wasted and soon aircraft leaving Germany and returning to England or the United States for inspections and maintenance also transported engines and other components for repair and rebuild. Then on their return to Germany they would bring back the rebuilt engines and other spare parts for the airlift aircraft.

One such aircraft was C-54 D, serial No. 45-543 which had been built in July 1945 and was assigned to the 48th Troop Carrier Squadrons (Heavy) (TCS(H)), 313th Troop Carrier Group (TCG) of the 9th Air Force, based at Bergstrom Air Force Base at Austin, Texas. The unit's C-54s were sent to the Rhein-Main Air Base on the 29 June 1948 and No. 45-543 was attached to the 61st TCG, comprising 14th, 15th, 17th, 53rd Troop Carrier Squadrons (Heavy) of the Combined Airlift Task Force (CALTF). The aircraft had been allocated to the 14th TCS (H) and had last been serviced on 23 November 1948 and when it took off from Rhein Main on the 7 January en route for Burtonwood for its 200 hour service, it was in fact some 38 hours overdue for this work.

The aircraft took off at 13.12, after a delay due to loading difficulties, for the estimated two hour forty-five minute flight via Amsterdam, Horsham St Faith and Shawbury. On board were four crew, two passengers and cargo believed to include a number of aircraft engines being returned via Burtonwood for major overhaul and medical supplies. The pilot, First Lieutenant Richard M. Wurgel had received a written report on the forecast weather conditions along the route, as well as a verbal briefing and in light of the expected conditions, the flight was recommended under Instrument Flight Rules (IFR). Although the C-54 was slightly over-loaded, this was not considered a problem as neither the pilot or Operations at the base regarded the additional 200 lb over the gross allowable weight, as excessive. The pilot was noted as having utilised the delay to good effect, completing the required paperwork in Operations prior to take-off, including adding details of a second passenger, Private R. E. Stone, who boarded the aircraft at the last minute and after the forms had been completed. At 16.28 the aircraft was past its estimated time of arrival, but all seemed well as it arrived over Shawbury and the radio operator Corporal Norbert H. Theis made contact with the Station and was given a bearing for Liverpool and told to make radio contact with Liverpool Approach Control. However his attempts to make contact were unsuccessful, but satisfactory contact was made at 16.30 with Burtonwood. The pilot, estimated his position using his instruments and the following conversation with the Air Traffic Service Officer,

Captain James E. Pound at Burtonwood Tower was recorded after one of the Tower operators had managed to gain clearance for the aircraft from Liverpool Control via the telephone.

"Burtonwood Tower this is 45543, over"

"45543 this is Burtonwood Tower. What is your present position and what are your flying conditions?"

"Tower, I am approximately 2 miles south of the field and have just broken clear of the clouds at 2200 feet. I will be completely VFR [Visual flight rules] in a few seconds, over"

"Roger 45543, this is Burtonwood Tower. Liverpool Control advises they have no known traffic in Control Zone and you are cleared into the Control Zone, over"

"45543 to Burtonwood Tower, Roger I am now completely VFR at 1700 feet"

"Burtonwood Tower, Roger. You are cleared to make a VFR approach. Advise tower before you encounter instrument conditions. For your information the Burtonwood Range may be used for homing purposes only on 214 kilocycles, over"

"Roger, 214 kilocycles"

The time was 16.42 and Captain Pound then turned the microphone over to the Chief Control Tower Operator on duty, Staff Sergeant Harold C. Skinner, for the local weather report and landing instructions to be given to the pilot. But the aircraft could no longer be raised, despite broadcasts on all transmitting frequencies. It later turned out that Liverpool Control had been monitoring the conversation between Burtonwood and 45-543, taking bearings on each transmission and had calculated that when the pilot had estimated his position as "approximately 2 miles south of the field [Burtonwood]", he was in fact between 10 to 15 miles to the north.

At approximately 16.40 witnesses on the ground near Garstang heard the aircraft's engines as it descended through the cloud and were surprised by the especially loud noise of an aircraft flying at such a low altitude. One witness, Mr Robert Salisbury, a delivery driver, was in the yard of a weaving mill at Calder-Vale, immediately below the flight path and startled by the noise, he looked up to see the plane appear out of the mist only some 80 feet above the ground. "As I looked up into the sky I saw an American Skymaster aeroplane directly over my head and the plane appeared to be about the height of the mill chimney". As the plane disappeared once gain into the cloud, he commented to a nearby workman that the plane would never clear the fells that it was now heading towards.

Just under 2 miles away, a Mr Edwin Rawlinson was in the yard of his farm at the foot of the fells on the edge of the Forest of Bowland, when his attention was also drawn by the noise of a plane flying unusually low. Both witnesses, however, noted that despite the unusual volume of the noise, they considered that the engines seemed to be running normally. Mr Rawlinson strained to see the direction in which the aircraft was travelling, but the mist and low cloud prevented him seeing even any lights as it passed overhead. Seconds later and probably before the pilot realised the danger of his situation, there was "a blinding red flash which lit all up, from the direction of Stake House Fell. The light did not last and gradually subsided and went clean out in a few seconds". Though the witness had heard no sound of a crash, due to the driving rain and strong winds, he realised that the flash he had seen through the mist was the C-54 exploding on impact. Also close to the impact was the Headmaster of the village school, Mr T.M. Muir and he also witnessed the flash and realised its significance, but, with the nearest telephone some distance away at the paper mill at Oakenclough, it was 17.23 before the alarm could be raised. Within 20 minutes of the call, some sixty men from Lancashire Constabulary and the County Fire Brigade were on the scene equipped with two-way radios, flares and portable searchlights and they made their way to the foot of the fell and began an organised search of the mist-shrouded moors. Some 2 hours later the first fragments of wreckage were spotted and the team, following this trail of debris, were soon confronted by the huge tail of the Skymaster lying on a steep slope just below the summit of the Fell. Two of the plane's occupants had been thrown clear of the wreck and lay some 100 yards from the shattered fuselage, the remainder of the crew were still trapped in the wreckage, but were obviously dead and due to the extreme weather conditions it was decided to leave the bodies where they lay until daylight.

Name	From	Position	Status
1st Lt. Richard M. Wurgel	Union City, New Jersey	Pilot	K.
1st Lt. Lowell A. Wheaton Jr.	Corpus Christi, Texas	Co-pilot	K.
Sgt. Bernard J. Watkins	Lafayette, Indiana	Engineer	K.
Cpl. Norbert H. Theis	Cunningham, Kansas	Radio Op	K.
Capt. W. A. Rathgeber	Portland, Oregon	Passenger	K.
Pte. Ronald. E. Stone	Mt. Sterling, Kentucky	Passenger	K.

The bodies of the Skymaster's crew and passengers were all recovered the following day by USAF personnel from Burtonwood, who also took over the task of guarding the wreck, the larger sections of which were later broken up and dragged off the moor after attempts to destroy it by burning apparently failed. Subsequent investigations into the cause of the crash found that a strong signal from a BBC radio station located to the North of the Burtonwood base was interfering with the Burtonwood Range signal. It was found that when set correctly, the radio compass on board an aircraft would continue to indicate that the base was further north even after the aircraft had passed to the north of the Range Station – following this incident the frequency was changed and the problem did not reoccur.

The final last-minute passenger who had boarded the C-54 in such a hurry at Rhein-Main for this fateful flight was twenty-year-old Private Ronald E. Stone, who had been previously stationed in Germany, but had been transferred to duties in England, where he had met and begun a relationship with a young lady. Having been called back to Germany on official business for a few days, he was naturally very keen to return to England to see his girlfriend as soon as was possible and to this end a friend pulled a few strings on his behalf, no doubt as a favour and got him on the next available flight back – C54 45-543! It seems that Ron Stone was coming to the end of his tour of duty and with a mind to the future had, in his letters home, expressed his desire to enter the clergy on his return. Sadly the dreams of this young man were not to be, as his life was tragically cut short on that bleak Lancashire hillside.

Pte. Ronald E. Stone, the last minute passenger on the fateful last flight of C54 45-543 (Gary L. Stone)

Despite being 2.5 miles from the nearest village it is known that many people visited the crash site shortly after the incident and that many items were taken from the wreck, apparently with the consent of the American servicemen guarding it. One of the first locals to reach the site the following morning described to us how the engines from the cargo lay scattered across the Fell together with many hypodermic syringes and glass medicine bottles. He also observed four bodies, laid out under one wing awaiting recovery, together with a dead dog – a pet of one of the passengers it would seem. The engines from the cargo and those from the plane itself (seven in total according to one witness) lay on the Fell for many years, until apparently recovered for scrap in the 1960s and medical supplies from the cargo were still to be found scattered below the crash up until several years ago. Today however, relatively little from such a large aircraft lies on the surface to remind us of the tragedy in 1949 and permission must be obtained from the estate manager, gamekeepers and farmer before visiting this site as it lies on a private grouse moor.

In October 2003 we set out to investigate rumours that substantial pieces of wreckage still lay at the crash site of this Berlin Airlift veteran. In the past we had taken as correct earlier reports that any remaining material had been removed by a local scrap merchant over 30 years ago.

Having obtained all the necessary permission to visit the site, we visited the farm at the foot of the Fell for last minute instructions on how to locate the site and advice on avoiding areas that had recently been sprayed with chemicals. On reaching the site there was indeed a surprising amount of aircraft remains lying in a hollow at the foot of a steep slope and difficult to see until we were almost upon them. Indeed one of our members who had attempted to locate the crash site, without success, on a previous occasion was amazed, as he had passed within 50 yards and not seen anything.

On examining the site, it became obvious that the plane impacted on a steep scree slope close to the summit of the Fell and had been dismantled and burned on the site, with the heavier items being rolled to the bottom and probably buried where they now lie, exposed by natural erosion.

No major engine parts remain at the site, these, it seems, having indeed been taken later for scrap and only four very rusty reduction gears were found. These appeared to have come from the aircraft's own engines, not those carried as cargo, as they had become separated from the engines when the reduction gear casings had been shattered on impact. All three undercarriage legs lie at the site, the two main oleos being intact and which are incredibly large and heavy forgings, with the smaller nose assembly being broken and only the upper section being visible on the surface. Finally, four stainless steel firewall and exhaust collector assemblies were found nearby, again believed to originate from the aircraft's own engines, as they all exhibit varying degrees of destruction, illustrating the force of impact at the time of the

135

The huge main undercarriage legs still lie at the base of the slope where the C-54 impacted.

crash. An examination of the loose scree slope revealed many small items jammed in amongst the rocks, including fragments of medicine bottles, melted radio valves (far too many to be from the aircraft's own radio equipment), cable tensioners, electrical components, cargo strap

Nearby engine firewalls, exhaust collector rings, propeller hubs and reduction gears, the gleaming stainless steel in stark contrast to the grey rock and heather covered moorland.

fittings and a stainless steel release cable from an airman's parachute.

During our research over the years, this particular crash site has often been mentioned by locals in the Forest of Bowland area, with an often-repeated tale of a visitor to the crash site being killed some years ago as a result of tampering with the wreckage. No dates or substantiated facts were ever given and we took these stories as good-natured warnings about the possible dangers of our hobby. Several quite different versions of the tale were recorded, usually involving a young farmer's daughter as the victim and the cause of her demise being exploding ordnance or toxic medical supplies from the cargo. Eventually, curiosity led us find out if there was any truth in the story and a tragic tale soon began to unfold that proved somewhat different from these accounts, but remains a sound warning none-the-less. The lady in question lived on a farm at Scorton, a few miles to the west of the crash site. Her brother had visited the wreck about a week after the crash and had found what he took to be a parachute pack, which he had brought home, presumably thinking that the fabric could be salvaged and put to good use. On the 23 January 1949, Miss Mabel Thompson, aged 42, began to unravel the parachute at her home at Clifton Farm, not realising that what she took to be a harmless bundle of fabric was in fact a phosphorous flare pack. When she reached the canister it burst into flames in her hands, causing serious burns. She was rushed to

Small fragments collected from the loose scree slope where the Skymaster burnt out, including: medicine bottle shards, radio parts and the release cable from a parachute.

hospital where her condition was described as 'very ill with severe burns' and she remained in the Royal Lancaster Infirmary until the 14 April when sadly she finally succumbed to her injuries.

On 12 May 1949 the Soviets agreed to lift the blockade on Berlin, but fearing further problems, the Airlift continued until 30 September 1949, when a C-54 Skymaster made the official last flight of the Berlin Airlift and Operation Vittles came to an end, with the city having received some 2,326,406 tons of supplies from the West. Today this remarkable humanitarian mission, in which memories of the recent conflict of World War II gave way to a new partnership, is commemorated by the Berlin Airlift memorial which stands in a small park at the Platz der Luftbrücke in front of Tempelhof Airport, Berlin. Inaugurated on the 10 July 1951, it is dedicated to the seventy-eight pilots and crew killed in crashes during the airlift. Their names are inscribed around the base of the memorial and a German inscription above reads: 'They gave their lives for the freedom of Berlin serving in the Airlift 1948 - 49'. The design of the monument is in the form of one half of an arch, dividing into three sections each representing the three air corridors along which the aircraft flew. A matching monument stands at the other end of the 'air bridge' at the former Rhein-Main Air Base, now Frankfurt Airport, completing the airlift arch. Among the thirty-one names of the United States casualties inscribed are six who whilst playing their part, lost their lives on that bleak Lancashire Fell in January 1949.

CHAPTER FIFTEEN

ABANDON AIRCRAFT!

The Boeing B-29 Superfortress is widely recognised as the largest and most powerful operational aircraft of World War Two. Designed as a replacement for the B-17 and B-24, it was the first to use a pressurised crew compartment, allowing it to maintain high altitudes out of reach of many of the fighters at the time. Also it featured remote-controlled turrets as defensive armament, allowing each gunner to take control of two or more turrets to concentrate firepower on a single target. However, its size and numerous innovative features meant that it was also one of the most sophisticated aircraft of its time and development problems delayed its introduction to combat service. Although it made its first flight in September 1942, it was April 1944 before the first operational B-29s were delivered and on 5 June of that year the first combat mission was flown, which proved to be the longest of the war to that date.

With the capture of islands closer to Japan, new airbases were set up and the B-29 came into its own, devastating much of Japan's industrial and economic infrastructure. However the B-29 is probably most remembered as the aircraft that delivered the first nuclear weapons used in combat, when on 6 August 1945, the B-29, serial number 44-86292 named *Enola Gay*, dropped an atomic bomb on Hiroshima, Japan. Three days later, another specially adapted Superfortress; named *Bockscar* dropped a second atomic bomb on Nagasaki, Japan. On 14 August 1945, the Japanese accepted Allied terms for unconditional surrender.

As the conflict came to a close, B-29s were used to drop food and clothing to inmates of prisoner of war camps, but all orders for new Superfortresses were cancelled and following the completion of several aircraft already partly built, production ceased in May 1946, with a total of 3967 B-29s having been built. The end of WW2 saw a large number of B-29s in the Air Force inventory, many 'war weary' and with most now considered to be rendered obsolete by the dawn of the new atomic age, what was to become of these armoured giants?

Pending the introduction of newly designed, long-range bombers, some sixty Superfortresses were modified to carry atomic weapons as a stop-gap measure, but for the majority of aircraft, new uses were found in the changing post-war environment. One of the more successful new roles for the B-29 was as the United States Air Force's first operational aerial refuelling aircraft with over 300 converted to various configurations as the techniques for in-flight refuelling developed. Other roles were soon found, utilising the B-29s extended range capability, with many converted as long range strategic reconnaissance aircraft and a few in the naval long-range maritime search role or as air-sea rescue aircraft with parachute dropped lifeboats. In 1950, in order to meet immediate British post-war needs for a long-range bomber, some eighty-seven B-29s were loaned to the RAF as another stop-gap measure, being designated as Washington Mk Is. These remained in RAF use as late as 1958, though they began to be returned in 1955 as the new 'V-bombers' entered service. Flying test-beds for new engines, crew trainers and even mother-planes for air-launch of experimental aircraft, accounted for a handful more. But one of the best remembered B-29 conversions was, perhaps, that of the WB-29 weather reconnaissance aircraft, as these aircraft were to be the last Superfortresses to be in service and continued in service, up until 1960.

B-29A serial No. 44-61600 was built in late 1944 at the Boeing plant in Renton, Washington, as part of Block Number 35 and designated the Contract Number 11077. It was one of 1119 of this variant of the Superfortress to leave the production line there. Powered by four 2200 hp Wright R-3350-57, eighteen cylinder radial engines, the B-29A was an improved version of the original B-29 production model and featured a new wing design, that gave greater strength, simplified and speeded up installation at the factory and made maintenance in the field easier.

By 1948 four Air Weather Service (A.W.S.) squadrons had been equipped with ageing RB-29s (reconnaissance versions of the B-29) and as no new aircraft were likely to be made available, the service began a programme of modernising and standardising the equipment carried by this fleet, resulting in the new designation of the WB-29. Equipped with additional fuel tanks and state of the art radar, radio and various meteorological analysis equipment, it is believed that just over 100 B-29s were eventually modified and refitted as WB-29s. One of the main distinguishing features of these aircraft was the prominent newly redesigned air sampling scoop now mounted on top of the rear fuselage, where the aft upper turret had been. Nick named the 'Bug-catcher' this apparatus was to test for airborne radiation levels after nuclear weapon tests conducted above ground and was initially used to test for radiation levels after atomic bomb tests at Bikini Atoll. However, the ability also to collect evidence of other nations weapons tests also was proved on 3 September, 1949, when an RB-29, on a daily weather reconnaissance track from Japan to Alaska, captured particles, which verified that the Soviet Union had detonated a nuclear weapon.

The 53rd Strategic Reconnaissance Squadron, Medium, Weather, had been re-formed as part of the US Air Force Air Weather Service, based at Kindley Field Air Force Base, Burmuda in early 1951 and had already acquired the nickname of the 'Hurricane Hunters'. In addition to its routine reconnaissance work, the squadron flew frequent missions to collect storm data in hurricanes, which had begun in 1946 when using an RB-29. They had been the first to fly into the top of a hurricane at 22,000 feet and in October of the following year they were the first to fly through one at low altitude (10,000 feet), again in an RB-29. Most of the squadron moved to Burtonwood Air Depot (later, RAF Burtonwood), near Warrington, in November 1953 and the unit was officially designated as the 53rd Weather Reconnaissance Squadron from February 1954. Their duties included carrying out daily, long duration, weather-recording flights, covering some 3686 miles and taking on average 15 hours. During these flights they recorded wind speed and direction, pressure, humidity, temperature, cloud conditions, visibility etc. and the data collected, was coded and sent back to the 53rd weather monitor at Burtonwood, relayed via Croughton radio station in Oxfordshire. Additionally the squadron carried out regular 'Falcon' flights, following designated tracks, some taking their aircraft north to the edge of the polar regions and it was on one of these flights in 1955 that a serious incident was to develop.

As early as 1943 US Weather Reconnaissance Squadrons had begun calling these regular weather tracks after bird names and by the 1950s this had become a tradition in the service, with tracks originating from the various airfields used in the UK therefore known as 'Falcon' flights. 'Falcon Coca #345' was a scheduled weather reconnaissance mission posted for the 24 October 1955 and an experienced crew commanded by Major Benjamin Hilkeman attended the regular briefing at 11:00 and began their pre-flight inspection of WB-29 44-61600 at 1500. During this check they found that number three main tank fuel booster pump to be inoperative and that there was a faulty connection on the aircraft's LORAN navigation receiver. The flight was postponed whilst the faults were corrected and the following morning the crew repeated the procedure and following a successful pre-flight inspection, during which it was noted that maintenance had been performed on the pump and all equipment was now operational, they took-off at 07:13. The flight was to take them out over the North Atlantic via Northern Ireland and with enough fuel for 19 hours flight on board, the crew settled into their routine. Apart from monitoring the on-board instruments, the crew also had to release parachute-deployed dropsondes at pre-designated points along the track. These devices, introduced circa 1950, comprised metal cylinders about 2 feet long, packed with weather sensing instruments that would transmit information including: wind speed, temperature, humidity, and atmospheric pressure, back to the aircraft as they fell.

Name	Position
Major Benjamin S. Hilkeman	Flight Commander
Captain James R. Bergevin	Pilot
Major Leo V. Sayre	Navigator
1st Lt Joseph F. Daly	Navigator
T/Sgt. Raymond. Smith	Flight Engineer
A/1C Weldon D, Wegner	Radio Operator
A/2C Virgil A. Herek	Radio Operator
A/1C Richard H. Sbrogna	Dropsonde Operator
S/Sgt. Harry S. Reynolds	Student Dropsonde Operator
T/Sgt. Juan De La Cruz Bou	Weather Observer
S/Sgt. William C. Akin	Scanner Operator

The aircraft reached the furthest limit of its flight, at 56 degrees north, 41 degrees west; a point 281 miles south of the tip of Greenland, without incident and Gander Oceanic Control (Newfoundland) gave clearance for the return leg of the flight at 9000 feet. However by this time it became clear to the crew that due to stronger headwinds than forecast, they were in fact 1 hour 15 minutes behind their flight plan. As the flight continued, the crew also began to experience problems with their radio equipment and although they continued to transmit their hourly position reports and weather observations, they noticed that the receipts for these messages were only received with great difficulty.

At around 16:00 44-61600 was at a point some 1200 miles west of the northern tip of Ireland, when the troublesome number three fuel pump failed again. As the aircraft continued, all engines were placed on direct tank to engine fuel supply and continued to operate satisfactorily, though intermittent fuel flow and pressure fluctuations were indicated on numbers one and four, the two outer engines. By the time the aircraft reached a point 196 miles from the west coast of Ireland, Major Hilkeman decided that a landing at Prestwick in Scotland would be prudent to refuel and check the problem, before returning to base. The crew then continued to the end of their weather track and as they set course for Prestwick, the flight engineer reported that there were two hours fuel remaining, not including the tank with the faulty pump, which held a further estimated 1000 gallons. After a further approximately twenty-five minutes, clearance was received to descend to 4000 feet, though again VHF reception was very poor and intermittent. Estimated arrival time at Prestwick was now calculated to be 22:30 and the navigator picked up a station passage indication showing that they were passing the radio beacon at Kintyre some 35 miles from their destination. However, on arriving over the Prestwick area, radio problems continued and the crew had great difficulty in locating the required radio beacons and could not establish any radio contact with: approach control, the tower, or the Ground Controlled Approach (GCA) facilities. Finally, intermittent contact was re-established with Scottish Centre Control and in view of the problems, particularly the lack of reliable navigation aids for an instrument approach landing, Hilkeman requested clearance from them for a change of flight plan, to continue back to their Burtonwood base.

With a calculated 1 hour and 30 minutes fuel remaining, the WB29 should have had no trouble making it home, but it was now that the crew began to experience more serious engine problems. The required report to Scottish Centre Control, as 44-61600 passed the New Galloway radio beacon was made with great difficulty, just before contact was lost completely. But then good clear contact was soon made with Preston Airways Control, as they passed the Dean Cross marker some 44 miles South of Prestwick. Just as they made contact, number one engine began to show signs of fuel starvation and the propeller was feathered as the engine was shut down. Although Preston was notified of this event, no emergency was declared. At the same time some icing of the aircraft was noted and over the next few minutes 44-61600 was allowed to settle to 4000 feet to counteract this and in order to maintain airspeed at 150 miles per hour. With the time now at 23:25, numbers two and four engines began to give indications of fuel starvation and Preston Airways was notified of this and that the crew intended to abandon the aircraft. Shortly before 23:30 the order was given to abandon the aircraft and the crew made a quick and orderly exit taking only some 30 seconds. The last to leave being Major Hilkeman, who noted that the aircraft was now at an altitude of 3200 feet and an indicated air speed of 130 miles per hour, only 13 mph above the WB-29's stalling speed.

Though the pilot would have set the stricken aircraft to fly out towards the sea, with two engines failing on one side and only one operational on the other it immediately began to turn and came down

143

in a slow spiral descent directly over the bale-out zone. No doubt much to the consternation of the eleven crew members now suspended by their parachutes below. Occupants of a local farm near Kirby Lonsdale heard the plane flying very low, followed shortly after by a terrific crash and the night sky lit up with an orange glow. The farmer, Mr George Richardson, rang the police and then rushed to the blazing wreck, meeting the first member of the crew with his parachute on the way. At the site he found five other airmen who informed him that everyone had baled out, though they were worried for the Commander who would have been the last to leave the aircraft. Before long the local ambulance and fire brigades arrived at the scene, though by this time, the fire had largely burnt itself out as the little remaining fuel had been consumed. Over the next couple of hours all the eleven crewmen were accounted for as calls were received from surrounding farms. All had made safe landings, though some had been more dramatic than others, with the Weather Observer, Technical Sergeant Juan Bou landing in a pig-sty and having to make a hasty exit and Navigator, First Lieutenant Joseph Daly, who was dragged through a barbed-wire fence by his parachute and suffered lacerations to his hand and a suspected broken finger. Otherwise a a few bruises, a lost wristwatch and shoe were the only misfortunes to befall the other crew members and following refreshments at the nearby farms, they were all picked up and taken to Westmoreland County Hospital at Kendal by ambulance to be checked over.

The following day only the massive tail of WB-29 44-61600 remained recognisable from the huge aircraft, still complete with it distinctive Bug-Catcher on top of the rear fuselage, the remainder being reduced to a debris field of millions of small fragments punctuated by the four massive Wright R-3350 Cyclone engines. Personnel from Burtonwood arrived and secured the crash site, collecting the personal belongings of the crew and other loose equipment scattered over the site and over the next few weeks supervising the massive clean-up operation to remove all the wreckage. The proximity of a reservoir used to supply local drinking water proved an immediate cause for concern, in case it had been contaminated by fuel or oil, but tests proved that all was well. No doubt this and a strong sense of the need to maintain good public relations, in the light of the massive press interest in the incident, meant that the recovery operation was indeed thorough; the wall was rebuilt and even the scorched grass reseeded, leaving nothing today to mark the site.

Despite the fact that previous investigations of the crash site of 44-61600 by enthusiasts appeared to confirm that the site had indeed been

The next morning, only the massive tail of the WB-29 remained recognisable, Note the distinctive "Bug-catcher" mounted on top of the rear fuselage to test for airborne radiation levels after nuclear weapon tests. *(Virgil Herek)*

completely cleared, we decided that in view of our extensive research into the incident, a few small representative pieces would be nice to complete the project and form part of a display at the museum. With this in mind half a dozen LAIT members equipped with modern metal detectors arranged to visit the site in November 2004, not the best time of year admittedly, but as is often the case, we needed to fit our activities in with the present use of the field for grazing purposes.

Having access to original photographs of the aftermath of the crash certainly helped us to plan a systematic search of the site, but we were initially disheartened to find that the main impact area, though clearly identifiable, was almost completely devoid of fragments. However, we continued with our search and were soon rewarded when a few recognisable fragments were soon unearthed including a couple of nice

The same spot today gives no clue to the dramatic events that took place just over 50 years before.

Ten of the crew looking somewhat relieved immediately after the crash - Major Hilkeman is back centre. (*Virgil Herek*)

component maker's plates. We were surprised to find that the area that was to yield the most fragments proved to be a short distance from any wreckage shown on the original photographs, but on examining the topography, it was obvious that this area was relatively sheltered from the prevailing wind and would have made the ideal spot to set up a temporary work area and tented accommodation for the recovery crew.

As the impact site is on an exposed fell-side, we were certainly cold enough after only a few hours detecting and the recovery crew 50 years before were there for a couple of weeks. Evidence of their endeavours was also found, with two snapped socket wrenches turning up during our search, perhaps weakened by the freezing temperatures they had to work in? Though a more surprising find was approximately twenty rounds of small calibre ammunition, still in the remains of their cardboard carton, jammed underneath the rebuilt dry-stone wall that the WB-29 had ploughed through. Each cartridge bore the headstamp 'WRA' indicating manufacture by the Winchester Repeating Arms Co. New Haven, Connecticut and the date 1944. By checking the cartridge dimensions these proved to be 0.30 calibre ammunition for the US M1 Carbine, which had been developed during WW2 by the Winchester Company in response to a need for a Personal Defence Weapon, with a more effective range and simpler to fire accurately, than the standard 0.45 calibre semi-automatic pistol or revolver. Some 6,000,000 of these guns were supplied between July 1942 and the end of the war and they saw use in all theatres, even as front-line weapons. Due to their small size and light weight they were carried in wartime B-29s as part of the survival kit and it seems that this provision was maintained on the WB-29s.

The 53rd Weather Reconnaissance Squadron maintain their

reputation as the Hurricane Hunters to this day as the only Department of Defense organisation still flying into tropical storms and hurricanes. Now an Air Force Reserve unit, their ten Lockheed-Martin WC-130 aircraft and crews are part of the 403rd Wing, based at Keesler Air Force Base in Biloxi, Mississippi. During the hurricane season from June 1 to 30 November each year, they provide surveillance of tropical disturbances and hurricanes in the Atlantic, Caribbean, and Gulf of Mexico for the National Hurricane Centre in Miami, Florida. They also may conduct aerial weather reconnaissance on storms for the Central Pacific Hurricane Centre in Honolulu, Hawaii. From 1 November to 15 April, the unit also flies through winter storms off both coasts of the United States in support of the National Centre for Environmental Prediction.

A selection of the many small fragments of 44-61600 collected from the crash site following a systematic detector search. Top left is a push rod tube from one of the Wright R-3350-57 engines, to its right is a main bearing shell and below a fire detector switch. Bottom centre are the rounds of small arms ammunition, to the right a fragment of a Perspex pressurised observation dome and above it, two broken socket wrenches left by the recovery crew.

CHAPTER SIXTEEN

FAILED TO RETURN

March 1941 saw a continuation of the Blitz with widespread heavy bombing across the country and the major ports proving frequent targets as the *Luftwaffe* tried to disrupt supplies reaching the UK from across the Atlantic. In fact this trend was causing the British authorities considerable concern and efforts were being made to strengthen the defences around these areas. Another worrying change of tactics was that the German raiders seemed to be concentrating their resources to attack a single target on a given night and then returning to the same target on successive nights. For Liverpool there had been something of a respite since the heavy Christmas raids of 1940, but now as weather conditions improved the *Luftwaffe* once again turned their attention towards the city and the night of the Wednesday 12/13 March saw a major raid against Britain involving some 373 aircraft, with 316 of them directed to attack the main target of the night – Liverpool!

Following the Battle for France, the *Luftwaffe* had reorganised and now had three *Luftflotte* (Air Fleets) facing Britain. *Luftflotte* 2, based mainly in northern France, Belgium and Holland was responsible for the bombing of south-east England and the London area, whilst *Luftflotte* 3, whose aircraft were now based on captured French airfields to the west of the River Seine was tasked to attack targets on the western side of Britain and as the campaign progressed they took much of the responsibility for the night Blitz. Finally *Luftflotte* 5, based in Norway, had responsibility for the north of England and Scotland.

One of the key units of *Luftflotte* 3, was *Kampfgeschwader* (KG, Bomber wing) 55 'Greif' (their aircraft being decorated with the red Greif [Griffon] badge). This *Geschwader* was one of the most active of the *Luftwaffe* of the entire war. Having fought in the campaign in Poland in 1939, they were sent to the west to join the fight, first against France in May of 1940, and in the air campaign against England during the rest of that year and into the next, before being moved east for the opening stages of Operation Barbarossa against Russia. *Kampfgeschwader* 55 comprised three *Gruppen* and a *Stab* (Staff) flight, with each *Gruppen* consisting of three *Staffel* (Squadrons) numbered consecutively within the wing and each with a nominal strength of twelve aircraft.

For the attack scheduled for the night of Wednesday 12/13 March raiding aircraft would be drawn from all three *Luftflotten*, with *Luftflotte* 2 unusually making the greater contribution for an operation that would normally have been the preserve of *Luftflotte* 3. Two specialist units were included in the attacking force, *Kampfgruppe* 100 (KGr100) equipped with *X-Verfahren*, and III *Gruppe*, *Kampfgeschwader* 26 (III/KG 26) operating *Y-Verfahen*, electronic navigation and bombing aids and collectively known as the *Beleuchtergruppen* (Fire-Starter Groups), serving as pathfinders for the main bomber force. However, for this raid KGr100 would be out of range of the radio beams necessary for the use of this complex equipment and they would have to locate their target visually, though III/KG 26, from *Luftflotte* 5, based at Stavanger in Norway, was able to use their equipment to locate their target – the docks at Birkenhead.

All three *Gruppen* of KG55, would supply HeIII aircraft for the raid and II *Gruppe* of this unit, although not officially recognised as a *Beleuchtergruppe*, would often assist KGr100, due to their considerable operational experience and skill at finding targets at night and would drop parachute marker flares to aid visual bombing. II/KG 55 was based at Chartres airfield to the south-west of Paris, though they had moved to Avord airfield near Bourges in central France on the previous day, mainly because the aerodrome at Chartres had become too soft, due to prolonged rain, for heavily loaded aircraft to take off. The move proved to be only a temporary one until Chartres had become serviceable again. One of the Gruppes aircraft was Heinkel He111P – 4A Werke No 2989, coded G1+CP of 6 *Staffel* KG55 (6/KG55 – the *Gruppe* number. being dropped when describing a *Staffel* individually). This P - 4A aircraft, which had been with the *Staffel* since before October 1940, featured specially strengthened external bomb racks to take heavy bombs of up to 1800 kilograms, in contrast to the He111P – 4B variant, which carried its bombs internally

At 19:23 on Wednesday 12 March 1941, G1+CP took off, from its temporary base at Avord along with four other Heinkel He111s of 6/KG55 in cloudless conditions and a full moon, giving good visibility over northern France, as the set course for their target. In command of the aircraft was *Hauptmann* Wolfgang Berlin, the observer and *Staffelkapitan* (Squadron leader) of 6/KG55, and it was piloted by *Oberfedwebel* Karl Single. The other crew members being; *Unteroffizer* Xavier Diem (wireless operator/gunner), *Feldwebel* Leonhard Kutznik (flight mechanic/gunner) and *Feldwebel* Heinrich Ludwinski (gunner). Their planned course took them over the coast at Dieppe then directly towards Merseyside at not less than 14,000 feet, though the actual attack was to be made at 10,500 to 11,500 feet. Their return course would have been via the radio beacon at Fecamp between Le Havre and Dieppe and onto Avord via further beacons at Chartres and Vierzon.

By 20:00 the radar stations along the south and south-east coasts of Britain had started to detect the raid forming and began to pass back plots on the aircraft coming in. As the raiders approached the English coast, a solitary obsolete Handley Page Harrow of No. 93 Squadron, based at Middle Wallop, was guided towards them and attempted to lay a 'Pandora' aerial minefield in front of the raiders. The specially modified Harrows carried a payload of 140 parachute mines, each comprising a 2 lb bomb attached to 2000 feet of piano wire suspended from a small parachute. The mines were released at intervals of 200 feet and towed across the path of the incoming raiders. This experimental form of defence was being used as part of an operational trial begun in October 1940, but it was found to be of little tactical value and on this occasion this unusual weapon once again proved unsuccessful.

After they crossed the coast, it was the turn of the night-fighters to go into action. Up to this point the interception of enemy raiders had largely been due to visual means as even the few Airborne Interception (AI) radar equipped aircraft had little success in locating them as the system was cumbersome and difficult to operate, requiring larger twin-engined aircraft, often of poorer performance. Efforts to utilise the system by fitting the AI equipped aircraft with powerful searchlights (Turbinlite) to illuminate the raiders and allow more conventional night-fighters working in association with them to attack the enemy, had also proved frustratingly ineffective. However from February 1941 developments such as the introduction of Ground Controlled Interception (GCI) radar stations and the first Bristol Beaufighters entering service would see a marked increase in the effectiveness of night-fighter operations. The Beaufighter was the first operational twin-engined aircraft that was suitable for installation of AI radar, yet had the performance required for use as a night-fighter. But it was to be the long awaited inland radar coverage provided by the GCI stations that would make the most significant difference at this stage, as the night-fighters could now be guided towards raiders and as tactics were improved, so did the effectiveness of Britains's night-fighter defences.

As the raiders made their way across southern England, radar equipped Beaufighter Mk-IF NFs of No. 604 Squadron and Defiants of No. 264 Squadron were already patrolling in the near cloudless moonlit sky, forming part of a record 260 night-fighters that flew patrols that night. Their first victim of the night was to be one of II/KG

55's HeIIIs, from 5 *Staffel*, which had taken off from Avord only some 45 minutes earlier and was brought down by one of No. 264's Defiants, using explosive/incendiary Dixon-De Wilde ammunition, at Ockley Surrey, with only one survivor.

The great majority of the raiders managed to get past the night-fighter patrols unscathed, however, and as they approached their targets, they found the Mersey dock areas were protected by a balloon barrage to prevent pin-point attacks from below 6000 feet. The first bombers arrived over Merseyside at around 21:00 and the ninety-six heavy anti-aircraft guns deployed in the area went into action and would fire over 3000 rounds that night. Afterwards the returning German aircrews reported their fire as being 'strong and accurate'. Immediately in front of and above the gun zone No. 96 Squadron, based at Cranage and tasked with the protection of Merseyside, patrolled in their Defiant and Hurricane night-fighters. They seem to have had little trouble locating their enemy that night, but as two of the squadron's Defiants got into firing positions on raiders, they were to suffer their guns jamming at the critical moment, allowing the raiders to escape. Return fire from one Heinkel wounded one of the pilots and as he lost consciousness the Defiant went into a spin, though fortunately he recovered enough to regain control and despite serious injuries he was able to land his aircraft back at Cranage.

Having reached Merseyside at around 22:00, the crew of HeIII G1+CP located their designated target, amid the burning city below and released their bombs over the docks at Birkenhead. Almost immediately the aircraft came under attack from behind, as one of No. 96 Squadron's Hurricanes, serial No. V7752, piloted by Sergeant Robin McNair, opened fire on the raider. In all McNair made three attacks on G1+CP, resulting in both engines stopping, though the stricken bomber did not catch fire. Wolfgang Berlin, the aircraft's commander recalled after the war,

There was only a little AA fire and not much searchlight activity. The weather was fine and clear and a bright moon was lighting up all of Southern England. If I remember correctly we were flying at about 3000 metres. After the attack on the docks at Birkenhead we turned for home and shortly afterwards our wireless operator/gunner, Unteroffizeier *Xaver Diem, reported on the interphone that a night-fighter was coming up from the lower rear. Only seconds later bullets ripped through the Heinkel, this first burst killed our gunner,* Feldwebel *Heinrich Ludwinski, and flight mechanic/gunner* Feldwebel *Leonhard Kuznik. The second and third bursts put both our engines out of action so I ordered the radio operator to bale out. However, he was unable to open either of the two rear exits because of damage inflicted by the fighter so had to crawl forward along the narrow passage between the bomb chutes to reach the cockpit. I opened the front emergency exit but by this time we were down to about 1000 metres and rapidly getting lower. We remaining three – pilot, radio operator and me – then got out. As I descended by parachute I could see below me the fenced meadows in the bright moonlight and men running in the direction of my point of landing which was in the middle of a field near a farm house. As soon as I landed the men arrived shouting "Hands Up!" They were members of the Home Guard, but I don't know how many. Then they guided me to the farmhouse and I was led into the living room where a homely fire was burning. It was very peaceful. The farmer then brought me a piece of buttered toast, so I knew I really was in England! My deep regret is that my schoolboy English was so poor, for I responded with "Thank you so much Madame"! Only the armed guard standing by the door reminded me that a war was going on.*

After a little while *Hauptmann* Berlin was escorted away by the police and then transferred under military escort to A.I.1(k) [the Air Ministry Intelligence section responsible for PoW interrogation] before proceeding to a PoW camp. He was later sent to Canada and was eventually repatriated to Germany in 1947.

Name	Position	Age	Status
Hauptmann Wolfgang Berlin	Observer/Aircraft Commander	27	U./POW
Oberfeldwebel Karl Single	Pilot	27	U./POW
Unteroffizier Xavier Diem	Wireless operator/gunner	23	U./POW
Feldwebel Heinrich-Johann Ludwinski	Gunner	26	K.
Feldwebel Leonhard Kuznik	Flight Mechanic/ Gunner	27	K.

Sergeant Robin McNair of No. 96 Squadron gave his account of the events in a Combat Report completed the following day.

I took off from Cranage at 20:35 hours, to patrol Liverpool at 12,000 feet'. I was patrolling [over] the fires when I suddenly sighted a Heinkel III travelling in a southerly direction. I was in a

Hurricane travelling N.E. I got under his tail at once, identified it as a twin engined aircraft by the two exhausts and approached to within about 75 yards astern. The aircraft was well in the sights and I gave it two bursts of four seconds each. My windscreen was then covered in oil and my machine enveloped in smoke. I broke away and noticed that the Heinkel's port engine was emitting a good deal of smoke. The port undercarriage was down and appeared to me to be hanging loose with the aircraft swaying about. I gave him another four seconds burst from 75 yards and then made a beam attack from the Port side at 50 yards using the rest of my ammunition. By this time the E/A was down to 3,500 feet'.

By that stage McNair was dangerously near the balloon barrage, so he gained height quickly and carefully manoeuvred himself out of the barrage and set a course for Cranage where he landed at 23:15, having flown a total of 2 hours and 40 minutes. In fact he had virtually no fuel left so by carefully nursing the engine and fuel he managed to touch down just before the engine cut out and his aircraft had to be manhandled from the runway.

By the time the three surviving crew members of G1+CP managed to bale out, the Heinkel had fallen from its bombing altitude of around 10,000 feet to around 3000 feet, now well within the effective height of the barrage balloon defences. The aircraft, with the two crew members who had been killed in the attack still onboard, continued to remain airborne for a short time before it struck a balloon cable belonging to No. 922 Squadron, "B" Flight, site No. 1 anchored on the works tip of McKechnie Brothers Ltd on Ditton Road. The balloon was being flown at 4500 feet, when at approximately 22:07 the He111, approaching from the west, struck the cable with its port wing tearing a section. The aircraft then slewed around to the north to crash three-quarters of a mile away into a ploughed field adjacent to the ICI recreation field, Widnes at 22:10, where it burst into flames and was completely burnt out.

Corporal Maddock was the NCO in charge of the site and stated in his report of the nights events:

At approximately 22.10 hours, I was in the hut when I heard machine-gun fire, about 1 minute later I heard the sound of an aeroplane which would be flying at approximately 3500 feet. The engines at this time were running quite smoothly and I dashed outside, to see if I could see the plane. As I got outside the engines were roaring much louder and sounded to be labouring, and the plane suddenly turned in a northerly direction. On investigation I found that the aeroplane had fouled the balloon cable, and the aeroplane had crashed into a ploughed field about 1 mile from this site. The lower D.P.L had fired, and was picked up on the field. The aeroplane was an enemy Heinkel Bomber, and was travelling from the west to an easterly direction.

The D.P.L. being the Double Parachute Link, which was an explosive cable cutter and a heavy-duty parachute, was attached to both ends of the cable. When an aircraft hit the cable, the shock of the impact triggered the explosive cutters and released a long section of cable. The cable would be dragged along behind the aircraft, opening a parachute at each end, which slowed the aircraft down and caused the pilot to lose control. The commanding officer of No. 922 Squadron, Squadron Leader F. C. Hornsby-Smith proceeded immediately to the scene of the crash and found that although the Police and Military were on the scene, no attempt had been made to recover bodies or salvage equipment etc from the wreckage, which was still burning. In addition to this about two hundred civilians were standing round in the glare in spite of heavy anti-aircraft fire and enemy aircraft overhead. He took control of the situation and organised for RAF personnel to be brought in and the civilians were soon cleared from the area and the bodies of Ludwinski and Kuznik, who was wearing an Iron Cross, were recovered. Also in order to prevent damage by fire, certain instruments were removed and

One local's souvenir of the defeated raider now in the LAIT collection is this personal identity disc fashioned from a fragment of aluminium and stamped to the reverse as a reminder of its origin. (*Mark Gaskell*)

handed to the police along with a despatch case, papers, identity discs and effects and an RAF guard was then posted at the site.

The three surviving crewmembers who had baled out were quickly rounded up from the surrounding area and taken into custody for interrogation. Xavier Diem and Karl Single came down in the grounds of Nazareth House becoming entangled in a tree facing the fire-watching post at Ditton Hall. Before they were cut free they were made to throw down their guns and were arrested by the local police, one of whom, Sam Marsh, was given a scarf by the pilot as a souvenir. The third, Wolfgang Berlin landed in Ash Lane, close to a barn at Bosco

Hall Farm, where he was captured by Tom Pemberton, the grandson of local farmer Tom Houghton, along with a group of Wardens armed with a shotgun. They were initially interviewed at Widnes Police Station by Pilot Officer Grey, the intelligence Officer at RAF Hooton, and were later taken under escort to Preston. The pilot, Karl Single had formerly been a fitter with Lufthansa, joining this unit a little more than six months previously as an *Oberfeldwebel*, having already done his ground training and he had carried out fifty-four operational flights against Britain. He would initially be held at the Warth Mills PoW camp at Bury, before being transferred to a camp in Canada in December 1941 and back to England in 1945, he was finally repatriated to Germany in June 1947. *Hauptmann* Wolfgang Berlin, was the *Staffelkapitan* and G1+CP had been the lead aircraft of 6 *Staffel*. He had taken part in the Polish campaign and been awarded the Eisernes Kreuz 1 (E.K.1 or Iron Cross, first class) in France. He had made at least ninety-two operational flights over Britain with KG55 although he had recently changed Gruppe from I/ KG55. Finally the Wireless Operator *Unteroffizier* Xavier Diem had made at least forty-eight operational flights over Britain, some thirty of which had been against London. He would also be held at the Warth Mills and sent to Canada, being transferred back to England in September 1944 and then repatriated to Germany in February 1947

On the ground most people were taking shelter as the bombing was so widespread and few people apparently felt confident enough to remain in the open to watch the proceedings. However, one such individual was seventeen-year-old Mr T. Condron from Widnes:

> *I stood on our doorstep with my father and another man; we were watching the planes going over to bomb Liverpool. It had been going on for some time. The planes were starting to return on their way home. There had been a lot of anti-aircraft fire, but it seemed to ease off. It was then that we [saw] machine-gun fire up in the sky. It was our aircraft and the German aircraft firing at one another. We [saw] a small fire on one of the aircraft. The aircraft turned and started to come down towards us, it was making a hell of a noise. In no time it appeared just above the houses on the other side of the road heading straight for our house. My father vanished along with his friend and I panicked and ran across the road.*

He then made for some open ground nearby, which turned out to be the recreation ground and he was 'amazed to see the aircraft flop into the field and burst into flames'. Initially his curiosity got the better of him

and he ran towards the plane: 'when I noticed that there were tracer bullets coming in all directions from the plane. It was then I decided to get way from it'. He later heard that one of the crew who had baled out had landed in a field near St. Michaels Church, Ditton.

Also watching the drama unfold was Mr Peter Gilhooley, who was on leave from his anti-aircraft gun unit in Scotland at the time and later recalled the events of that night.

I had come home on leave on the 11 March and on the night of the 12th which was a very clear night I had stayed up top during

The Heinkel crash site today, the new concrete panel fence and high hedge obscures the buildings visible in the 1941 photo, which are just visible to the extreme left, making an exact comparison difficult.

the raid to watch it being used to this kind of thing. I noticed that the guns had stopped firing and this meant a night-fighter was approaching, I was looking up Oxford Street and saw the aircraft firing at each other circling the town towards Ditton, the starboard engine was blazing and I could see swastika markings on the aircraft. The aircraft stuck a barrage balloon cable next to the offices of McKechnie Brothers Ltd on Ditton Road tearing a part of the wing off and it then plunged down, cartwheeling across the field next to the ICI Recreation Field with wreckage flying everywhere and nearly hitting the houses at the bottom of Green Lane. During this time I had jumped on a bicycle and rode to the scene of the crash and was one of the first on the scene along with an officer and three gunners from the heavy anti-aircraft gun site at Heath Road who asked who I was, and as I was a fellow gunner on leave I was asked to help keep the crowds back as the ammunition was going off and flying in all directions. The following day I saw the crew being collected from Widnes Police station in a Army truck.

The fellow gunners he had encountered were in fact from 'P' site No. 334 Battery of No 107 Heavy Anti-Aircraft (HAA) Regiment Royal Artillery (RA), who recorded in their war diary that an aeroplane had crashed in flames near their 'Q site' on that night.

The following morning crowds of sightseers gathered to view the now guarded wreck of G1+CP, which was widely scattered over the playing field, with only the shattered and partially burnt tail unit still being recognisable. RAF Air Intelligence personnel examined the remains and reported that; 'The cause of the crash was night-fighter action, one [bullet] strike was found at the bottom of the engine case. The aircraft was totally burnt out on crashing and no plates were recovered. The aircraft also hit balloon cables'. Both engines were found embedded in the ground and were recovered along with four MG 15 machine guns, though all the aircrafts instruments were found to have been destroyed, except for one *Loft 7C* bombsight, recovered in poor condition. Bullet holes were also noted in the starboard wing and propeller and a length of mangled balloon cable 400 feet long was also found beside the wreckage. The port wing was missing from the engine nacelle outwards and was thought to have fallen into one of the many chemical works slurry ponds, that lay between where the balloon had been struck and the crash site. For the next few days locals continued to flock to the site trying to catch a glimpse of the aircraft through the ICI recreation field's railings, unfortunately the cricket square got rather damaged due to the procession of sightseers crossing it, much to the annoyance of the groundsmen. It was noted that the exploding ammunition at the time of the fire was ricocheting of this fence, leaving marks on the iron railings. However, the fence has subsequently been replaced by a concrete panel type one, leaving no trace of the events this night. The wreckage, which was guarded by the Army, was left as it was for a few days to allow the examination to be completed and was then cleared away within two weeks. After which the local children descended on the site looking for souvenirs, but unfortunately for them very little was to be found apart from a few small pieces in the brook at the edge of the field.

The two unfortunate airmen were both buried on the 15 March 1941 at Widnes cemetery in an area laid aside for war casualties, the arrangements were kept quiet and only a few early morning visitors were aware the two crewmen were being interred. A detachment from No. 922 Squadron, in the charge of Squadron Leader F. C. Hornsby-Smith arrived at the cemetery by lorry, and formed a guard of honour for the RAF tender and escort under the command of Pilot Officer A. M. Jamieson which bore the two plain oak coffins, upon which was a laurel wreath bearing the national colours of red, black and white. These wreaths, which were bought by the squadron, were carried by Squadron Leader F. C. Hornsby-Smith and Warrant Officer Martin. Following a short, simple service around the graveside conducted by the Rev F. W. Haworth, an RAF Chaplin, the coffins were lowered into their resting place in view of the guard of honour, the civilian bystanders and a detachment of police. The wreaths were later placed on top of the burials and bore the simple inscription   'Feldwebel

Members of No. 922 squadron, 'B' Flight, site No 1, Barrage balloon crew pose proudly with their trophy from the downed Heinkel (*Maddock family*)

[Name], German Air Force. Killed in action, March 12th 1941. RIP'. Whilst they remained buried in Widnes cemetery, a local woman, Mrs Beswick, who had lost her own son during the war, tended their graves until 1962 when they were exhumed and reburied. *Feldwebel* Heinrich Ludwinski is now buried in block No. 3, grave No. 152 next to

Feldwebel Leonhard Kuznik in grave No. 153 at Cannock German Military Cemetery in Staffordshire.

The Air Ministry reported the following day: 'Last night the moon being full and the weather clear, the enemy attempting his first large scale raid for some time attacked Merseyside in force. On this occasion, however the damage and casualties bore no relation to the scale of the attack and very little was achieved beyond serious damage to a number of private houses'. In fact this was the heaviest raid so far in 1941, with over 300 enemy aircraft estimated to have been over Merseyside dropping 303 tons of high explosive bombs and 1782 incendiary canisters (36 x 1kg magnesium and thermite bombs per canister = 64,152 incendiary bombs). Birkenhead had been the focus of the raid where over some six hours, 180 high explosive bombs, forty parachute mines and thousands of incendiary bombs were dropped. Around two-thirds of the bombs dropped had fallen well outside the target area, many on residential areas and casualties were high with 264 killed in Birkenhead, 198 in Wallasey and forty-nine in Liverpool. Throughout Merseyside there was widespread damage and over 500 fires were reported having been started by the numerous incendiary bombs. Although no ships had been sunk, a few smaller craft were damaged and many dockside installations were damaged and warehouses set on fire. There was also significant damage to utility services and the railways as well as further disruption due to the numerous unexploded bombs that littered the area. The *Luftwaffe* losses for this raid, though relatively light, at three HeIIIs and two Ju88s destroyed and two further HeIIIs damaged, did demonstrate that RAF night-fighters were becoming more effective at locating the raiders and as tactics developed the German losses would soon increase significantly.

As with many such projects, we are often surprised how snippets of information relating to an incident that we are researching seem to crop up in unusual places and such was the case with the Widnes Heinkel. The first surprise was in a letter from a local who recalled how two of the crew who baled out, came down in the grounds of a local convent, one becoming entangled in a tree, but she also drew our attention to the well-known public information booklet *Roof over Britain* published by HMSO in 1943, a publication that many enthusiasts, myself included, probably have a copy of. This wartime propaganda work, with its striking cover graphics depicting an upward facing helmeted serviceman at night, silhouetted by rockets and searchlights, describes how the defeat of the *Luftwaffe* over Britain by the RAF had been achieved through cooperation between the ground based defence forces and night-fighter squadrons. A prime example of this joint effort, outlined early on in the text, describes somewhat dramatically the circumstances of this very incident, citing the bomber's uncontrolled headlong crash into the balloon cable as an instance of 'the full-flower of co-operative function'!

The second surprise occurred one evening whilst browsing on the Internet for information on RAF losses over France, when a familiar aircraft serial number attracted my attention. The article referred to No. 137 Squadron (a Typhoon unit) based at Eindhoven in the Netherlands during December 1944. It seems that this unit retained an ageing Hurricane for use as the Squadron hack – the serial number being V7752! The same aircraft McNair had been flying that night in March 1941, though sadly it was destroyed on the ground during Operation Bodenplatte, the *Luftwaffe's* last ditch major offensive against Allied forward air bases in Europe on 1 January, 1945.

Though we have pinpointed the area, it has not proved possible to carry out any physical investigation of the crash site of G1+CP as the playing field is still in use and the surface of the cricket pitch obviously needs to be maintained to a high standard and cannot be disturbed. Our research has shown, however, that little is likely to remain at the site in any case and our investigations into this incident have in themselves proved more than enough to maintain our interest. Most rewarding has been the opportunity to speak to eyewitnesses who recalled the events of that night as well as relatives of Sergeant McNair. McNair died on the 18 May 1996 aged 77, leaving a widow Estelle whom he married in 1940, seven children and eighteen grandchildren.

Robin John McNair was born the 21 May 1918, he joined the RAFVR in February 1939 and joined the RAF in September of that year. Following training he was posted to No. 3 Squadron stationed at Wick and then on 15 September to No. 249 squadron based at North Weald and helping to defend the South East and London during the remainder of the Battle of Britain, with its Hurricanes. He went on to join No. 96 Squadron flying night operations in the defence of Liverpool. He moved to No. 87 Squadron in 1942, again flying Hurricanes where he took part in the disastrous Dieppe raid, providing air cover. For this action, and for his night-fighter activities, he received the Distinguished Flying Cross, having flown some 110 operational sorties. In 1943 he moved onto Typhoons, now as a Flight Lieutenant; he was flight commander of No. 245 Squadron, part of the Second Tactical Air Force attacking targets in preparation for the D-Day landings and flying-bomb launch sites. In 1944 Robin McNair was appointed Squadron Leader and commanding officer of No. 247

Squadron, still flying Typhoons and playing a key role in the Normandy invasion, based at the temporary airfield, B6 at Coulombe, just south of Caen in France and performing ground attack missions on enemy transport. He was subsequently awarded a bar to his DFC having flown a further 170 sorties. Before leaving the RAF in December 1945 he commanded No. 74 Squadron, one of the first RAF squadrons to be equipped with Meteor jet fighters. He then settled in Ealing and began a career in civil aviation at British European Airways (BEA) retiring in 1979. McNair a devout Roman Catholic, worked tirelessly for local and national charities and was heavily involved in the community.

Though now widely regarded as one of the leading British fighter pilots of World War II, McNair was very modest about his contribution and in the words of his son, 'would have been surprised and probably embarrassed by his recognition today'. There are a number of memorials to this brave pilot in the form of three roads named after him; McNair Close, Selsey, Chichester, West Sussex, McNair Court, Portland Road, Hove, Sussex and McNair Road in Ealing (with blue plaque), London UB2. On 20 November 1988 his son Duncan McNair visited Widnes to meet the Mayor of Halton, and talk over the events of that night the 12 March 1941. This close association with Widnes was commemorated on the 17 March 2000, when an English oak tree with plaque was planted on land to the rear of Liverpool Road/Stewards Avenue to remember Robin McNair. The Mayor of Halton, the RAF association and the Ball O' Ditton Royal British Legion planted the tree and unveiled the plaque near the Heinkel crash site. The guest of honour at the ceremony was Robin McNair's son Duncan and he thanked the town for its tribute to his father, 'My Father led a full life', Duncan said, 'They say cats have nine lives but I think my father had a multiple of nine lives. This was one incident he was lucky to live through. He was a man of great humility' and that 'he attended mass at the nearest church after a battle to say a prayer for his enemies'.

CHAPTER SEVENTEEN

OUT OF FUEL AND OUT OF TIME

During the Battle of France many Czech airmen, who had fled their own country as it was overrun by the Germans, fought alongside their French counterparts in the Armée de l'Air, taking an active role in the short-lived Battle of France. The subsequent rapid fall of France led to some 4000 Czechoslovak soldiers and airmen arriving in Britain, where they were keen to continue to play their part in the battle against Germany. With the RAF now in need of as many trained aircrew as it could muster, the invaluable combat flying experience of these Czech airmen was recognised and they were soon incorporated into the RAF. Initially two Czech Squadrons were formed: No. 310 Czechoslovak Fighter Squadron, at Duxford On 10 July 1940 and No. 311 Czechoslovak Bomber Squadron at Honington on 29 July. Soon after No. 310 became operational on the 17 August, a second Czech fighter squadron, No. 312 was formed on 29 August 1940 at the Czech aircrew depot at RAF Cosford. The home base of the new squadron was to be RAF Duxford, where No. 310 (Czech) Squadron was already based. Two days later their first nine used MkI Hawker Hurricanes were flown into Duxford and on the 4 September 1940 a Mk.I Miles Master joined them. The Czech airmen, flying personnel and ground staff, arrived at RAF Duxford during afternoon of 5 September 1940. As with No. 310, the new squadron was based around experienced pilots, who already had combat experience during the Battle of France and many of whom already had more then one victory.

On 6 September 1940, the pilots began their theoretical preparation for conversion to flying the Hurricanes, as well as training flights on the Master. This was to prove a slow process due to the fact the unit had just the one trainer aircraft! To speed things up, another Master was loaned from No. 310 Squadron. After nearly a month of intensive training, on the 26 September, the squadron moved to its new home, the RAF station at Speke airport, Liverpool. There the unit completed its retraining and in the last days of September obtained further Hurricanes. On the 2 October 1940, No. 312 (Czech) Squadron was declared operational and tasked with the protection of the Liverpool area from enemy raids. The squadron's motto was, *Non multi sed multa* – 'Not many but much' and the squadron badge was a Stork volant.

The stork in their badge relating to the French *l'escadrille des Cigognes* with which the original pilots of the squadron had flown prior to coming to Britain. Initially things went well for the new squadron, when on only 8 October 1941, they scored their first victory, a Junkers Ju88, Wk. No. 4068, coded M7+DK, of 2 *Staffel Kampfgruppe* 806 (2/KGr806). This lone raider had taken off from its base at Caen-Carpiquet in France to bomb the Rootes aircraft factory at Speke and photograph the results. However, it was spotted over the Mersey, just as No. 312's Yellow Section were taking off for a patrol. They were ordered to intercept and all three Hurricanes, piloted by Flight Lieutenant D.E. Gillam A.F.C, Pilot Officer A. Vasatko and Sergeant J. Stehlik attacked the bomber, which crashed on reclaimed land on the far side of the river Mersey. The victory, shared by the three pilots, was witnessed by many locals and they became celebrities for a while and one of the pilots cut the insignia from the fallen enemy as trophy, which was hung in the flight hut at the squadron dispersal.

However following such a glittering start, the events of the rest of October, must have had a sobering effect on the pilots of No. 312 Squadron. The first of these came only two days later, when on the 10 October 1940, Sergeant Otto Hanzlicek, took off from Speke in Hawker Hurricane I, serial No. L1547 (the first production Hurricane built) along with Pilot Officer Dvorak, to carry out practice enemy aircraft attacks in the Liverpool area. At 14.15 the engine of his aircraft caught fire and he was forced to abandon his aircraft near Oglet, but the wind blew him out over the River Mersey, and after problems with his parachute, due to baling out too low, he fell into the River Mersey and was drowned. His body was eventually found 5 miles to the east of Speke at Widnes on the 1 November 1940. With 930 flying hours to his credit and having been awarded the *Croix de Guerre* in France, the loss of this experienced 29-year-old pilot, the squadron's first casualty, must have been a severe blow. The next incident, came just three days later, early on the evening of the 13 October, when Squadron Leader Ambrus, Flight Lieutenant Comerford and Sergeant Stehlik believed that two aircraft they sighted whilst on patrol over the Point of Air, were in fact enemy raiders and opened fire. Squadron Leader Ambrus attacked first, followed by Flight Lieutenant Comerford who fired a short burst and Sergeant Stehlik also fired a short burst at about a distance of 1100 yards. The aircraft initially attacked, then fired two red flares, the recognition signal of the day, but it was too late, as at the same time the other aircraft, Blenheim No. L6637 of No. 29 Squadron burst into flames and crashed into the sea at Hoyle Bank in the River Dee estuary at 18:20. Realising that they had made a dreadful mistake, the Hurricanes then escorted the damaged aircraft, Blenheim No. L7135 back to its base where it landed safely with no injuries to its crew; Pilot Officer J. D. Humphreys, Sergeant E.H. Bee and Aircraftsman 2nd class J.F. Fizell. None of the crew of the stricken L6637 were seen to leave the aircraft and a naval vessel called in to search the area found no trace of the airmen, though a tunic containing identity card no. 742992 and a driving licence made out for R.E. Stevens was found on the 24th. The pilot, Sergeant R.E. Stevens, Air Gunner Sergeant O.K. Sly and AI Operator Aircraftman 2nd Class A. Jackson were all missing presumed killed. Aircraftman Jackson's body washed ashore at a later date and he now lies in Mexborough cemetery, Yorkshire, the other two airmen being commemorated on the Air Forces Memorial at Runnymede.

Tragedies such as this were unfortunately not uncommon at this time and in fact during the period 1939 to 1942, some twenty Blenheims were shot down and nineteen damaged through mis-identification by RAF pilots and anti-aircraft fire, resulting in the deaths of thirty-two aircrew and seven others injured. An investigation determined that this case was caused by 'a culmination of a succession of faults, each of minor character' and that 'Evidence disclosed a lack of teamwork and co-ordination between Sector and squadron', referring it seems to the fact that Squadron Leader Ambrus had not been informed that any British aircraft may be present in his patrol area.

Not all Fighter operations during the period of the famous Battle of Britain involved contact with the enemy concluding with a dogfight. Many involved long routine patrols guarding Britain's shores, without so much as a sighting of an enemy aircraft. After the chaotic air battles over France, that many of No. 312's pilots would have taken part in, such duties must have seemed mundane. But they were not without their own dangers as a flight of Hurricanes from the Squadron found out as they were patrolling the coast of Lancashire. Tuesday 15 October 1940 saw some 550 enemy fighters and bombers attacking London, the Thames Estuary and Kent in five waves and that night an even heavier assault on the capital as some 300 bombers, in the light of a full moon, gave Londoners a foretaste of the Blitz to come. But for now this intense activity was focused to the south and early that evening two flights of Hurricanes, Red and Yellow Sections of No. 312 Squadron, took off from Speke at 17:30 for a dusk patrol over the Lancaster area, with instructions to return at 18:25. Red section did indeed land as instructed, but there was no sign of Yellow Section consisting of Squadron Leader Jan K. Ambrus flying No. V6846, Pilot Officer T.

Vybiral flying No. V6811 and Flight Lieutenant H. A. G. Comerford in Hurricane No. V6542.

It appears that Yellow Section became lost over the sea in deteriorating weather conditions and the failing light, after Squadron Leader Ambrus, who knew his position, followed Flight Lieutenant Comerford, who he believed had sighted an enemy aircraft. Though the

flight was fortunate in regaining the coast, they found themselves once again over land on the Barrow peninsular, their fuel situation was becoming critical and both Comerford and Vybiral were soon forced to abandon their aircraft. Flight Lieutenant Comerford ran out of fuel and baled out at 19:00, landing near Dalton-in-Furness, with slight injuries having struck his head on the tail of his aircraft as he left it. His aircraft dived vertically into farmland at Gleaston narrowly missing a cottage by only 20 yards. Flight Lieutenant Comerford was subsequently rendered non-effective for a while due to his injuries.

At about the same time Pilot Officer Vybiral also ran out of fuel and baled out, leaving his aircraft to crash into farmland near Dalton-in-Furness. He landed close-by at Whinfield Farm Lindal, where it appears that he was mistaken for a German airman, due to his accent by the farmer's wife and not being able to convince her otherwise, he found himself locked in a barn until his identity was confirmed. The flight had been observed by a number of local witnesses in the Dalton-in-Furness area who recalled seeing the aircraft flying overhead and then observed two of them fly into the ground, but most were soon relieved to see two parachutes.

A local police officer saw one of the pilots in his parachute and armed with a .303 rifle, he commandeered a Ribble bus to take him to the spot where the pilot landed. This is believed to have been Pilot Officer Vybiral and on arrival at the farm, the policeman found himself 'rescuing' the unfortunate airman, having quickly established his true identity. Squadron Leader Ambrus continued flying until his fuel ran out and then carried out a well executed wheels-up forced landing on

Pilot Officer Tomas Vybiral. (*Pavel Vancata*)

farmland south of Over Kellet, near Carnforth at 20:00 leaving a furrow across the field. He was not injured and the aircraft was not too badly damaged and was subsequently repaired. The official enquiry into the incident later concluded that the flight should have kept sight of land and landed 20 minutes before blackout as instructed, no further action was taken against the pilots and this was to be the squadron's last accident of the Battle of Britain period.

Forty-one year old Squadron Leader Jan K. Ambrus had served with the French *Section de Liaison et d'Entraînement* (Training and Liaison Section) at Chartres during the battle of France, until June 1940 when he came to Britain and joined No.310 Squadron on 12 July. Following a brief period of training at No. 6 O.T.U. in August he was posted to command No. 312 Squadron at Duxford on 9 September 1940, but on 12 December, perhaps in light of the events of October, he left the squadron and started work as an officer at the Czechoslovak Inspectorate General in London, remaining in this position until the end of 1941. In 1942 he was promoted to the rank of Wing Commander and sailed to Canada, where he worked as Czechoslovak Air Attaché in Ottawa until the end of war. After the war he returned to Czechoslovakia, where he was promoted to the rank of General in 1946 and on 19 April 1947 he was awarded the Order of the British Empire (OBE). Following the events of February 1948 when the Communists took power in Czechoslovakia, he emigrated to Canada and later he moved to USA where he lived until his death in Chicago during 1994.

Pilot Officer Tomas Vybiral had also served in France as a lieutenant with the *Groupe de Chasse* I/5 (GC I/5), Flying Curtiss Hawk H-75s from their operational base at Suippes near Reims and had been credited with seven confirmed victories, making him effectively an 'ace' even before the Battle of Britain commenced. With GC I/5 having its roots reaching back to the famous SPA 3 (WW1 French units were designated according to the aircraft they were using – in this case the Spad) *l'Escadrille Guynemer*, its aircraft still bore the prestigious Stork Passant emblem. On arriving in Britain, he was assigned to No. 312 Squadron at Duxford in September 1940, becoming commander of B flight on 5 June 1941 and leaving for No. 41 squadron on 19 June 1942. He returned to command No. 312 as Squadron Leader on 1 January 1943 remaining in this position until November of that year. In February 1944, the three Czechoslovak fighter squadrons; Nos. 310, 312 and 313 were assembled into No. 134 (Czech) Wing of the Second Tactical Air Force (2nd TAF) at Mendlesham, Suffolk and led by the now Wing Commander Tomas Vybiral. He was awarded the DFC in July 1944 and the DSO in

December 1944; after the war he left the RAF and died in London in 1981 aged 69.

Flight Lieutenant Harry Alfred George Comerford had joined the RAF in 1927, trained at Digby and was posted to No. 28 Squadron at Ambala, in India. In October 1934 he transferred to the Reserve of Air Force officers, being recalled on active service at the beginning of the war, he was then posted to No. 312 Squadron at Speke in September 1940. He became Flight Commander of the Squadron's A Flight on 30 September and remained so until 15 November 1940. He was awarded the AFC in 1941 and resigned his commission in 1943. Flight Lieutenant Comerford is also known to have spent time as a test pilot at Vickers-Armstrong and whilst there he was one of the forty-nine test pilots involved in the development of the various Marks and Variants of the Spitfire.

As for the aircraft involved in this incident: Hawker Hurricane Mk.Ia serial No. V6846 was repaired and returned to service, eventually being struck off charge on 30 June 1944 in India. It was reported that a derelict Hurricane, displayed in Indian Air Force markings, that was photographed at the Panta Air Base in India in 1973, was in fact V6846 and rumours persist that this aircraft is still in existence there. Flight Lieutenant Comerford's aircraft, serial No. V6542 was completely destroyed when it dived vertically into farmland and the crash site was relocated in 1977 by the Warplane Wreck Investigation Group from Merseyside, assisted by local aviation enthusiast John Smallwood. They carried out a full excavation on the 14 November, using a JCB machine during which the propeller hub and a few other fragments were recovered; these items are currently on display in the Fort Perch Rock Museum at New Brighton. It seems that this group also attempted to locate the crash site of Pilot Officer Vybiral's Hurricane serial No. V6811, but although they narrowed down the location, permission was not given for a dig to be carried out at that time.

In November 2004 a small group from the Lancashire Aircraft Investigation Team resumed the search for the crash site of V6811, also assisted by Mr Smallwood and tracking down one of the individuals involved in the earlier search certainly saved us a lot of time. The aircraft had impacted on the lower slopes of a hill above a fairly steep drop to a small lake below and we soon located several, shallow detector finds including a cockpit lamp holder with the remains of the bulb still in place and a .303 calibre round dated 1939, with the rusted remains of a link attached indicating that it was from a machine gun. As usual these finds were systematically marked with pegs and a

Plenty of onlookers for our excavation of Hurricane V6811 in March 2005, but then its not often you get to dig on a genuine Battle of Britain crash site today!

Willing volunteers carry out the initial cleaning and sorting of the recovered artefacts at the dig site.

distinct shallow depression became apparent at the centre of the area indicated. This spot gave a clear medium strength signal from our Fisher Gemini and several distinct readings from the Forster, indicating that moderate remains lay more deeply buried. A sketch map of the site was made and a GPS reading taken and following further talks with the landowner, an MoD permit was applied for.

Having dealt with all the formalities, on the 19 March 2005 members of the Lancashire Aircraft Investigation Team and the RAF Millom Museum gathered at Dalton-in-Furness for our first full excavation of 2005. Using a small tracked excavator, as the slope of the site made a larger or wheeled machine impractical, we began by stripping away the topsoil and soon started to see evidence of the crash in the form of corroded aluminium fragments and parts of copper radiator cooling fins. Digging proved difficult, as the original RAF

recovery crew appeared to have back-filled the crater with many large stones and there were few finds to be seen after these were removed. However, at a depth of about 7 feet below the surface there was cache of aircraft remains, including some engine ancillaries such as the generator, a large section of main wing spar and one of the main undercarriage legs. Below this was the rudder counter-balance weight and a few small finds kept emerging in the next few feet, mainly consisting of broken engine casing and one cylinder liner, indicating that the Merlin engine must have shattered on impact. Finally at

The only major part of V6811 found, a main undercarriage leg, in remarkably good condition after 65 years burial.

about 10 feet below the surface the red sandy soil gave way to boulder clay level and a rusted spam tin and an intact glass pop bottle of 1940s vintage and from a local firm were found in this before clean clay was reached at about 13 feet. Surprisingly few parts from the cockpit were found, perhaps indicating that the forward fuselage survived the impact with the sandy soil relatively intact and was dragged clear in one piece, though the face from the airspeed indicator and the emergency kick-down lever for the main landing gear were found whilst checking through the spoil before back-filling. It appeared that the aircraft had penetrated the ground to a depth of about 10 feet where the engine probably broke up as it hit the boulders and the RAF recovery crew then seem to have made a remarkably thorough job of the subsequent clean up operation, even disposing of their own rubbish carefully!

CHAPTER EIGHTEEN

BOMBERS IN THE MARSH: THE WARTON INVADERS

In common, I suspect, with other Aviation Archaeology groups, particularly those who maintain a presence on the Internet, we have been approached several times with regard to the possibility of filming our projects for television. It seems that there are few groups remaining active these days and even fewer with major excavation projects in this country in the pipeline. Although at any one time we often have several ongoing research projects and usually one or two that are likely to lead to an excavation, we had felt that none of the proposals put to us aroused our interest.

It was towards the end of 2003 that, whilst sorting through the daily collection of 'spam' that any website seems to generate, I spotted a message with the distinctive '@Timeteam' suffix – not an uncommon event for us, but being a fan of the programme I am always curious of what they are up to! It came as no surprise to hear that they were looking for an Aviation Archaeology project for their next series – we had been in discussion with them earlier in the year concerning another of our projects when unfortunately the landowner's circumstances changed and the dig was called off at the last moment.

This time we had no particular project in mind but it seems that the researchers at Time Team had obviously considered carefully the previous two aviation archaeology projects that they had been involved in and had come up with a set of criteria for their ideal site. Obviously some mystery behind the incident was crucial as usual, but also they had become concerned as to the depth below ground many of our excavations seem to require and also, as the programme aims to bring aspects of archaeology to a general audience, they wanted recognisable aircraft remains to work on, certainly a tall order! After some discussion we decided that we were still interested in taking part in a joint project, as we did indeed have the perfect site, though with one slight complication – it was nearly 1 mile from solid ground on a marsh! However, after explaining that the site potentially held an almost intact WW2 aircraft still lying where it had fallen 60 years before, their interest was aroused and a meeting to view the site was arranged. This took place early in 2004, with the not altogether inconspicuous arrival of the famous Time Team Land Rover Discovery at Freckleton. On the walk out to the site, accompanied by a representative of the Lytham and District Wildfowlers Association, who own and manage the marsh. We had plenty of time to describe the background to the incident and relate how we believed at least one of the two aircraft lay almost intact only a few feet below the surface! I confess this may have seemed pretty far-fetched at first, but the sight of the tattered vertical fin poking through the grass soon vouched for our story and the initial planning stage of the project began.

From original photographs of the crash scene in 1944 we had a rough idea of where the remains of the two aircraft lay in relation to each other, but due to the size of the area to be covered we were asked to locate and plot as much of the wrecks as possible and also began the task of collating our research notes and tracking down any surviving witnesses or relatives of the crews.

The aircraft involved were two A-26B Invaders: 43-22298 and 43-22336. Both had been built only a month apart at the Douglas plant at Tulsa, Oklahoma and flown to the UK probably via Prestwick during October or November of that year. Production records indicate that the two aircraft differed slightly – a factor that would prove important to us 60 years later. They were then transferred to the American Base Air Depot 2 (BAD2) at Warton where they joined others being prepared and waiting to be allocated to front line units of the Ninth Air Force, in replacement for A-20 and B-26 aircraft. One of these units was the 641st Squadron of the 409th Bombardment Group who since September had been based at Station A-48, Bretigny, Seine Oise, France, flying regular combat sorties, mostly against close support

Hubbard's shattered Invader 43-22298 is examined by personnel from BAD 2 as it lies on the foreshore as the tide recedes after the crash. (*USAF Historical Division*)

The severed tail of 43-22298 lies at the high water mark, where for years it remained a visible reminder of the tragedy, before it was overcome by the marsh. (*USAF Historical Division*)

targets in their A-20s. From mid-November they began converting to the A-26 and later that month a group of pilots from the squadron flew their old A-20s to Warton in order to familiarise themselves with their new charges and fly them directly back to their base.

Just after 12.00 on the 29 November 1944 the A-26s began taking off from BAD2 and forming up over the airfield ready for the return flight to France. Witnesses recall some twenty aircraft being in the air above the base where the Invaders were forming up in four flights of six aircraft – 43-22298 was being flown by 2nd Lt. Kenneth E. Hubbard accompanied by Corporal John F. Guy, a crew chief. Hubbard was forming up as No. 6 in the first flight, when his aircraft collided with 43-22336 flown by 2nd Lt. Norman Zuber who was unaccompanied. Witnesses recall that one aircraft exploded on contact and a fellow pilot from Hubbard's flight recalls he saw a ball of flame with a propeller protruding from it as it fell. He was so shocked that he continued the flight out of formation, keeping a secure distance from the other aircraft. The second aircraft was seen to fall out of control with one wing missing outboard of the engine. It all happened so fast that the witness statements at the time seem confused as to what had actually occurred.

Both aircraft fell on tidal mudflats in the Ribble estuary close to the base and at first there seemed hope that there could be survivors and as crowds gathered at the waters edge, some thought they saw

2nd Lt. Kenneth E. Hubbard
(Hubbard family)

movement inside one of the fuselages. Many servicemen from BAD2 had witnessed the tragedy and one of them; Sgt Stanley C. Begonsky immediately began to wade and then swim out to the burning aircraft, being the first to reach them. At the first aircraft the fire had by now died down, but as he looked into the cockpit he realised that the two crewmen inside were beyond help. He then waded to the second still burning plane, but at first he could see little through the thick smoke. Crouching down he chopped his way into the cockpit where he found the pilot amidst flames and began to drag him out, but sadly again he was beyond help, having been killed instantly in the impact. By this time several lifeboatmen arrived at the scene in the local lifeboat boarding boat – the lifeboat itself being out of action whilst undergoing repairs. They recovered the two bodies from the first aircraft with the help of Sgt. Begonsky, who showed them how to gain access to the cockpit and then returned amid exploding flares and burning fuel to recover the third body and transported them all back to the shore.

As these dramatic events were unfolding, it was of course still night time back in the United States and Hubbard's fiancé was startled to be awoken from her sleep by the sound of his voice calling her name. Unsure of the meaning of this event, she wrote down the time and date and later she found it would have been the same time that the crash had taken place and his untimely death, thousands of miles away across the Atlantic.

Sgt. Begonsky and the ten lifeboat men involved that day were later to receive awards for gallantry for their rescue attempts. For some reason the wrecks of the two Invaders were left where they had fallen, gradually disappearing from view as the marsh began to consolidate and the level of accumulating mud rose to cover them. Only the tail of 43-22298 remained visible by the 1950s, providing occasional shelter during inclement weather for the few hardy wildfowlers who ventured out onto this part of the marsh.

By the time of our next visit at the end of February we had spent many hours poring over photographs from the crash report and aerial surveys at the local Record Office, attempting to workout exactly where the various sections would lie – now we would see if theory would translate into practice! Two of our team recalled an expedition to the site in the 1980s when two propeller blade tips had also been visible, but these too had apparently vanished. However, the preparation paid off and by the time we packed up, we had located and had GPS references for both aircraft and all four of their engines – the prop tips were still there, hidden in the grass – as we discovered when tripping over one of them! Planning now began in earnest with permit applications being submitted to the MoD and consultation with regards to the equipment and logistics that would be required to carry out an excavation in such difficult terrain. Things were not to run smoothly however, as preparations progressed it became clear that the essential MoD permits were not forthcoming and after numerous enquiries it finally transpired that a permit could now not be issued without English Nature consent, the site being SSSI designated and we had been awaiting MoD consent before approaching English Nature!

As with all such projects the date set seemed to arrive all too quickly and before long we were again at the site, this time as preparations for

End of "Day One" and as the light fades, the first R-2800 engine is recovered and briefly takes to the air after 60 years underground.

the dig started two days before filming – tracks across the marsh had to be marked out, tidal gutters bridged and plant equipment moved out to the site. The incident room was set up at the BAe Warton Sports Club and the on-site catering arrived – certainly a bit different from our usual dig arrangements! Access to the site was to be via two Hagglund BV206 all-terrain personnel carriers. Other specialist equipment included: a third trailer and crane equipped Hagglund, a six wheeled all-terrain crane-equipped Supacat, two high flotation tracked 20 ton excavators, one with long reach arm and a 12 ton tracked dumper – plenty of toys to play with! Various 'experts' were brought in by Time Team including Guy De La Bedoyere and Air Crash Investigator Steve Moss, as well as an RAF 'crash and smash' team and EOD (Explosive Ordnance Disposal).

Day 1 arrived and saw the first two trenches opened on the tail section of 43-22298 and one of the detached engines that we had identified. 'Geophys' were busy surveying the areas that we had indicated – no doubt glad that we had narrowed down the area for them from the 20 or so acres we had started off with for our grid search months earlier. Progress on the engine was rapid with the excavator carefully avoiding the upright propeller blade that had protruded only a couple of inches above the surface. Once the engine was reached the excavation continued by hand and with a nearby gutter dammed, the excavation stayed surprisingly dry. Unfortunately, the same could not be said over at the tail where almost constant ingress of water made conditions very sticky indeed, but Phil Harding was on the case and determined not to be beaten. The engine proved remarkably undamaged and cylinder heads, exhaust stacks and ignition harness were soon revealed as well as the still attached propeller with all three blades intact. Though moving back towards the ancillary section revealed a different story – the magnesium supercharger and accessory casings had completely disappeared leaving ancillary assemblies lying loose, including a superbly preserved carburettor. The same was found to be the case with the reduction gear casing, where, of course, the engine maker's plate would have been, meaning identification of which plane this engine had originated from would be difficult. Fortunately one of the modifications known to have been incorporated on one of the aircraft was the fitting of R-2800-71 engines, with an improved ignition system using the distinctive General Electric 'Turtleback' combined distributor magneto units and as the mud was cleared one of these units was uncovered still in place and clearly bearing its GEC logo cast into the casing. This engine was therefore from 43-22336 flown by 2nd Lt. Norman Zuber and perhaps this was the propeller seen 'protruding from a ball of flame' 60 years before? As the day drew to a close and the film-crew seemed happy with their coverage of the excavation of the engine it was decided that it could now be lifted whilst there was sufficient light to film the operation.

Following a final check of the engine trench for any missed loose artefacts, Day 2 saw what was to be one of the biggest ever trenches on Time Team, opened on the remains of 43-22298. Geophys had already produced a remarkably aeroplane – shaped printout after passing their instruments over the site – complete with wings – much to the amusement of an incredulous Tony Robinson. However, it came as no surprise to us having spent so much time studying the crash photos and aerial surveys, we were already convinced of what lay below, but what condition it would be in after 60 years no one could predict. As the cockpit area began to emerge, the first signs appeared promising, with solid skinning to the fuselage sides and wing roots, but then we realised that we were in fact looking at the additional thick duralumin cladding applied as extra protection against small-arms fire when attacking ground targets at low level. In fact as the wings and remains of the rear fuselage began to emerge we realised that we were looking at a 20th Century 'fossil' with much of the metal being replaced by crystalline corrosion products and concreted mud. Still it looked amazing as the distinctive outline of a Douglas Invader began to emerge. Conditions were sticky to say the least as we cleared the final layer of mud from around the fuselage by hand to avoid damage and

2nd Lt. Norman Zuber (centre) poses with his crew in front of their A-20 (*Russell Brown*)

trying to excavate inside the constricted fuselage was really slow going. Another problem was sinking into the glutinous morass and I noted that TT Supervisor Kerry Ely had found a nice solid object to stand on and save him from losing his wellies, until I politely pointed out to him that his handy foothold was in fact a 0.50 calibre Browning machine gun! This was the EOD team's cue to emerge from their tent and with the film crew in position, the gun was removed to their custody to be X-rayed to ensure no live ammunition was present.

As the day progressed we reached the relatively hard sand which had formed the original surface the aircraft had landed on 60 years before and another surprise awaited us. The uncovered fuselage proved to be only some 3 to 4 feet high – it had obviously impacted flat with almost no forward momentum, the sides of the fuselage ballooning out as if it had been squashed flat. In fact the gunners control position in the rear fuselage had completely collapsed, no longer having the structure of the severed tail unit to support it. The sides had burst

As the cockpit of Hubbard's A-26 is slowly uncovered, Tony Robinson is filmed watching as a .50 calibre Browning machine gun emerges from the mud. (*Andrew Boardman*)

The intact remotely controlled upper gun turret, complete with its guns was a surprising find, considering the apparent accessibility of the wreck immediately after the crash.

outwards and the glazed escape hatch, once set in the top of the fuselage, was found lying on the sand, pinned down by a large and heavy cylindrical object that had fallen from the upper section of the rear bomb bay. Uncovering the perforated cooling sleeves of the twin 0.50 Brownings protruding from the domed cover quickly identified this object as the remotely-operated upper gun turret, part of one of the most sophisticated airborne fire control systems of WW2.

Back at the tail section, the trench was by now taking on the appearance of a small lagoon, with the now fully exposed rear fuselage still clearly marked with its 'Star & Bar' insignia. However, hopes of lifting this section in one piece were diminishing rapidly, with a serious crack from the impact now opening up, coupled with a large section of the underside having been torn out as the lower turret obviously fell away when the plane broke up in the air. The turret itself was found in a tidal gutter between the two sites.

As with all TT projects, Day 3 promised to be pretty hectic, though we had discussed the possibility of excavating a complete aircraft, the reality was something else! The tail section had yet to be lifted, pending the decision on cutting it into two parts – recovery of this section had originally been scheduled for Day 1! We continued to clear the fuselage of 43-22298, revealing the full length of the starboard

Graphic evidence of the catastrophic collision between the two Invaders in the form of the twisted wing spars, where the port wing was torn off Hubbard's A-26. (*Mark Gaskell*)

wing and the shattered spars protruding from the torn off port wing. The rear fuselage, though now flattened, was found to extend to the point where the separated tail section began, but beyond it a further section of airframe began to come to light. This proved to be the starboard nacelle, which had been swept from the wing by the force of the impact and the rear end fairing showed clear evidence of an internal explosion at the site of the de-icing fluid reservoir. Priority was given to clearing the cockpit and centre fuselage, the latter proving almost impossible due to the burnt and shredded remains of the centre self-sealing fuel tank. The cockpit also showed signs of a brief but intense fire, with plenty of charred wiring, but no signs of any instrumentation or flying controls. Also obviously absent was the complicated hydraulic systems behind the pilot's position. It became clear that although the wreck had not been recovered, there had been a thorough and systematic stripping out of most of the avionics – hardly surprising as the A-26 was probably the technical equivalent in its day of the Eurofighter Typhoon, which constantly over-flew the site throughout the 3-day dig, often so low it was obvious that they were trying to get a better look at the dig! Digging further into the cockpit revealed dramatic evidence of the impact, as the folded nose wheel assembly,

A-26 Invader 43-22298 completely uncovered for the first time in over 60 years. (*Andrew Boardman*)

complete with intact wheel and tyre, had been forced up through the cockpit floor. With the lift of the tail finally completed, albeit in two sections, more diggers were freed to finish clearing the incredibly intact airframe. The upper turret was lifted in one piece, though largely held together with mud and the starboard engine was cleared ready to lift, proving that it too had broken away from its mounting and in fact lay several feet in front of its original position.

As the filming drew to a close the experts began piecing together the evidence to come up with their theory on how the two A-26s came to collide. In the past people had noted the position of the then visible wreckage, in relation to the alignment of the main runway at Warton, assuming that this was a simple take-off accident. The front aircraft either developing a fault and slowed down or the rear aircraft applied too much power and ran into the back of the former. Our research had already showed that the aircraft were in fact circling the airfield whilst they got into their assigned positions to fly in close formation to their destination, as was the normal procedure at the time.

The A-26 was a brand new aircraft and had only just gone into operational use, but a major problem had already emerged – that of

Engine makers plate from the first R2800 recovered, confirming that this engine in fact originated from Zuber's aircraft.

pilot visibility beyond the prominent engine nacelles. A revised canopy arrangement had quickly been drawn up at least partly to alleviate the problem, but revising the production line and modifying aircraft already delivered was giving Douglas further headaches. In fact they did attempt to introduce the new design by hand building the modified section in lieu of a major revision of the line, but this obviously slowed production and no provision for field modification was put in place. Hubbard's aircraft appeared from the records to have been fitted with the original style of canopy and this was confirmed during the excavation. Zuber's on the other hand should have had the revised canopy, perhaps this why Hubbard was accompanied by a flight engineer and Zuber not? In the event it made no difference. A large gouge in the top of the tail section appeared to indicate that first contact had been made in this area (in contradiction to TTs findings!). The propeller would have sliced into the gunner's compartment and the damage to this weaker, glazed section of the airframe, together with the weight of the ventral turret behind this position must have led to the break-up. In fact the evidence seemed to point to the two aircraft having become almost locked together – the two wrecks coming down within 80 feet of each other and collision damage being clearly visible on the blades of the engines from both aircraft (another fact overlooked).

The following day, with filming finished, we were given permission

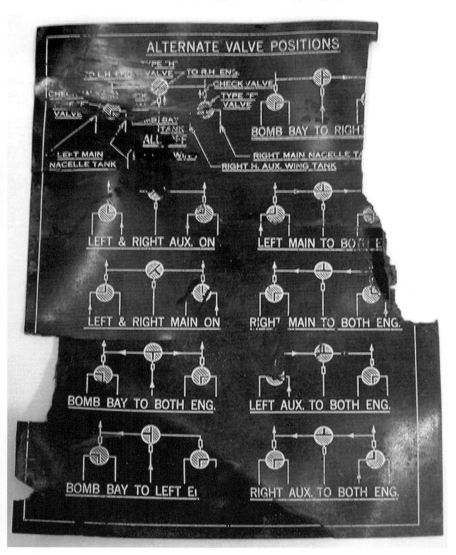

Due to the complexity of the new A-26, pilot's were provided with "Aide-memoire" cards for reference in the cockpit. This one from Zuber's aircraft covers the many positions of the main fuel valves and indicates which tanks would be supplying the engines.

to use the equipment, when it was not required landscaping the filled-in TT excavations, to continue our recovery work. We discussed the options and decided to excavate the second aircraft, as we knew from study of the crash report photos that this was already largely destroyed in the impact and subsequent fire. We reasoned that any attempt to disturb Hubbard's aircraft would have simply resulted in its disintegration, leaving us with little more than a lorry-load of individual components. As we were dealing with identical aircraft it seemed disrespectful to commit such vandalism when the second aircraft was probably little more than individual components anyway. Progress was rapid and as the mud was scooped clear, our theory proved

"Day Four" and with filming finished, our excavation of 43-22336 gets underway as the nosewheel leg and surrounding structure are lifted clear.

correct with the wings having been reduced to little more than a pair of girder-like spars, though an intact main oleo unit was recovered, still attached to a section of main spar and complete with its charred tyre. The upper gun turret was next, minus it guns, but this was almost entirely reduced to crystalline corrosion products and rapidly disintegrated when moved, leaving only its stainless steel traversing gear ring recognisable amid a heap of white powder. It did reveal the well-preserved bomb racks below and these were duly recovered. Moving aft we found no substantial remains of the tail section, despite this being visible in the wartime photographs of the wreck, so we then followed the trail of wiring forward. This soon brought several duralumin cladding sections from the cockpit to light, but this time there was no aircraft structure behind them. The only substantial remains of the airframe found was the cockpit floor section, which had embedded in the wet sand and escaped the fire. This still had the complete nose wheel assembly folded into its well underneath – the magnesium alloy wheel had long since disappeared but the tyre was unmarked.

Other smaller finds included: Batteries, radios, both rudder pedals, control column, an amazingly intact pilot's seat and the pilot's ashtray! Next to this was a printed fibre aide-mémoire card for the fuel valve settings – it seemed strange to think of the pilot surrounded by hundreds of gallons of high-octane fuel being allowed to smoke, but perhaps considering the danger these guys faced on a daily basis, the need for such comforts outweighed the risk? Our records of this second excavation included a sketch of where the various components had been found in relation to each other and study of this showed that Zuber's aircraft had in fact come to rest, broken in half with the tail at 90 degrees to the forward fuselage – again indicating a weak point around the gunners position, as well as facing Hubbard's aircraft, nose to nose! This together with the scatter of the remaining engines gives a distinct impression of the two planes spiralling down out-of-control following the collision – sadly too low for any chance of baling out.

In the final analysis there seems little point in trying to attribute blame for this incident, it serves no purpose, there is no doubt that both pilots were very accomplished and experienced, each having completed some fifty missions, but both were inexperienced on the type. Reading Hubbard's last letter home to his relatives, dated 25 November 1944 and

The author (right) and LAIT member Russell Brown contemplate the pilot's seat from 43-22336, last occupied by 2nd Lt. Norman Zuber on that fateful day 60 years before. (Mark Sheldon)

addressed simply 'France', paints a picture of a pilot who was growing tired of the war; the excitement was gone and replaced by a sense of duty, seeing his missions as merely work to be done. However, there is no complacency evident, he clearly knew that the war, in Europe at least, was coming to a close and he was determined to live through it and return to his fiancé in the States. He goes on to relate that he 'hasn't been raising much hell lately' and had been getting plenty of sleep and it certainly seems safe to assume that he would have in no way taken any unnecessary risks. Though we know less about 2nd Lt. Norman Zuber and Corporal John F. Guy, it is likely that they were of a similar outlook, certainly Guy had joined the 641st in November

This pilot's ashtray from Zuber's A-26 must surely be a unique find from a WW2 combat aircraft?

1943, coming over to England with the squadron in April 1944 and had been awarded the Purple Heart, with Zuber being assigned in June 1944. Whatever the circumstances, the visibility problems inherent to the design of the A-26 cockpit, which had already been identified, particularly with regard to close formation flying, was undoubtedly the critical factor. But actually establishing which plane was the cause of the accident proved impossible to ascertain and perhaps it is better to leave it that way. We felt from the start that determining the cause of the crash was never really a suitable mystery to be solved and perhaps Tony Robinson introducing the project with the line: "Could there really still be an intact WW2 Bomber, lying below just our feet?" would have sufficed for most viewers and allowed everyone to concentrate on the excavation itself.

For us, the most important outcome of this project, was the opportunity to uncover and properly record one of the most intact aircraft wrecks in the UK, whilst there is still enough of it left to examine. The extremely advanced state of corrosion surprised everyone – not even the virtually anaerobic conditions present in the marsh could prevent the highly reactive aircraft alloys disintegrating, providing a graphic warning that much of the wreckage at all crash sites will eventually succumb, leaving fewer and fewer artefacts to be uncovered as time moves on. The recovered engines and tail section hopefully can be successfully conserved and form a dramatic memorial at the RAF Millom Museum.

The cleaned engines and a main undercarriage leg now form a dramatic memorial outside the museum at Millom.

APPENDIX I: AIRCRAFT INCIDENTS

DATE	AIRCRAFT	SERIAL NO.	LOCATION	REASON	PILOT	UNIT
26/06/17	Avro 504K	D7001	Wirral	Spun in	P/O E Pentland	5 FTS
27/01/18	Sopwith Dolphin		In River Mersey off Hooton Park	Dived in	2/Lt. John Daniel George Brendel	4 TDS
3/03/19	SE5A		IOM			
2/05/23	Avro 504	H7530	Blacon, Cheshire, near Chester	Lost control & crashed		5 FTS
1/06/28	Avro 504N	J8542	Ledsham, Cheshire, Two Mills	Engine failed at 1000ft. After take off & crashed		5 FTS
6/11/28	AW Atlas I	(AW289)	? Preston Moor, Yorkshire	Crashed		26 Squadron
23/7/29	Avro 504K	H2618	Agden, Altrincham, Cheshire	Attempting F/L & spun in		5 FTS
10/25/31	AW Atlas I ?	(AW296)	Aldford, Cheshire, near Chester	Struck ground attempting F/L in bad weather		26 Squadron
16/07/36	Hart	K6474	Speke	Force landed due to engine failure	F/O Peter Stanley Salter	611 Squadron
19/09/36	Hart	K3044	Speke	Taxying/Landing accident	F/O Peter Stanley Salter	611 Squadron
8/11/36	Hart		Nr Northwich from Speke	Force landed	F/O McComb	611 Squadron
5/12/36	Hart		Nr Kingsley, Cheshire from Speke	Force landed	F/O Peter Stanley Salter	611 Squadron
12/12/36	Heyford II	K4874	Oldham, Lancashire	Crashed		102 Squadron
12/12/36	Heyford III	K6898	Disley, Cheshire	Crashed		102 Squadron
12/12/36	Heyford III	K6900	Hebden Bridge, Yorkshire	Crashed into hill		102 Squadron
12/02/37	Hart	K4931	Wrexham, North Wales	Crashed		5 FTS
19/03/37	Hawker Hind	K6617	Lowca, Whitehaven	Engine failure	R Vaughan, Cpl WA Ballett	98 Squadron
4/06/37	Vildebeest	K4607	Penrith, Cumbria	Crashed		42 Squadron
5/06/37	Vickers Vilderbeast III	K4607	Shelter Crags	Flew into Hillside	Sgt F Wilkinson	42 Squadron
5/06/37	Hawker Hind	K6614	Threshthwaite Cove, Ulverston	Flew into Hillside	Sgt S Mitchell	98 Squadron
22/07/37	Heyford III	K6875	Edale, Derbyshire	Crashed		166 Squadron
26/11/37	Hawker Hind	K6632	Workington	Engine failure	P/O E A Hunt	218 Squadron
6/12/37	Audax	K5159	Everton, Liverpool	Crashed		5 FTS
10/06/38	Bristol Blenheim	L1157	IOM			
22/07/38	DH60 Moth	K1890	Barton, Lancashire	Failed to pull out of dive		5 FTS
6/08/38	Hector	K9759	?Pennines	Crashed on high ground		13 Squadron
30/08/38	Blenheim Mk I	K7067	Near Redesdale Camp,	Icing	Major Edwards, H.I. (Aus)	
21/10/38	Harrow II	K7019	3 miles NE of Speke, Nr Halewood	Engine failed at 4,000ft	Sgt E F Lines 564865	115 Squadron
3/01/39	Gloster Gladiator	K7998	Great Corby	Fuel Shortage	P/O G Evans	25 Squadron
20/01/39	Fairy Battle		Seascale	Mechanical Failure		
30/01/39	Blenheim	L1476	Sykes Moor	Flew into high ground		64 Squadron
20/05/39	Lysander II	L4784	Ringway	Stalled at low speed	Stanley John Daly Robinson	26 Squadron
28/05/39	Hart	K3864	?Dene Valley, Cheshire	Crashed		28 ERFTS

Date	Aircraft	Serial	Pilot	Cause	Squres Gate	Unit
7/06/39	Henley I	L3294		Belly landed in error	Carrington Moss, Lancs	1 AACU
27/06/39	Tiger Moth II	N6470		Stalled on forced landing and tipped up		17 ERFTS
12/07/39	Hind T	L7214		Damaged in Hanger Fire	Speke	
18/07/39	Spitfire Mk I	K9888	Sgt Mitchell	Hit ground in rain storm	5 miles NE Knock, Cumbria, Appleby	611 Squadron
28/07/39	Hudson I	N7260		Broke up in air & crashed	Thurstaston, Wirral from Speke	Lockheed
10/10/39	Hart Trainer	K6482	Mycroft, T	Spun into ground, cause unknown	Cheviot Hill, Northumberland	
20/10/39	Master I	N7415	SD Flt Perth		?Burton Meadows, Cheshire	5 FTS
8/11/39	Blenhiem	P4848		Flew into hill in bad visibility	Kirbyshie, North Wales	
9/11/39	Henley	L3391			IOM	
28/11/39	Battle	K7628			IOM	
29/11/39	Wellington	L4388		Collided with L4389	Silloth	22 MU
29/11/39	Wellington	L4389		Collided with L4388	Silloth	22 MU
1/01/40	Handley Page Hampden	P1260	P/O Horace McGregor	Flew into hillside	Snaefell, IOM	7 Squadron
8/01/40	Audax	K5151		Ranaway backward downhill after forced landing	IOM	
8/01/40	Harvard I	P5820			Ambergate nr Birkenhead	15 FTS
11/01/40	Oxford	N6263		Baled Out	IOM	
15/01/40	Avro Tutor	K3422		Lost in fog & abandoned	Nr Slaggie Ford	
15/01/40	Tutor	K4820		Forced Landing	Alston, Cumbria	
25/01/40	Avro Tutor	P4223	S/L G V Williamson	Crashed on high ground	Alston	500 Squadron
23/02/40	Swordfish	K4800	F/Lt G A B Cooper	Oil pressure dropped	Holmfirth, Derbyshire	22 MU
2/03/40	Avro Tutor	X9325		Forced Landing	Bowness on Windermere	
4/03/40	Hornet Moth	K6758	Ward-Hunt, P	Crashed	Penrith	
5/03/40	Hind	N5094	P/O Armstrong	Emergency Landing	Hoylake, Cheshire, on beach	5 FTS
6/03/40	Anson Mk I	K6655		Force Landed	Alwinton, Northumberland	9 AONS
13/03/40	Hawker Hind	N5385			Cockermouth	
17/03/40	Anson	L4063	Ayres, VJ		On beach at Bispham	
8/04/40	Hampden Mk I	L9039		Flew into mountain in cloud	Cocklawfoot, Roxburghshire	
19/04/40	Blenheim IV			Force Landed	Bethesda, North Wales	13 OTU
	Oxford			Force Landed	Burtonwood	
30/04/40	Whitley IV	K9039		Low on fuel, Bad weather, crashed in F/L	Slaidburn, Burnside Fell	51 Squadron
7/05/40	Tutor	K3308			Edale, Derbyshire	Avro
23/05/40	Hampden	L4055		Ran out of fuel & crashed	Holme Moss	83 Squadron
3/06/40	Fairy Battle	P2157	A/C Okie	Crash Landing - unqualified pilot	Kingstown	15 FTS
8/06/40	Whitley	N1356			IOM	
9/06/40	Master I	N7477		Dived into ground	Holly Bush, North Wales	5 FTS

Date	Aircraft	Serial	Location	Cause	Crew	Unit
10/06/40	Battle	L4951	Outside boundry of Squires Gate	Landing accident	F/L A Chalmers	13 OTU
13/06/40	Wellington	N3012	IOM			
14/06/40	Battle	P6753	IOM			
19/06/40	Blenheim	L1154	IOM			
17/07/40	Miles Magister	P6412	River Esk	Flew into power cables		15 FTS
22/07/40	Miles Magister I	T9738	Kingstown	Crash Landing		15 FTS
22/07/40	Miles Magister I	L6124	Mossband	Crash Landing		15 FTS
25/07/40	Blackburn Botha I	L8336	Cockermouth	Mechanical Failure	P/O Bradshaw	
26/07/40	Miles Magister I	L7963	Kingstown	Heavy Landing		
1/08/40	Anson	P2073	IOM	Undercarriage collapsed		
2/08/40	Hampden	K7141	Burtonwood			
5/08/40	Blenheim	N1411	IOM	Emergency Landing		
7/08/40	Whitley	AS981	Squires Gate	Engine failure	P/O E G Libbey	271 Squadron
23/08/40	HP 42 Horsa	AS426	Moresby Parks	Engine failure	Plt Off M N Hesketh	4 FPP
24/08/40	Buffalo	L6160	Few miles short of Burtonwood	Crashed at Night	P/O D Alexander 9093	1 OTU
8/24/40	Blackburn Botha I	N2945	Silloth			
28/08/40	Wellington	L6203	IOM	Crashed		1 OTU
2/09/40	Blackburn Botha I	K7249	Silloth	Damaged during test		
3/09/40	Whitley II	P5011	Burtonwood	Overshot on take off into trees.	P/O Honeyman	51 Squadron
3/09/40	Whitley V	X4159	Adjacent to RAF Dishforth	Oygen failure, Crashed	Pilot Sgt Edgar	7 OTU
5/09/40	Spitfire I	P9563	Tatton Hall, Cheshire	Crashed		64 Squadron
12/09/40	Spitfire	?L2929 or L2629	Hartington	Engine failed, abandoned over high ground	P/O D R Strachan	4 FPP
15/09/40	Skua	N7456	Bentham, Lancashire	Stalled recovering from dive & hit ground		5 FTS
18/09/40	Master I	N7936	Tattenhall, Cheshire	Failed to pull out of dive		5 FTS
22/09/40	Master I	L8076	Dodleston, Cheshire	Flying Accident		15 FTS
22/09/40	Miles Magister I	T9713	Kingstown	Flying Accident		15 FTS
22/09/40	Miles Magister I	V6668	Kingstown	Force landing		
24/09/40	Hurricane	N7944	Waddington, Near Clitheroe	Abandoned in spin in cloud & crashed into river		5 FTS
27/09/40	Master I	L5672	Dee River			
27/09/40	Fairey Battle	N9095	IOM			
28/09/40	Hereford	N8010	IOM	Engine failure	S/L Stefan Laszkiewicz	308 Squadron
29/09/40	Miles Master	N3640	Baginton	Crash Landing		7 Squadron
29/09/40	Short Stirling	K6236	Barbon	Short of fuel & crash landed		
30/09/40	Stirling I	L4189	Hodder Bridge, Cumbria, near Kirkby Lonsdale			
30/09/40	Anson I	L5671	Blackpool, on South Shore	Crashed in forced landing		1 SGR
110/40	Hampden		Black Edge			106 Squadron
	Fairey Battle		IOM			

3/10/40	Master I	N7442	Lanford Tool Works, Burtonwood, Latchford, Warrington, Burtonwood ?		Crashed	5 FTS
5/10/40	Westland Lysander II	N1295	Minera, 4.5 miles W of Wrexham	P/O H Thomas	Flew into hill in bad visibility	
6/10/40	Boston		Kirby Sephen		Emergency Landing	Lockheed
6/10/40	Audax	P6750	Speke Airport		Bomb damage	
6/10/40	Fairey Battle		Speke Airport		Bomb damage	
7/10/40	Hurricane I		IOM		Bomb damage	312 Squadron
8/10/40	Ju88	4068	Bromborough, Wirral	Helmuth Bruckman	Shot down	KG2/806
10/10/40	Hurricane I	L1547	Off End Runway 8 in the River Mersey at Speke Airport, Liverpool, Lancashire	Sergeant Otto Hanzlicek	Engine Failure	312 Squadron
13/10/40	Blenheim	L6637	Point of Ayr	Sergeant Robert Edard Stevens	Shot down in error	29 Squadron
15/10/40	Hurricane I	V6542	Near Dalton-in-Furness, from Speke	F/L HAG Comerford	Crashed ran out of fuel	312 Squadron
15/10/40	Hurricane I	V6811	Near Dalton-in-Furness, from Speke	P/O T Vybiral	Crashed ran out of fuel	312 Squadron
15/10/40	Hurricane I	V6846	Near Carnforth, from Speke	J K Ambrus	Forced landed ran out of fuel	312 Squadron
16/10/40	Henley I	L3317	Liverpool Bay		Engine Failure	1 AACU
16/10/40	Hurricane	P3399	Near Baginton	S/L Davis	Hit Ballon Cables	308 Squadron
16/10/40	Hurricane	V6859	Baginton	F/L Young	Landing accident	308 Squadron
17/10/40	Vickers Wellington Ic	L7857	Penrith		Baled Out	75 Squadron
23/10/40	Blenheim I	L1272	Kirkby Malzeard, Yorkshire		Control lost in cloud & dived into hill	600 Squadron
24/10/40	He111 ?		Liverpool Bay		Hit ballon barrage	
25/10/40	Bristol Blenheim	K7154	IOM			15 FTS
26/10/40	Miles Magister I	R1846	Carlisle		Hoar Frost on wings	15 FTS
26/10/40	Miles Magister I	R1850	Carlisle		Hoar Frost on wings	15 FTS
26/10/40	Miles Magister I	R1853	Carlisle		Hoar Frost on wings	15 FTS
26/10/40	Miles Magister I	R1904	Carlisle		Hoar Frost on wings	15 FTS
26/10/40	Miles Magister I	T9736	Carlisle		Hoar Frost on wings	15 FTS
30/10/40	Whitley	P4957	Slaggyford		Crashed	10 Squadron
31/10/40	Wellington	N2755	Squires Gate		Forced Landed	4 FPP
3/11/40	Magister I	L8154	Gisburn, Lancashire		Stalled in forced landing & hit tree	15 FTS
7/11/40	Spitfire IIA	P9330	Hooton Park		Overturned on Landing on boggy ground.	610 Squadron
11/11/40	Blenheim	L1200	Speke	P/O Cohen	Crashed	8 RSS
11/11/40	Hurricane I	P3810	Near Speke airport	Sgt Otto Spacek 787671	Forced landed with engine failure	312 Squadron

Date	Aircraft	Serial	Location	Cause	Crew	Unit
13/11/40	Boulton Paul Defiant	N1682	IOM			10 FTS
14/11/40	Westland Wallace	K5076	IOM	Flew into hill in bad visibility		2 OTU
14/11/40	Anson I	N9858	Macclesfield, Wildboarclough			4 FPP
17/11/40	Blenhiem	L6800	Monyash			
17/11/40	Spitfire	P7596	The Roaches			
26/11/40	Boulton Paul Defiant	N1624	IOM			
26/11/40	Master I	N7839	Speke, In Mersey	Crashed into river after take off		57 OTU
26/11/40	Avro Anson I	W1790	Kingstown	Crash Landing		
27/11/40	Blenhiem	T1884	Stockport, Greater Manchester	Abandoned & aircraft destroyed		105 Squadron
28/11/40	Blenhiem	T1884	Harrop Edge			105 Squadron
2/12/40	Boulton Paul Defiant	L7035	IOM			
3/12/40	Blenhiem	K7172	Woolley Bridge			29 Squadron
6/12/40	Spitfire I	L1049	Speke	Crashed on Landing		57 OTU
7/12/40	Westland Wallace	K4342	IOM			
9/12/40	Henley I	L3370	On beach at Blackpool, Lancs	Engine cut and belly landed	McGregor, H.B	1 AACU
11/12/40	Spitfire Mk IA	P9451	Nr Eglingham, Northumberland			
11/12/40	Spitfire Mk1	X4649	Nr Eglingham, Northumberland	Ross, A.R		
14/12/40	Hurricane I	V6810	Crossens, Southport, from Speke	Force landed	P/O H C Gundry	312 Squadron
14/12/40	Hurricane IB	V6924	Crossens, Southport, from Speke	Force landed	Sgt J Janeba 787707	312 Squadron
17/12/40	Westland Wallace	K6073	IOM			
17/12/40	Lysander III	R9062	Hooton Park	Undershot and hit tree		13 Squadron
17/12/40	Lysander III	R9063	Hooton Park	Spun In		13 Squadron
20/12/40	Hawker Henley	L3325	IOM			
21/12/40	Hampden	X3154	Rushup Edge		Michael Hubbard	106 Squadron
22/12/40	Hampden	X3154	Chapel en le Frith, Derbyshire	Crashed into hill	P/O Hubbard	106 Squadron
23/12/40	Boulton Paul Defiant	N1641	IOM			
23/12/40	Hurricane	V6862	Squires Gate	Taxiing Accident	P/O Leggett	96 Squadron
24/12/40	Hampden	P2071	Nantwich,Cheshire	Abandoned & crashed	Sgt Snowden	106 Squadron
28/12/40	Hurricane	P3899	In sea of Squires Gate	Crashed in Sea during practie night flight	P/O L M Sharpe	96 Squadron
29/12/40	Spitfire	L1045	Squires Gate	Overshoot landing in trench and overturned		9 FPP
31/12/40	Magister I	L8355	Ullswater lake, Cumbria, 3 miles SW of Pooley Br.	Hit water low flying & dived into lake		15 FTS
1/01/41	Defiant	N3432	Windermere, Cumbria	Flew into hill in mist		
1/01/41	Anson I	R3305	Beach at Hoylake, wirral	Wing hit ground in turn		60 OTU
2/01/41	Hawker Hart	K3866	IOM			48 Squadron
7/01/41	Botha I	L6126	Irish Sea of Whitehaven	Ditched		

Date	Type	Serial	Location	Circumstance	Crew	Unit
9/01/41	Defiant	N3315	Squires Gate	Taxied into a ditch	P/O R. Smok	307 Squadron
10/01/41	Defiant	N1684	Squires Gate	Hit by taxiing aircraft		307 Squadron
10/01/41	Defiant	N1699	Squires Gate	Taxied into parked		307 Squadron
10/01/41	Defiant	N3401	In sea near Barmouth	forced landing	Sgt L. Mironczuk.	307 Squadron
10/01/41	Hurricane I	P3522	?Calberth Moor, Yorkshire	Flew into hill in cloud	Sgt A. Joda	213 Squadron
14/01/41	Lysander II	R2000	Runcorn, Cheshire	Hit balloon cable in bad visibility & crashed		6 AACU
15/01/41	Blackburn Botha	L6126	IOM			15 FTS
16/01/41	Bristol Blenheim	K7131	IOM			15 FTS
16/01/41	Magister I	R1843	Solway Firth	Engine failure	D M Crook,	220 Squadron
21/01/41	Magister I	T9687	Kingstown	Overturned		307 Squadron
22/01/41	Hudson II	N3320	Scath Nick, Osmotherly, Lancs	Flew into high ground	Sgt J. Milszo.	9 FPP
23/01/41	Defiant	R3399	Down Holland, Lydiate	Force landed		
23/01/41	Anson		Nr Marshside Road, Southport	Emergency Landing/Pilot Error	Flight Lieutenant Dennis Brian Brooks	
26/01/41	Blenheim I	K7076	Masham, Yorkshire	Flew into high ground		54 OTU
26/01/41	Blenheim	Z5746	Ox Stones	Stalled on approach and undercarriage collapsed		2 Squadron
29/01/41	Botha I	L6228	Squires Gate	Force Landed		3 SGR
31/01/41	Wellington	R1391	Cockerham	Force Landed		149 Squadron
1/02/41	Spitfire I	K9890	Hooton Park, River Mersey	Landed out of fuel in river		AST
1/02/41	Hurricane I	P3658	Newby	Engine failure		258 Squadron
4/02/41	Defiant	L4479	Squires Gate	Damaged during landing		307 Squadron
4/02/41	Beaufort	R1298	Morecombe Beach	Force Landed		3 OTU
4/02/41	Wellington	T7055	Middlewich, Cheshire	Hit balloon cable & crashed		18 OTU
4/02/41	Tiger Moth II		Kingstown	Overturned		
4/02/41	Hurricane	V7078	Speke, Liverpool, River Mersey	Crashed into river in bad visibility	Sgt John Arbuthnott 564104t	229 Squadron
5/02/41	Fulmar	N4076	Wrexham, Minerva mountain	Crashed on mountain	S/L S G Burden	Station Flight
10/02/41	Magister I	N3951	Bolton, Lancashire	Hit wall in forced landing on road		
12/02/41	Wellington	P3588	Greyrigg	Ran out of fuel		
13/02/41	Hurricane I	V6885	Ashton Field Colliery, Walkden, Lancs. From Speke.	Engine failure	P/O (acting F/Lt) J F F Finnis	229 Squadron
13/02/41	Hurricane I		Talacre near Prestatyn, North Wales, from Speke	Dived into ground during a diving turn	Pilot Officer Jindrich Bartos 83220	312 Squadron
17/02/41	Anson	K6283	Bradnop	Crashed during forced landing		23 ANS
17/02/41	Hector	K9754	Near Ringway	Rolled & dived into ground		CLE
17/02/41	Defiant	N3314	Wrea Green, Lancashire			307 Squadron
21/02/41	Botha		Jurby IOM	Engine Failure		
22/02/41	Botha		Sealand, Chester	Engine Failure		
22/02/41	Hurricane I	P3612	Penrhos	Crashed on take off	Sgt F Kruta 787674	312 Squadron

Date	Aircraft	Serial	Location	Cause	Name	Unit
23/02/41	Hawker Henley	L3332	IOM	Crashed on beach		1 GDGS
23/02/41	Botha	L6506	Beach at South shore Blackpool	Crashed on landing		
25/02/41	Westland Wallace	K6068	Ronaldsway IOM	Mechanical Failure		
26/02/41	Battle		Methop			6 AACU
26/02/41	Battle I	L5011	Low Meathop, Grange over sands	Engine cut and hit ground	F/O Callington	
3/03/41	Tomahawk	AK126	Squires Gate	Landing accident	S/Lt P Constable	
3/03/41	Botha	L6319	Squires Gate	Taxiing Accident		
4/03/41	Master I	N7782	Crewe, Cheshire	Hit balloon cable & crashed		5 FTS
8/03/41	Botha I	L6262	Millom	Crashed		
11/03/41	Handley Page Hereford	N9094	IOM			
12/03/41	He111	6236	ICI sports field, Widnes	Shot down/hit baloon cable	F/L W P Green	6/KG55
13/03/41	Botha	L6505	Squires Gate	Blown onto nose by wind	S/Lr D E Gillam DFC AFC	
13/03/41	Hurricane	V7726	Near Wrea Green	Engine failure		9 group
13/03/41	Walrus	W2705	Squires Gate	Landing accident		
16/03/41	Bristol Blenheim	L1318	IOM			
17/03/41	Handley Page Hereford	N9074	IOM			
18/03/41	Botha	N3836	Squires Gate	Engine failure		15 FTS
18/03/41	Magister I		Kingstown	Engine failure		
20/03/41	Hawker Hurricane		IOM		P/O F Kornicki	315 Squadron
20/03/41	Hurricane IB	V7675	Speke	Force landed		
21/03/41	Hurricane		Hawkshead	Ran out of fuel		
25/03/41	Wellington 1c	T2712	Frizington, Cumbria	Engine failure	Sgt J Malton 748082	21 OTU
25/03/41	DH89A Rapide	X9448	Standish Near Wigan	Crashed during force landing		11 SFF
26/03/41	Hereford	L6075	Ballacain, IOM	Engine fire		5 BGS
27/03/41	Hurricane	P3936	In sea near Fleetwood, from Speke	Ran out of fuel	F/O Wolinski	315 Squadron
27/03/41	Handley Page Hampden	P4313	IOM			
27/03/41	Magister I	R1966	Solway Firth, foreshoe at Silloth	Forced Landing	1st Off G W Holcomb	1 FPS
27/03/41	Master I	T8822	St Bees Head, Cumbria	Flew into High Ground	Sgt Paterek	315 Squadron
27/03/41	Hurricane	V7187	Irish Sea near the BAR Lightship	Collided with V7188	F/O Szulkowski	315 Squadron
27/03/41	Hurricane	V7188	Irish Sea near the BAR Lightship	Collided with V7187	P/O Holden	315 Squadron
27/03/41	Hurricane	V7656	In sea near Fleetwood	Dived into sea	P/O Dewar	315 Squadron
30/03/41	Hurricane	V6872	In sea of Prestatyn from Speke	Mid air collision with W9307	P/O Du Vivier	229 Squadron
30/03/41	Hurricane	W9307	In sea of Prestatyn from Speke	Mid air collision with V6872		229 Squadron
31/03/41	Magister I	N3856	Monkhill	Engine failure		
31/03/41	Anson	N9912	Bolsterstones			25 OTU
31/03/41	Hurricane I	V6987	Birkdale Fell	Flew into High Ground	P/O T C Smith 61251	
31/03/41	Hurricane I	V7537	Scarr Craggs	Flew into High Ground	F/O J W Seddon	
3/04/41	Hurricane II	Z3166	Nr Tarleton, Lancashire	Flew into ground in bad weather		1 FPP
5/04/41	Botha	L6143	Squires Gate	Landing accident	F/O R N H Courtney	

Date	Aircraft	Serial	Location	Cause	Crew	Unit
6/04/41	Hurricane	P2974	Speke	Landing accident	F/O Eugeniusz Fiedorczuk	315 Squadron
7/04/41	Ju88	8138	Banks Marsh, Lancashire	Shot down		11/KG54
7/04/41	Botha	L6304	Squires Gate	Taxing Accident	F/L P D Dear	256 Squadron
7/04/41	Defiant I	N1694	Behind Lowlands Farm, Hallsal, Nr Southport	Abandoned in flight due to radio failure.	Flight Sergeant J Stenton	256 Squadron
8/04/41	He111H		In Ribble of Lytham St Annes	Shot down		11/KG54
8/04/41	Defiant	N3424	Blackpool,Squires Gate - Manton	Lost height and crashed on take off	Sgt J D H Cunningham	256 Squadron
9/04/41	Spitfire	N3250	Tattenhall, nr Chester	Crashed in force landing		57 OTU
10/04/41	Hurricane I	L1670	Keld, Yorkshire	Caught fire in air & abandoned		55 OTU
12/04/41	Defiant	N1766	Rowlee Pasture	Engine cut & abandoned	Paul Rabone	96 Squadron
12/04/41	Hurricane I	P3831	Longtown	Baled Out	F/O B W Vickers 42282	
12/04/41	Oxford II	T1201	Keswick	Flew into High Ground	F/O C W R Sawer 41212	
13/04/41	Blenheim	L6780	Squires Gate, Docrays Farm	Take off accident	F/L T R Kitson	245 Squadron
14/04/41	Magister I		Lowther Park	Ran out of fuel		
14/40/41	Botha I	L6283	Millom	Crashed in force landing		2 BGS
10/04/41	Magister I	R1967	Kingstown	Mechanical Failure		
15/04/41	Battle I	L5785	Millom	Mid air collision		
15/04/41	Botha I	L6431	Millom	Mid air collision		
16/04/41	Hawker Henley	L3404	IOM			
18/04/41	Magister I	L8328	Southwaite	Engine failure		6 AACU
19/04/41	Leapod Moth	W5783	Ringway	Flew into ground		5 FTS
20/04/41	Magister	L8139	Meerbrook			
25/04/41	Hurricane		Kingstown	Engine failure		59 OTU
25/04/41	Spitfire	K9972	Rhyl	Crashed in force landing		57 OTU
25/04/41	Handley Page Hereford	L6040	IOM			
25/04/41	Handley Page Hereford	N9077	IOM			
26/04/41	Handley Page Hereford	L6075	IOM			
26/04/41	Beaufighter	R2271	Bagillt	Dived into ground		30 MU
26/04/41	Botha	L6311	Squires Gate	Landing accident		6 FPP
1/05/41	Botha	L6326	Sea off Ronaldsway Harbour IOM	Engine Failure	F/O J W L Bruxner-Randall	
2/05/41	Magister I	P2470	Kingstown	Crashed into T9687		15 FTS
2/05/41	Magister I	T9687	Kingstown	Crashed into P2470		15 FTS
4/05/41	He111		Liverpool Bay	Hit ballon barrage		
4/05/41	Bristol Blenheim	L1152	IOM			
4/05/41	Hudson I	N7304	Solway Firth	Crashed	P/O M S Smith 89356	
6/05/41	Botha	L6265	Anglesey, In sea of Puffin Island	Engine failure	F/O R A C MacDonald	
6/05/41	Hurricane I	V6921	Fraggs Craggs, Burnbank	Flew into High Ground	Sgt B V Votruba 787435	312 Squadron

Date	Aircraft	Serial	Location	Cause	Crew	Unit
8/05/41	He111P-4	2871	Hazel Grove, Stockport, Torkington Golf Course	Shot Down	Oberleutnant Adolf Knorringer	KG55
8/05/41	Ju88	6213	Roach End			KG 76
8/05/41	Supermarine Spitfire	BL351	IOM			256 Squadron
8/05/41	Defiant I	N3500	Micklehead Green, Nr St Helens	Shot Down		
11/05/41	Bristol Blenheim	L1338	IOM			
14/05/41	Handley Page Hampden	AD758	IOM			
14/05/41	Bristol Blenheim	K7142	IOM			
14/05/41	Spitfire II	P8161	Colne, Lancashire	Hit high ground in mist	Sgt Charles Edward Bell	9 MU
15/05/41	Defiant	T3955	Carnforth, Lancashire	Dived into ground		256 Squadron
17/05/41	Blenheim	V5565	Morecambe Bay, in sea 5 Miles off	Crashed into sea		17 OTU
18/05/41	Magister I	R1852	Burnfoot	Crashed	J Szabunienica	15 FTS
20/05/41	Fairey Battle	L5084	IOM			
20/05/41	Hurricane I	V7043	Kingstown	Crashed		
21/05/41	Blenheim IV	L9388	Dalton in Furness, Cumbria	Flew into high ground in bad visibility		17 OTU
24/05/41	Hurricane	R4122	Speke	Landing accident	P/O Fiedorczuk	315 Squadron
31/05/41	Bristol Blenheim	Z6266	IOM			
4/06/41	Hurricane I	V6632	Carlisle	Crashed	D E Fletcher	
5/06/41	Magister	R1845	Kingstown	Engine failure		15 FTS
7/06/41	Hurricane I	W9131	Kingstown	Landing accident		59 OTU
8/06/41	Hurricane I	P3034	Kingstown	Landing accident		59 OTU
8/06/41	Hurricane I	R4098	Kingstown	Landing accident		59 OTU
10/06/41	Bristol Blenheim	L1298	IOM			
10/06/41	Blenheim	V5850	Squires Gate	Crash landing	F/O G A Pettit	3 SGR
11/06/41	Spitfire I	R6834	Snowdonia, North Wales	Crashed, DBF		57 OTU
14/06/41	Hurricane	V7024	Hawes, Yorkshire, Redshaw Moss	Flew into hill in bad visibility		55 OTU
15/06/41	Hurricane I	W9217	Crofton	Crash landing		55 OTU
18/06/41	Hurricane I	W9131	Craggs	Flew into High Ground	Sgt A P Kitherside	59 OTU
20/06/41	Bristol Blenheim	L9238	IOM			
20/06/41	Spitfire I	N3265	Kingstown	Overshot		
22/06/41	Defiant I	AA306	Gilsland	Crashed		6 FPP
23/06/41	Handley Page Hampden	L4199	IOM			
25/06/41	Whitley III	K8974	Kingstown	Taxiing accident	A Habola	
25/06/41	Magister	L8084	Carlisle	Structural Failure	J B Spangler	
25/06/41	Hurricane I	V7044	Kershopefoot	Crashed	F/O R N H Courtney	59 OTU
26/06/41	Botha	L6210	Squires Gate	Crash landing		
26/06/41	Hurricane I	V6669	Ivegill	Crashed		59 OTU
30/06/41	Bristol Blenheim	Z6269	IOM			

Date	Aircraft	Serial	Location	Event	Crew	Unit
1/07/41	Bristol Blenheim	L6753	IOM	Taxiing accident		15 FTS
1/07/41	Magister	N5432	Carlisle	Engine failure		15 FTS
1/07/41	Tiger Moth II	T7730	Beaumont	Engine failure		1 AACU
2/07/41	Henley I	L3289	1m SE of Squires Gate	Hit hill desending in cloud		57 OTU
3/07/41	Spitfire I	K9892	?Raubon, North Wales	Hit hill in cloud		57 OTU
3/07/41	Spitfire I	K9894	Wrexham, North Wales, ?Raubon	Hit hill desending in cloud		57 OTU
3/07/41	Blenheim IV	X4167	?Raubon, North Wales			6 AACU
3/07/41	Hurricane I	Z5870	Crowden, Mill Hill	Crashed	Sgt F G Ninke 1375405	59 OTU
4/07/41	Botha	V6996	Carlisle	Crashed	P/O E Partridge	
5/07/41	Hurricane	L6255	Squires Gate	Taxiing accident		
7/07/41		P2827	Speke	Struck airport boundry when coming into land.	F/O Jerzy Michal Czerniak P1283	315 Squadron
8/07/41	Bristol Blenheim	L1258	IOM	Spun in		15 FTS
8/07/41	Magister I	V1081	Thursby	Overshot landing & crashed,	Cpl M Peszynskie	15 FTS
10/07/41	Spitfire I	R6601	Ledsham, Cheshire, Two Mills	DBF		57 OTU
14/07/41	Whitley I	X6748	Anthorn, Nr Solway House	Forced Landing		
16/07/41	Battle I	L5775	Solway Firth, Blackshaw Bank	Crashed	LAC W Weatherburn 640401	10 BGS
16/07/41	Whitley V	P4971	Silloth	Crashed	Sgt C Odonell	
17/07/41	Magister I	R1844	Kingstown	Stalled		15 FTS
18/07/41	Hurricane I	V7534	Appleby	Crashed	P/O J K Roberts	59 OTU
21/07/41	Hawker Hurricane		IOM			
22/07/41	Magister I	R1968	Kingstown	Crashed		15 FTS
23/07/41	Hurricane I	V7674	Kingstown	Overturned		15 FTS
24/07/41	Hurricane I		Burnfoot	Crashed		15 FTS
24/07/41	Tiger Moth II	N5447	Hooton Park	Collided with P5316 Hampden		19 EFTS
24/07/41	Hampden I	P5316	Near Hooton Park	Collided with Tiger Moth		
24/07/41	Magister I	R1905	Burnfoot	Crashed		15 FTS
25/07/41	Magister I	P6398	Kingstown	Landing accident		15 FTS
25/07/41	Magister I	T1968	Kingstown	Overshot		
28/07/41	Hudson II	T9268	Skinburness	Crashed	F/O C T Dacombe 43199	
29/07/41	Hurricane I	L1870	Aspatria	Crashed		59 OTU
29/07/41	Hurricane I	V7255	Esk Bridge	Crashed	Sgt H S Jacques 968333	59 OTU
31/07/41	Wellington	W5719	Upper Tor, Edale, Derbyshire	Flew into high ground		150 Squadron
1/08/41	Anson I	N5093	Appleby	crashed		ATA
3/08/41	Defiant I	N1736	Penrith	Crash landing	P/O Cragg,	2 EPP
7/08/41	Hampden	P2073	Burtonwood	Crashed on landing	Plt Off Baynham,	
8/08/41	Bristol Blenheim	N6218	IOM			5 AOS
9/08/41	Blenheim IV	V6320	Barrow, in Sea, Peel Channel	Ditched in Sea		
11/08/41	Spitfire	X4065	Irish Sea 3 miles from Prestatyn	Lost control and dived into sea	P/O S.J. Juszczak	303 Squadron
12/08/41	Hurricane I	V6565	Scafell	Flew into High Ground	P/O Z Hohne P0875	55 OTU
12/08/41	Hurricane I	V7742	Scafell	Flew into High Ground	Sgt S Karubin 793420	55 OTU

Date	Aircraft type	Serial	Location	Description	Crew	Unit
13/08/41	Hurricane I	R4112	Heathergill	Crashed	Sgt M C Tagseth	59 OTU
15/08/41	Botha	L6354	Off coast of Barrow	Ditched in Sea		2 AOS
15/08/41	Magister I	T9687	Kingstown	Overshot		15 FTS
16/08/41	Botha	L6315	East boundry of Squires Gate	Crashed due to engine failure	P/P E W Patridge	
16/08/41	Magister I	L8174	Kingstown	Landing accident		15 FTS
16/08/41	Spitfire I	X4710	Carlisle	Mid air collision		3 FPP
16/08/41	Spitfire I	X4834	Carlisle	Mid air collision		3 FPP
16/08/41	Vickers Wellington	X9803	IOM			
18/08/41	Defiant I	N1651	Marshaw, Lancs, 1.5 miles NW of	Flew into hill in cloud	P/O N J Sharpe	256 Squadron
19/08/41	Bristol Blenheim	V5374	IOM			
19/08/41	Lysander III	V9403	1m N of Crewe Resevoir, Cheshire, Slate Pit Moss	Flew into high ground		6 AACU
21/08/41	Magister I	V1023	Kirkbrampton	Crashed	Sgt F H Oakley	
22/08/41	Botha I	L6416	Castle Moss	Crashed	Sgt W Walisewki	2 AOS
24/08/41	Master I	T8739	Stapleton	Crashed at night	Lt T P G Baste	
25/08/41	Magister I	L8345	Burnfoot	Landing accident		15 FTS
25/08/41	Hurricane I	R4099	Crosby	Flew into Hillside	Sgt R J Davies	59 OTU
26/08/41	Tiger Moth	N6937	Mold, North Wales	Abandoned after control lost	P/O A. A. Horne	19 FTS
27/08/41	Botha I	L6509	Blackpool, on Rly station	Collided with Defiant N1745 & crashed		3 SGR
27/08/41	Defiant I	N1745	Blackpool, Reads Avenue	Collided with Botha L6509 & crashed	Sgt L. J. Ellmers	256 Squadron
29/08/41	Defiant I	N3378	Glossop, Derbyshire	Flew into hill in cloud	P/O James Craig	255 Squadron
1/09/41	Hurricane I	W9202	Dalston	Engine failure		
2/09/41	Oxford	V3210	Chapel en le Frith, Derbyshire	Flew into hill in fog		2 FTS
4/09/41	Defiant I	V1177	Blackpool, Squires Gate	Hit trees on approach		456 Squadron
4/09/41	Hurricane I	V6862	Penrith	Mechanical Failure		59 OTU
5/09/41	Botha	L6295	Squires Gate	Undercarriage failure	P/O Gilmore	
5/09/41	Spitfire I	X4622	Soulby	Forced Landing	H Carter	
8/09/41	Hector	K8096	Red Pike	Flew into Hillside	F/O J A Craig	ATA
9/09/41	Bristol Blenheim	L8693	IOM			
9/9/41	Hudson I	N7337	Irish Sea	Crashed into sea	Cpl R J Clarke	
9/9/41	Hurricane I	P3880	Micklewaite	crashed	Sgt E De-Sapgay	
10/09/41	Tiger Moth	R5077	Biston, Wirral, Haddon Lane	Spun into ground whilst low flying	P/O A V Saunders 778252	MSFU
12/09/41	Botha	L6503	Squires Gate	Taxiing Accident	Sgt N F Grinham	
12/09/41	Tiger Moth	N6723	Kingstown	Landing accident		
12/09/41	Hurricane I	V7251	Warwick Bridge	Crashed	Sgt A M L Withers	
14/09/41	Blenheim	V5432	Squires Gate	Undercarriage failure	Sgt A I Rowe	3 SGR
17/09/41	Magister I	L8073	Lowther Park	Crashed		15 FTS
17/09/41	Magister I	N5432	Kingstown	Hit by landing aircraft		15 FTS

Date	Aircraft	Serial	Location	Remarks	Crew	Unit
17/09/41	Tiger Moth II	N5454	Grange over Sands, on beach	Stalled and dove in		1 AACU
17/09/41	Tiger Moth	T6498	Kingstown	Landing accident		15 FTS
18/09/41	Hurricane II	V6998	Crosby	Crashed	W/Cdr D P H Boitel_Gill	59 OTU
20/09/41	Battle	P2181	Kelsic			
20/09/41	Magister I	T9740	Longtown	Crashed		15 FTS
21/09/41	Hurricane I	P63623	Westlington	Crashed	Sgt W Brownlie	59 OTU
22/09/41	Magister I	L8055	Kingstown	Undercarriage collapsed		15 FTS
22/09/41	Magister I	L8337	Kingstown	Undercarriage collapsed		15 FTS
25/09/41	Botha I	L6277	Millom	Crashed		
26/09/41	Spitfire I	X4843	Snowdonia, North Wales	Hit mountain		57 OTU
27/09/41	Hampden		Millom	Undercarriage collapsed		
29/09/41	Master III	W8594	Bewcastle	Flew into Hillside	Sgt G F Hillier	ATA
1/10/41	Oxford IV		Rockcliff	Flew into Hillside	P/O R A McAnney	
1/10/41	Oxford	V3435	4m N of Carlisle	Spun in		1 OTU
4/10/41	Spitfire Vb	AB987	Kirkbride	Landing accident		
6/10/41	Boston	DG555	Burtonwood	Crashed due to engine problem,	F/Sgt Rocky Sim	Repair Depot
8/10/41	Hurricane 11B	Z3253	Snaefell Mines , IOM	Flew into hillside	P/O Roy Stout	133 Squadron
8/10/41	Hawker Hurricane	Z3253	IOM			
8/10/41	Hawker Hurricane	Z3457	IOM			133 Squadron
8/10/41	Hurricane	Z3677	North Laxey Mine , IOM	Flew into hillside	P/O Hugh McCall	
8/10/41	Hawker Hurricane	Z3781	IOM			
8/10/41	Wellington	Z8424	Snaefell, IOM	Flew into hillside	First Officer Kenneth M. Seed	9 FPP
10/10/41	Beaufighter If	T4797	Silloth	Landing accident		20 FTS
15/10/41	Tiger Moth II	N6812	Stainburn, Yorkshire	Spun into ground		2 AOS
16/10/41	Botha I	L6425	Ravenglass	Engine failure		96 Squadron
16/10/41	Defiant	T3921	Shining Tor	Dived into house during low level aerobatics		SFP
17/10/41	Tomahawk	AK191	Bolton, Lancashire			
20/10/41	Hampden I	P2127	Westfield	Crashed	Sgt A Raw	12 MU
20/10/41	Spitfire Iia	P7678	Kirkbride	Landing accident		ATA
22/10/41	Spitfire IIA	P7880	Near Frodsham. From Speke	Engine failed and crash landed	Sgt Z Horn, 782489	306 Squadron
28/10/41	Hurricane I	V7236	Kingstown	Hit trees	Sgt S D Fassino	59 OTU
30/10/41	Defiant I	N3376	Gatley, Cheshire, Park Rd.	Abandoned after engine failure at night		96 Squadron
31/10/41	Botha I	L6321	Squires Gate	Engine Cut and crash landed		3 SGR
2/11/41	Oxford I	AT486	Caw Fell	Flew into Hillside	Sgt C A Des-Baillets	
2/11/41	Magister I	N3840	Kingstown	Landing accident		15 FTS
3/11/41	Defiant I	N1575	Wrexham, North Wales	Caught fire & abandoned		96 Squadron
3/11/41	Hurricane	V7461	Southwaite, Cumbria	Abandoned after control lost		59 OTU
3/11/41	Hurricane IIB	Z3150	10 miles N of Kielder		Mehta, H.C.	

Date	Aircraft	Serial	Location	Remarks	Crew	Unit
4/11/41	Anson	T4053	Thornton Cleveleys, on shore	Baled out due to engine trouble		15 FTS
5/11/41	Magister I	L5925	Kingstown	Landing accident		15 FTS
5/11/41	Magister I	T9948	Kingstown	Landing accident		15 FTS
7/11/41	Hampden I	P5396	Field adjacent to Burtonwood	Dived into ground on Overshoot	1st Officer I Paredes	3 FPP
8/11/41	Magister I	L5988	Kingstown	Emergency Landing		15 FTS
8/11/41	Magister I	N3779	Carlisle	Forced Landing		15 FTS
10/11/41	Hurricane I	W9342	Westnewton	Crashed		59 OTU
11/11/41	Westland Wallace	K3906	IOM			
11/11/41	Hurricane I	R4080	Westlington	Crashed	Sgt J W Moreux	59 OTU
12/11/41	Tiger Moth II	T6497	Kingstown	Landing accident		15 FTS
13/11/41	Westland Wallace	K3912	IOM			
13/11/41	Magister I	N3987	Kingstown	Landing accident		15 FTS
13/11/41	Magister I	V1097	Kingstown	Landing accident		15 FTS
13/11/41	Defiant I	V1175	Blackpool, Lancashire, Squires Gate	Spun into ground on approach		153 Squadron
14/11/41	Hudson	AM536	Solway Firth	Crashed into Sea	Sgt J A Stark	3 FPP
15/11/41	Airacobra I	AH598	Kirkbride	Engine failure	Capt W Handley	12 FTS
16/11/41	Oxford	V3626	Longnor, Derbyshire, near Buxton	Flew into hill in bad visibility		15 FTS
17/11/41	Magister I	N5432	Kingstown	Landing accident		15 FTS
17/11/41	Magister I	R1855	Kingstown	Landing accident		15 FTS
18/11/41	Handley Page Hampden	P1355	IOM			
19/11/41	Oxford I	AT478	Wigton	Flew into Hillside	P/O R A L White	2 AOS
19/11/41	Hampden I	L4076	Kirkbride	undercarriage collapsed		25 OTU
22/11/41	Anson 1	AW939	Lofthouse, Yorkshire	Abandoned whilst lost at night		15 FTS
22/11/41	Spitfire	L8174	Kingstown	Ran out of fuel		131 Squadron
22/11/41	Hurricane I	P7560	Harpur Hill	Flew into Hillside		59 OTU
25/11/41	Magister	T9524	Brampton	Controls Jammed		15 FTS
25/11/41	Hurricane I	T9973	Kingstown	Crashed		59 OTU
27/11/41	Spitfire Vb	P3228	Harker	Overturned		ATA
27/11/41	Magister 1	VL412	Kirkbride	Overturned		15 FTS
28/11/41	Botha I	T9871	Kingstown	Crashed	Sgt J R Jones	2 BGS
28/11/41	Dominie	W5053	Millom	Crashed into Lake	Sgt C G A Tarbor	
28/11/41	Henley	X7402	Derwentwater	Landing accident		15 FTS
29/11/41	Supermarine Spitfire	L3254	Kingstown	Hit by landing aircraft		
29/11/41	Lysander IIIa	P7445	IOM	Overshot		15 FTS
1/12/41	Blenheim	V9589	Squires Gate	Crashed		
1/12/41	Hector	K9729	Millom			
1/12/41	Spitfire	P7503	Force landed on beach at Glinby, 4 miles north east of Workington.	Force landing	Sgt Rozworski	306 Squadron

Date	Aircraft	Serial	Location	Crew	Cause	Unit
1/12/41	Supermarine Spitfire	P8380	IOM		Crashed into sea	
3/12/41	Hurricane I	AF985	Mawbray	Sgd Ldr T G Pace		306 Squadron
5/12/41	Supermarine Spitfire	P7502	IOM			
5/12/41	Spitfire IIA	P7749	playing fields of King Edward VII School, Lytham. From Speke	Sgt Otton Pudrycki 782879	Crashed in bad weather	
5/12/41	Bristol Blenheim	V6036	IOM	Burtnick. L.		
5/12/41	Hurricane Mk I	W9199	Ovingham, Northumberland	P/O H.J.Armstrong 406022	Crashed in snow storm	57 OTU
7/12/41	Spitfire I	L1042	Picton, Cheshire, Hill Farm	F/O R A Payne	Engine failure	1401 met flight
7/12/41	Spitfire	X4502	Squires Gate		Cable breakage	
8/12/41	Horsa Glider		Arnside		Hit trees	ATA
9/12/41	Hurricane	BM955	Lunecliffe	Second Officer Alfred Edward Green		
10/12/41	Botha	W5103	Round Hill	1st Officer T W Rogers	Flew into high ground	7 FPP
10/12/41	Hurricane I	W9342	Westnewton		Crashed	59 OTU
13/12/41	Proctor III	R7537	Millom		Overturned	ATA
14/12/41	Hudson	N7223	Silloth	Sgt A J Birchwood	Crashed	
14/12/41	Boston III	Z2299	Kendal	F/O J F Wolfe	Ran out of fuel	
15/12/41	Hector	K9760	Millom		Engine failure	
17/12/41	Anson I	N9842	Millom	Sgt W M Pepper	Crashed into sea	
17/12/41	Spitfire I	R7126	Chester, Cheshire, Parkgate Road	P/O J Marrey	Crashed, total wreck	57 OTU
19/12/41	Hampden I	L4076	Kirkbride		Undercarriage collapsed	ATA
19/12/41	Master III	W8479	Sedbergh		Flew into Hillside	
20/12/41	Hurricane I	R4086	Irthington	Sgt K F Peters	Mid air collision	59 OTU
20/12/41	Hurricane I	V7601	Irthington	P/O D F Meachann	Mid air collision	59 OTU
21/12/41	Hudson V	AM624	Dent Fell	Sgt E D Parrish	Engine failure	1 OTU
21/12/41	Spitfire	P8183	Ribble Estuary, from Woodvale		Crashed	
21/12/41	Spitfire I	X4059	Kirkbride	P/O E Krawczynski	Overturned	308 Squadron
28/12/41	Hudson V	AM789	Maryport		Forced Landing	
29/12/41	Wellington	P7905	Fisher Tarn		Crashed	1 OTU
31/12/41	Supermarine Spitfire		IOM	R W Allsop		
1/01/42	Defiant I	N3432	Troutbeck		Flew into Hillside	96 Squadron
4/01/42	Bristol Blenheim	N3602	IOM			
4/01/42	Wellington II	W5389	Kirkbride		Swung of runway	
7/01/42	Anson	R3409	Sedbergh, Cumbria, Cantley Crag, Brant Fell		Iced up & abandoned	1 AOS
9/01/42	Hurricane	BJ445	Dufton Fell	1st Officer John Charles Fisher	Engine Failure	6 FPP
9/01/42	Curtiss Mohawk	L5935	Astley, Lancashire, near Wigan		Forced Landing	
9/01/42	Magister I	N3936	Kingstown		Engine Failure	15 FTS
9/01/42	Magister I		Carlisle		Engine Failure	15 FTS
9/01/42	Spitfire IIa	P8206	North of Formby point, from Woodvale	S/L Marian J Wesolowski	Mid air collision, entered flat spin	308 Squadron

Date	Aircraft	Serial	Location	Cause	Personnel	Unit
9/01/42	Proctor I	R7491	Kirkbride	Taxiing accident	Sgt M H Wadham	50 Squadron
10/01/42	Anson	536	Millom	Crashed into Sea	Sgt S Earnshaw	
10/01/42	Hampden I	AE250	Brampton	Crashed		
10/01/42	Beaufighter If	T4884	Kirkbride	Taxiing accident		
13/01/42	Magister I	P2468	Carlisle	Crashed		420 Squadron
16/01/42	Hampden I	AE393	West Burton, Yorkshire	Flew into hill		
17/01/42	Avro Anson	N5030	IOM			15 FTS
17/01/42	Magister I	R1849	Carlisle	Forced Landing		50 Squadron
21/01/42	Hampden I	AE381	Kinder Scout, Derbyshire	Flew into high ground at night		308 Squadron
25/01/42	Spitfire IIa	P8142	Warton from Woodvale	Crashed	pilot F/O Mensall	
28/01/42	DH82A Tiger Moth	BB752	Garston, near Speke ?			15 FTS
28/01/42	Magister I	L5928	Rockcliff	Crashed	Sgt B Astley	ATA
28/01/42	Magister I	T8614	Stainmoor	Crashed	Section Officer R H Winn	18 OTU
30/01/42	Wellington	N2848	Buckden Pike, Yorkshire	Flew into hill in cloud		1 OTU
31/01/42	Hudson I	T9308	Great Corby	Crashed	P/O D M C Burgess	55 OTU
1/0242	Hurricane I	Z4575	Kingstown	Engine Failure		398th BG
2/02/42	B-17G	43-38944	Wildboarclough, Macclesfield,	Crashed into Hillside	1st Lt Donald J DeClene	ATA
6/02/42	Hurricane I	L1638	Kirkbride	Crashed		1 FPP
6/02/42	Boston	W8254	Ringway	Crash landing		12 Squadron
6/02/42	Wellington	Z8491	White Edge Moor			3 SGR
7/02/42	Botha	L6249	New Brighton Beach	Forced Landing	F/O Jackson smith	256 Squadron
7/02/42	Defiant I	V1116	Lytham, Lancashire, in sea off pier	Hit sea low flying		3 DF
8/02/42	Spitfire	BL520	Squires gate	Forced Landing	Sgt K R Middlehurst	101 Squadron
8/02/42	Wellington	L7869	Squires Gate	Overshot	Sgt House	22 OTU
8/02/42	Wellington	T2714	Skidaw	Flew into Hillside	E G Jenner	
8/02/42	Anson I	W1793	Stainmoor	Flew into Hillside	W J Elliot	
9/02/42	Oxford II	P1920	Rochdale, Lancashire	Crashed forced landing in bad weather		6 FTS
9/02/42	Supermarine Spitfire	P8576	IOM			
12/02/42	Avro Anson	N5346	IOM			
12/02/42	Lysander III	P9125	Kirkbride	Overturned		ATA
13/02/42	Avro Anson	AX411	IOM			
13/02/42	Spitfire Vb	BL585	Aspull, Nr Wigan, Lancs	Baled out after blacking out	Flying Officer Boleslaw Paley	308 Squadron
13/02/42	Stirling I	N6075	Merryton Low, Derbyshire	Flew into hill in bad visibility		101 CF
14/02/42	Spitfire Vb	BL898	Kirkbride	Landing Accident		ATA
14/02/42	Gloster Gauntlet	K5335	IOM			
16/02/42	Halifax	L9619	Keld	Struck High ground	F/Sgt Lloyd	10 Squadron
16/02/42	Defiant TT III	N1764	Great Orton	Emergency Landing		
18/02/42	Hudson V	AM825	Solway Firth	Crashed into Sea	P/O T R Godfrey	
22/02/42	Magister		Lytham	Force Landed		
23/02/42	Anson I	AX565	Millom	Mid air collision	Sgt J D D White	

Date	Aircraft	Serial	Location	Incident	Pilot / Crew	Unit
23/02/42	Spitfire	R7173	Kirkbride	Landing Accident		10 AGS
23/02/42	Dominie I	Z7256	Millom	Mid air collision		
27/02/42	Avro Anson	DG841	IOM			
2/03/42	Handley Page Hampden	N9090	IOM			
8/03/42	Supermarine Spitfire	BL491	IOM		Sgt Duncan	781 Squadron
8/03/42	Defiant I	N1811	Barrow, Cumbria, 3 miles S of	Stalled and dived into ground		
8/03/42	Bristol Blenheim	Z6363	IOM			
9/03/42	Albacore	X9055	Pilling	Force Landed	Sgt L C Storey	
12/03/42	Botha	L6314	Isle of Man	Flew into high ground		
12/03/42	Oxford II	X7185	Kirkbride	Undercarriage Collapsed		
15/03/42	Hudson V	AM774	Kirkbride	Landing Accident		
15/03/42	Bristol Beaufort	N1017	IOM			
15/03/42	Spitfire	X4817	Cark Airfield	Landing accident	Sgt Grainger	3 SGR
17/03/42	Bristol Blenheim	N3575	IOM			
21/03/42	Spitfire	P9543	Squires Gate	Landing accident	Sgt Jones	3 SGR
24/03/42	Westland Wallace	K6064	IOM			
24/03/42	Anson	K6274	Squires Gate	Overshot	P/O W W Lomas	3 SGR
24/03/42	Westland Wallace	K8695	IOM			
25/03/42	Hudson I	N7392	Solway Firth	Crashed into Sea	Sgt M C Taylor	15 FTS
26/03/42	Magister I	N3830	Kingstown	Engine Failure	3rd Officer P J Frisby	ATA
27/03/42	Tutor	K3310	?Warton, Lancashire	Crashed in forced landing	F/O Newmark	
27/03/42	Hurricane II	Z3401	Silloth	Collided on take off		
28/03/42	Magister I	R1959	Kingstown	Undercarriage Collapsed		15 FTS
28/03/42	Wellington	W5623	Squires Gate	Fired on by convoy	P/O G B Afke	3 OTU
28/03/42	Blenheim	Z7983	Irish Sea	Missing at Sea	Sgt K J Johnson	13 OTU
2/04/42	Westland Wallace	K3568	IOM			
2/04/42	DH Tiger Moth (Queen Bee)	V4742	IOM			
8/04/42	Bristol Blenheim	V6024	IOM			
13/04/42	Hudson	W6940	Kirkbride	Landing Accident		1 OTU
13/04/42	Lysander	Z4103	In sea off Fleetwood	Ran out of fuel	P/O H W Trilsbanch	10 AGS
13/04/42	Hurricane I	Z7150	Kirkbride	Mid air collision		59 OTU
13/04/42	Hurricane I	P5161	Kirkbride	Mid air collision		59 OTU
14/04/42	Lockheed Hudson		IOM			
16/04/42	Supermarine Spitfire	AB243	IOM			
16/04/42	Spitfire Vb	BM478	Burtonwood	Overshot on landing	Sgt R Ross-Jay	6 FPP
16/04/42	Botha	L6331	Squires Gate	Landing accident		

Date	Aircraft	Serial	Location	Remarks	Crew	Unit
16/04/42	Handley Page Hampden	P1207	IOM			
21/04/42	Spitfire	X4268	Weeton, Swarbrick's Hall Farm	Engine fire	P/O R Clarke	3 SGR
22/04/42	Botha I	L6210	On Beach, Blackpool, Lancs	Engine cut and crash landed		3 SGR
22/04/42	Anson	N5372	Squires Gate	Collision	Sgt Cunningham	3 SGR
22/04/42	Spitfire	R7128	Squires Gate	Overshot	P/O O'Gorman	3 SGR
24/04/42	Botha	L6210	Blackpool foreshore	Lost control	Sgt R T Smith	
27/04/42	Proctor III	DX225	Kirkbride	Overturned		
3/05/42	Spitfire	AD537	5m NNW of Fleetwood	Brought down by enemy action		
3/05/42	Botha	L6330	Sandbank off Lytham St Annes	Engine failure	P/O H J Appleford	
3/05/42	Botha I	L6331	On sand bank off Blackpool	Engine cut and forced landed		
5/05/42	Anson	W2631	Barrow, Cumbria	Hit balloon cable & crashed		11 RS
6/05/42	Blenheim	K7091	?Standingholme, Yorkshire	Crashed after control lost at night		10 AFU
6/05/42	Botha	L6141	12 miles W. of Squires Gate	Engine fire	Act F/L K F Scotney	20 OTU
7/05/42	Spitfire Vb	AB171	Kerrow Kneale, IOM	Fire in flight	Pilot Officer Whillans	457 Squadron
7/05/42	Hurricane II	P3116	Penton	Crashed		
7/05/42	Anson I	R9757	Millom	Engine Failure	Sgt V T Wolfe	
8/05/42	Supermarine Spitfire	AB244	IOM			ATA
10/05/42	Botha	L6508	Squires Gate	Blown over	F/L J N Mulder	
10/05/42	Wellington III	Z1722	Millom	Engine Failure		
16/05/42	Botha	L6512	Squires Gate	Landing accident		
19/05/42	Botha	W5051	Wigton	Crashed	Sgt B K Blatchford	
20/05/42	Halifax	DG2	Padeswood, 2 miles SE of Mold	Force Landed after engine failure	P/O D W J Reynolds	Rootes
22/05/42	Hurricane IA	V7166	Speke airport	Stalled		MSFU
22/05/42	Wellington	Z1566	Grindon	Crashed into Sea	F/O R W Rollalson	75 Squadron
24/05/42	Hudson V	AM794	Millom	Hit trees	Sgt G E Barden	
26/05/42	Master	N7884	Wreay			6 AACU
30/05/42	Lysander	V9729	Cronkstone	Control lost during dive		6 AACU
31/05/42	Master I	N7553	Ringway	Throttle jammed on approach, hit Wellington X3926		256 Squadron
1/06/42	Master I	R2256	Blackpool, Squires Gate	Parachute dummy caught in tail and crash landed		
3/06/42	Albemarle	P1386	Near Ringway			AFEE
5/06/42	Hurricane	MF	Appleby	Crashed	W/Cdr Lucas	601 Squadron
6/06/42	Halifax II	W7668	Methop	Ran out of fuel		78 Squadron
8/06/42	Armstrong Whitworth Whitley	N1356	IOM			
9/06/42	Hudson I	N7307	Silloth	Crashed on runway when taking off	Sgt E A Jefferson	
11/06/42	Magister I	R1851	Dalston	Crashed	P/O J Bramely	15 FTS

Date	Aircraft	Serial	Location	Cause	Crew	Unit
15/06/42	Hurricane	P7899	Kirkbride	Undercarriage Collapsed		57 OTU
16/06/42	Spitfire		West Kirby	Engine failure & force landed	Sgt G D Weir	
16/06/42	Tiger Moth II	T6812	Carlisle	Crashed		
20/06/42	Magister I	HM569	Appleby	Ran out of fuel		
23/06/42	Dragon	K7084	Squires Gate	Undershot	F/L Gilmore	
25/06/42	Bristol Blenheim	N2666	IOM			
25/06/42	Hurricane I	Z6191	Easton	Crashed	Sgt S Allcock	55 OTU
25/06/42	Bristol Blenheim	L7927	IOM			
26/06/42	Avro Anson	P2877	IOM			
26/06/42	Hurricane I	AD570	Black How, Cleator	Dived into ground	Sgt B Nicholls	59 OTU
29/06/42	Supermarine Spitfire		IOM			
29/06/42	Hampden I	AD848	?Moorend, Yorkshire	Engine failed, attempted forced landing	S/L J A Willcox	14 OTU
29/06/42	Roc	L3119	Ainsdale, sand dunes	Caught fire & abandoned		776 Squadron
1/07/42	Hurricane	V7660	?Corly, Cumbria	Undercarriage Collapsed		59 OTU
5/07/42	Hurricane I	BW481	Millom	Hit trees		
5/07/42	Hurricane I	P2684	Appleby	Hit tree whilst low flying	L D Rymoer	601 Squadron
5/07/42	Hurricane	R2684	Appleby, Cumbria, .5 miles S of	Controls failed & crashed		59 OTU
6/07/42	Whitley III	K9013	Wilmslow, Cheshire	Structural Failure		PTS
7/07/42	Master I	T8411	Kelsick	Crashed	Sgt J Tresiter	55 OTU
8/07/42	Hurricane I	AG125	Easton	Engine Failure and forced landed	Sgt A L Gane	55 OTU
8/07/42	Henley I	L3357	Bootle ,Lancs			1 AACU
8/07/42	Hurricane I	Z7077	Solway	Crashed into sands	Sgt T R Robieson	55 OTU
11/07/42	Battle II	L5717	Solway Firth	Crashed into Sea	Kpl J Krzystoszek	1 OTU
13/07/42	Stirling	N6075	Merryton Low	Abandoned after bomb hung up		101 HCU
14/07/42	Halifax II	W7761	Knaresborough, Yorkshire	Crashed	Sgt T Nawrocki.	35 Squadron
16/07/42	Spitfire V	W3628	Dunsop Bridge	Lost wing & crashed		315 Squadron
17/07/42	Hudson I	N7253	Tyn-y-Bryne, North Wales	Crash landing		24 Squadron
17/07/42	Avro Anson	R9640	IOM			
17/07/42	Hurricane I	W9324	Aspatria	Engine Failure		59 OTU
18/07/42	Wellington	Z8980	Rudd Hill	Spun into ground		27 Squadron
19/07/42	Hurricane I	V7008	Penrith	Crashed		55 OTU
20/07/42	Master III	W8474	Hyde, Cheshire			16 FTS
20/07/42	Hurricane I	R4217	Dowthwaite Head			59 OTU
23/07/42	Botha	W5142	Moel Wnion North Wales	Flew into high ground		
24/07/42	Hurricane I	P2901	Lessonhall	Emergency Landing		55 OTU
24/07/42	Spitfire	EN856	Squires Gate	Collision		315 Squadron
28/07/42	Oxford	V3727	Squires Gate	Collision		5 OTU
28/07/42	Bristol Blenheim	P4918	IOM			
28/07/42	Douglas Boston	W8291	IOM			
29/07/42	Oxford I	AT671	Denton, Manchester	Crashed in forced landing		11 PAFU

Date	Aircraft	Serial	Location	Cause	Crew	Unit
29/07/42	Hurricane	L1870	Aspatria	Forced Landing		59 OTU
1/08/42	Master		Pooley Bridge	Emergency Landing		Burtonwood Flight Test
4/08/42	Bristol Beaufighter	T4715	IOM			MSFU
7/08/42	C-61	42-13574	Winter Hill, Near Bolton	Collision with object in flight	Lt Adolf Kurek	
9/08/42	Hurricane IA	P3385	Bleaenau Ffestiniog from Speke	Hit Hillside in cloud	P/O R B McIntyre	55 OTU
10/08/42	Hurricane		Kirkbride	Mechanical Failure		55 OTU
13/08/42	Hurricane	V7496	Kingstown	Engine Failure		55 OTU
13/08/42	Hurricane I	V7744	Penrith	Belly Landing		55 OTU
14/08/42	Spitfire	AA929	Squires Gate from Woodvale	Emergency Landing after combat with Ju88	Sgt Malek	315 Squadron
14/08/42	Hurricane I	V6857	Longtown	Blacked Out	Sgt D R S Dixon	55 OTU
14/08/42	Hurricane I	W7496	Kirkbride	Low oil pressure		
15/08/42	Spitfire V	BL751	Birkdale Sands,	Hit obstruction	Pilot F/O E Fiedorczuk	315 Squadron
16/08/42	Hurricane	P4318	Arkengarthdale Moor, Yorkshire,	Flew into hill in cloud		14 OTU
19/08/42	Avro Anson	N4902	IOM			
20/08/42	Wellington 1c	T2715	Millburn	Crashed	Sgt B G Crew	25 OTU
20/08/42	Hurricane I	Z4874	Silloth	Landing Accident		
22/08/42	Lancaster I	L7584	Masham, Yorkshire	Flew into high ground at night		44 Squadron
23/08/42	Armstrong Whitworth Whitley	BD417	IOM			
23/08/42	Botha	L6318	Tal-y-Fan nr Conway	Flew into high ground	Sgt H Pendell	3 SGR
23/08/42	Hurricane I	Z7074	Kelsick	Engine Failure	Sgt Nice	55 OTU
24/08/42	Hurricane I		Wath Head	Mechanical Failure		10 SLG
25/08/42	Hudson V	AM676	Silloth	Crashed into Sea	Sgt R D McKenzie	1 OTU
26/08/42	Botha I	L6245	Cark	Engine Failure		ATA
26/08/42	Bristol Blenheim	Z6268	IOM			
27/08/42	Hudson I	N7226	Millom	Crashed into Sea		1 OTU
31/08/42	Spitfire I	N3265	Millom	Landing Accident		
1/09/42	P-38F	41-7669	Hurstwood Village	Dove in after avoiding hill in overcast sky.	Pilot 2nd Lt Lyle L Williams	
1/09/42	Defiant	T3923	RAF Woodvale	Hit motor roller		285 Squadron
2/09/42	Wellington I	Z8808	Pateley Bridge	Crash landed		11 OTU
3/09/42	Wellington IC	DV718	Pateley Bridge, Yorkshire	Flew into hill		11 ot
4/09/42	Wellington 1c	DV600	Keswick	Flew into Hillside	Sgt D E Derbyshire	25 OTU
5/09/42	Hurricane I	Z4577	Armthwaite	Forced Landing	Sgt L E Leavson	
6/09/42	Hudson I	N7325	Appleby, Cumbria, Cross Fell	Crashed on high ground in cloud		10 OTU
6/09/42	Hudson I	N7725	Cross Fell	Flew into Hillside	P/O P A Bourke	1 OTU
7/09/42	Spitfire		Kirkbride	Forced Landing		1 OTU
9/09/42	Spitfire Vb	ER138	Kirkbride	Emergency Landing	1st Officer I S Fossett	154 Squadron
15/09/42	Wildcat IV	FN108	Millom	Mechanical Failure		ATA

Date	Aircraft	Serial	Location	Cause	Crew	Unit
16/09/42	Hurricane I	EP983	Wigton	Mechanical Failure		55 OTU
17/09/42	Spitfire V	N1214	Chester, Cheshire, Saighton	Crashed		3 FPP
18/09/42	Lysander II	N4869	Cark in Cartmel, Lancs	Engine cut and hit hedge		6 AACU
20/09/42	Anson II	AM608	Muncaster Fell	Flew into Hillside	Sgt C Kemp	
21/09/42	Lockheed Hudson	P3255	IOM			59 OTU
21/09/42	Hurricane		Cark, Cumbria	Stalled in bad weather & spun into ground in circu		
22/09/42	Halifax II	W1272	?Middle farm, Yorkshire	Spun into ground		46 OCU
23/09/42	Beaufighter VI	X8201	Brayton Park	Crashed		219 Squadron
25/09/42	Spitfire I	X4234	Alsager, Cheshire	Wing failure in spin, crashed		57 OTU
26/09/42	Wellington IC	DV821	Pateley Bridge	Crashed in forced landing		26 OTU
26/09/42	Hurricane XII	JS303	Kirkbride	Hit petrol bowser		ATA
28/09/42	P-38	12371	Burtonwood	Undercarriage collapsed		
30/09/42	Botha	L6498	Squires Gate	Take off accident		4 AOS
1/10/42	Anson	DJ410	Barrowdale, Green Gable, Cumbria	Flew into high ground out of cloud		
2/10/42	Avro Anson	L7960	IOM		Station Officer P T Robinson	ATA
3/10/42	Hurricane I	AG116	Silloth	Crashed on runway when taking off		
3/10/42	Hurricane IIc	BN382	Wylie Syke	Crashed	F/Sgt B C Williams	539 Squadron
4/10/42	Mustang I	AM168	?Preston Moor, Yorkshire	Spun into ground out of cloud		63 Squadron
4/10/42	Hurricane	BN205	Burscough, Lancashire	Spun during aerobatics and dived in	Roy Timewell	539 Squadron
4/10/42	Hurricane IIC	BN382	Gilsland, Cumbria, 3 miles NE of	Dived into ground out of low cloud		539 Squadron
4/10/42	Beaufighter VI	T5286	Crosby	Mechanical Failure	F/O E Lyon	90 OTU
6/10/42	Botha	W5080	Squires Gate	Landing accident	P/O Appleyard	15 FTS
8/10/42	Tiger Moth II	T6559	Rockcliff	Crashed	P/O Berry	
11/10/42	Botha		Squires Gate	Pilot Error		5 PAFU
12/10/42	Master	W8455	Kings Sterndale			
14/10/42	Beechcraft		Coniston	Flew into Hillside		613 Squadron
14/10/42	Mustang I	AG509	Settle, Yorkshire, 1 mile N of	Flew into high ground in bad weather	G W Branson	
14/10/42	Hurricane I	P3034	Carlisle	Emergency Landing		55 OTU
14/10/42	Spitfire II	P7533	Parkside, Birkinhead, Wirral	Caught fire and Abandoned & crashed		57 OTU
15/10/42	Anson I	L7968	Buxton, Derbyshire, NW of, Moss Ridge, Long Hill	Flew into high ground		CNS
17/10/42	Wellington IC	L7857	Penrith, Cumbria, 5 miles N of	Ran out of fuel & abandoned		75 Squadron
21/10/42	Mustang	AM241	IOM			
23/10/42	Hotspur II	BT723	Hollylodge School, Queens Drive, Liverpool, Lancashire	Lost tow in cloud and crash landed		GPEW

Date	Aircraft	Serial	Location	Cause	Crew	Unit
23/10/42	P-400	BX-418	Burtonwood	Landing Accident	Urban, John A	10 AGS
24/10/42	Defiant	N3328	Gisburn	Dived into ground in bad weather		
26/10/42	Supermarine Walrus	W3037	IOM			
27/10/42	Botha	L6192	Squires Gate	Landing accident	P/O R A N McCready	4 Squadron
27/10/42	Botha	W5141	Squires Gate	Landing accident	F/O S P Marlett (Canada)	
29/10/42	Mustang	AP208	Holdron Moss	Flew into high ground	Sgt M S Gilbert	
30/10/42	Master I	T8770	Penrith	Flew into Hillside		
31/10/42	Wellington	BK234	Near Bangor, N Wales	Mid air collision	S/L Roger De-Winton	256 Squadron
31/10/42	Beaufighter 1F	X7845	Bangor N Wales	Mid air collision	Kelsall Winlaw	
5/11/42	Avro Anson	R9756	IOM			
10/11/42	Hudson V	AM608	Martindale	Crashed	P/O I Jones	
10/11/42	P-400	BX-250	Burtonwood	Landing Accident	Melvin E Jarvis	
11/11/42	Argus I	FK359	Kirkbride	Taxiing accident		
12/11/42	Wellington III	BK517	Millom	Engine Failure		25 Squadron
13/11/42	Master	MB238	Speke	Ran of runway	Sgt Brown	ATA
13/11/42	Seafire Iic	N7207	Kirkbride	Mechanical Failure	F/O R A Gibson	
13/11/42	Hudson I	V6696	Silloth	Crashed into sea	Sgt J Fisher	
13/11/42	Hurricane I		Allerton Golf Course, Liverpool	Hit trees	F/O S A Fannon	MSFU
14/11/42	Hudson	X4621	Kirkbride	Swung of runway		1 OTU
14/11/42	Spitfire I		?Ridgley, Cheshire	Failed to recover from dive		61 OTU
15/11/42	Anson		Kirkham			3 SGR
15/11/42	Proctor III	HM353	Kirkbride			
16/11/42	A-20B	41-2999	Hooton	Overturned	Gulick Spencer H	
18/11/42	Hampden I	P1356	Millom	Engine Failure		
20/11/42	Spitfire Vb	AD544	Martindale	Flew into Hillside	F/O R S Strzak	222 Squadron
20/11/42	Mustang I	AG505	?Moldsworth, Cheshire	Flew into high ground in bad weather		41 Squadron
20/11/42	Wellington	Z1744	Near Leek	Flew into Hill		27 OTU
22/11/42	Stirling I	BF404	Kirkbride	Engine Failure		
22/11/42	Airacobra	BX195	Nr Scalebar Force, Goxhill	Crashed		
22/11/42	P-39	BX-195	Settle	Engine failure	Lieutenant Cecil Rhodes	1 FG
22/11/42	Anson	DJ637	Richards Field, 1/4 mile from RAF Weeton	Iced Up	P/O Finley	5 AOS
26/11/42	P38-F	43-2087	Warton	Belly landing		
28/11/42	P-38F	41-2371	Burtonwood, Tinkerhall Site	Landed on nose,	Robert T Schwabe	12 Photo
28/11/42	Anson	DJ635	Caernarvon, near lake Cwellyn	Flew into high ground		9 AFU
28/11/42	Defiant I	N3319	Timperley, Cheshire	Engine cut, stalled attempt F/L & dived into grnd.		14 FPP

Date	Aircraft	Serial	Location	Incident	Name	Unit
29/11/42	Mustang I	AP208	Holdron Moss, Trough of Bowland	Struck Hillside	Flying Officer Sholto Paton Marlatt	4 Squadron
30/11/42	Hudson I	N7207	Silloth	crashed in sea	Sgt Brunton	
1/12/42	Spitfire V	AB914	Ormskirk, near military hospital	Force landed	Sgt E. Kostanski	315 Squadron
6/12/42	Hurricane I	R4230	Carlisle	Crashed	Sgt C R F Shackell	
9/12/42	Wellington	DV810	Broomhead Moor			21 OTU
11/12/42	B-17G	42-31268	Warton	Taxing accident		311 ferry Sqn
14/12/42	Oxford II	HN428	Silloth	Hit trees		ATA
15/12/42	Mustang I	AG586	Pateley, Bridge, Yorkshire	Abandoned in bad weather	Staion officer H Thomas	613 Squadron
15/12/42	Hector	K9760	Millom	Engine Failure		
16/12/42	Avro Anson	R3432	IOM			
16/12/42	Wellington III	X3336	Carside Fell, Skiddaw	Flew into Hillside	T S Bellew	23 OTU
17/12/42	Hurricane I	AG282	Kirkbrampton	Crashed	Sgt K Holden	55 OTU
21/12/42	P-400	AH-609	Burtonwood	Forced Landing	Richard J Drayton	
21/12/42	Anson	EG211	Squires Gate	Landing accident	Sgt Blashford	
21/12/42	Battle I	P6638	Cark	Hit towing cable		
21/12/42	Boston III	W8273	Kirkbride	Undercarriage Collapsed	F/O C W Totto	
24/12/42	Anson	EF877	Squires Gate	Fire damage		
27/12/42	Lysander III	T1674	Millom Bay	Mechanical Failure		
28/12/42	Spitfire Vb	AD230	White Moss, Bleasdale,	Crashed after becoming lost in clouds	Lt W Pucek	317 Squadron
28/12/42	Hurricane I	AG150	Longtown	Mid air collision		
28/12/42	Hurricane I	P3899	Blackpool, Squires Gate	Crashed into sea after night takeoff	Sgt G H Walsh	96 Squadron
28/12/42	Hurricane I	W9233	Longtown	Mid air collision	Sgt A V Marshall	55 OTU
28/12/42	Spitfire	X4276	?	Collided with X4650 & crashed	Pilot F/L Deere	54 Squadron
28/12/42	Spitfire	X4650	?	Collided with X4276 & crashed	Sgt Squires	54 Squadron
1/01/43	Anson I	AX145	Glengale, Cumbria	Missing & later found crashed		1 AFU
1/01/43	Anson I	W2629	Skidaw	Flew into hillside		1 AFU
2/01/43	Anson I	W2629	Caldbeck fell, Cumbria	Crashed into high ground		1 AFU
3/01/43	Spitfire I	R6769	Hatton, Cheshire, Halton Hill Farm	Crashed low flying		61 OTU
4/01/43	Hudson I	N7308	Solway Firth	Crashed into Sea	D J Wearne	
4/01/43	Hurricane	P3176	Garstang	Ran out of fuel	Sgt J D Knowles	55 OTU
9/01/43	Lancaster I	ED394	Brampton	Crashed into House	W/O G Sunley	50 Squadron
9/01/43	Spitfire Vc	JG953	Kirkbride	Landing Accident		ATA
10/01/43	Beaufighter Ic	T5103	Crosby	Undercarriage collapsed		9 OTU
11/01/43	P-400	BX-283	Burtonwood		Edwin Fuller	122 Squadron
13/01/43	Tiger Moth II	BB755	Burnfoot	Collided on runway		
13/01/43	Tiger Moth I	T6499	Burnfoot	Collided on runway		
13/01/43	Hudson I	T9322	Silloth	Crashed	Sgt C Ring	1 OTU
14/01/43	P-400	AP-292	Burtonwood		C R Brown	

Date	Aircraft	Serial	Location	Cause	Crew / Personnel	Unit
14/01/43	Anson I	EG110	Lake Dulyn, North Wales	Flew into high ground		90 AF
15/01/43	P-38G	42-12920	Croston 1m west, close to the River Douglas, from Burtonwood	Forced landing	Kennth Burnett	13 Photo
15/01/43	Master	W8840	Bottom House			5 PAFU
20/01/43	Skua	L3408	Haverigg	Mechanical Failure	W Mougeridge	
20/01/43	Henley	AF959	Methop	Engine Failure	Second Officer R H Badhe	ATA
21/01/43	Hurricane I	DE925	Skidaw	Crashed	Sgt D L Baker	55 OTU
21/01/43	TIGERMOTH	DE-925	Balderton		Jack R Timney	
21/01/43	Tigermoth		Balderton		Jack R Timney	
21/01/43	Halifax	DT581	Hoarside Moor	Crashed into high ground		51 Squadron
21/01/43	Spitfire IIa	P7889	Kirkbride	Overturned		ATA
26/01/43	P-38	42-12905	Dunsop Fell, Trough of Bowland	Collision		78 FG
26/01/43	P-38	42-12928	Baxton Fell, Trough of Bowland	Collision		78 FG
26/01/43	Wellington	X3348	Blackden Edge			427 Squadron
27/01/43	Beaufort II	DD880	Longtown	Crashed	Carl Taylor	
28/01/43	Halifax II	W1146	Thwaite, Yorkshire, 6 miles N of	Flew into hill in cloud	Sgt L F Sinpson	1659 HCU
29/01/43	Botha I	L6184	Silloth	Undercarriage collapsed		ATA
30/01/43	Wellington	R1011	Birchen Bank Moss			28 OTU
30/01/43	Wellington	R1101	Birchen Bank Moss			28 OTU
30/01/43	Wellington	R1538	Cellerhead			28 OTU
1/02/43	Spitfire Vb	N3507	RAF Valley	Overturned on Landing	F/O Birtus	317
1/02/43	Defiant		Askam, Cumbria	Dived into ground		10 AGS
2/02/43	Skua	L2892	Astley Bridge, Lancashire.	Engine failed, Force landed and exploded on impact	S/L A J Newton	776 Squadron
3/02/43			The Delph, Springfield Lane, in resevoir en route to Speke from Woodvale			
3/02/43	P-39M	42-4833	Warton	Destroyed by fire	2nd Lt Potts	
3/02/43	Spitfire Mk I	R7202	Hepple, Northumberland		Moureaux, H.R.E	
3/02/43	Spitfire I	X4411	Kirkbride	Destroyed by other aircraft		
5/02/43	Mustang	AP216	Prestatyn, North wales, into sea	Hit pole & crashed into sea	Sgt W H Meakin	41 OTU
7/02/43	Defiant	V1134	Plumley, Cheshire	Struck ground on diving attack exercise		285 Squadron
8/02/43	Anson I	AX293	Millom	Crashed into Sea	F/Sgt H Smith	
8/02/43	Dominie	X7522	Burtonwood		Clarence E Robinson	
9/02/43	Beaufighter	V8457	Irish Sea off Squires Gate	Crashed		256 Squadron
10/02/43	Tiger Moth I	T5955	Solway Firth	Mechanical Failure	F/L D Toone	
11/02/43	Lysander	V9666	Fleetwood, Lancashire, in sea off	crashed		10 AGS
13/02/43	Anson	DJ466	Grisedale Pike, Cumbria	Flew into high ground	Sgt W A Szott (Polish)	10 AFU
13/02/43	Wellington X	HE466	Snowdon	Flew into high ground in bad visibility		30 OTU
14/02/43	Anson	EG434	In sea, Cardigan Bay, North Wales	Ditched in Sea	F/O J H Spurgeon	
14/02/43	Defiant II	N1551	North of Barrow, Lindel, Lancs	Baled out after contol lost.	Station Officer R W Reisent	6 FPP

Date	Aircraft	Serial	Location	Cause / Notes	Name	Unit
14/02/43	Beaufighter	V8551	?Poherbeck, Treleth, Lancashire	Crashed into hill in bad visibility		219
15/02/43	Anson II	DJ464	Hobcarton End	Flew into hillside	F/Sgt A J Jeague	
16/02/43	Anson		Cross Fell	Crashed	1st Officer M A Murtagh	ATA
17/02/43	Tiger Moth II	T1712	Binsey Hill	Crashed	F/O A E Woodley	15 FTS
18/02/43	P-39M	42-24734	Burtonwood	Take off accident	Walter O West	
18/02/43	Anson	DJ453	Cron? Fell, Cumbria	Flew into hill in cloud		4 AOS
18/02/43	Typhoon	EJ909	Close to RAF Woodvale	Crashed	Pilot Sgt Lindsay Fisher, J.	
19/02/43	Mustang Mk I	AG617	5 miles N of Bellingham, Northumberland	Dived in		
22/02/43	P-47C	41-6244	Speke en route to Burtonwood	Engine cut out; nosed over	James A Goodson	
24/02/43	Wellington X	MF571	Millom	Overturned		
26/02/43	Hurricane I	P8813	Bewcastle fell	Crashed	Sgt R V Kennady	55 OTU
28/02/43	Hurricane I	V6573	Blackford	Mid air collision	Sgt R D Fatig	
28/02/43	Hurricane I	W9170	Blackford	Mid air collision		
1/03/43	Wellington IC	X3171	Bellingham, Northumberland	Icing	Barley, D.L.	
2/03/43	Tiger Moth II	N9462	Solway Firth	Ditched in Sea		15 FTS
3/03/43	Avro Anson	EG300	IOM			
3/03/43	Tiger Moth II	T8033	Kingstown	Taxiing accident		15 FTS
7/03/43	Defiant I	AA353	Farndon, Cheshire	Abandoned		285 Squadron
8/03/43	Proctor III	HM367	Kirkbride	Overturned		
9/03/43	Typhoon	DN474	RAF Woodvale	Crashed	Pilot Sgt Jones	
9/03/43	Beaufighter Vic	T5158	Brampton	Crashed	F/O R D Jones	
10/03/43	Lysander II	N1302	Speke	Swung and under carriage collapsed	S/L P Johnston P68139	Station Flight
10/03/43	Beaufighter	X8026	RAF Woodvale	Crashed on sports field after engine failure	P/O Henery Peter Harrison-Yates	256 Squadron
12/03/43	Boston III	AL269	Nearby field to Burtonwood	Engine failure	Fg Off C C A Fuchs	226
12/03/43	Lancaster I	ED614	Kirkbride	Mechanical Failure		
12/03/43	Wellington X	HX713	Millom			ATA
13/03/43	Blenheim	V6099	Snowdonia	Missing later found on high ground		13 OTU
21/03/43	Bermuda	FF562	Speke	Crashed on landing	Mr John Patrick Wakelin Topham	Lockheed
21/03/43	Master	W8761	Camp Hill			16 PFTS
22/03/43	P-47C	41-6244	Speke			
22/03/43	Mosquito II	DD750	Keighley, Yorkshire	Flew into hill at night		25 OTU
22/03/43	Blenheim IV	V5727	Speke	Crashed whilst taking off	F/Sgt Evans	77 Wing
25/03/43	Dornier Do217E-4	5432	Hethpool, Northumberland		Kalbfeisch, F.	KG2
25/03/43	Spitfire Mk IIB	P8587	Cheviot Hill, Northumberland		Brown, E	
26/03/43	Westland Lysander	T1444	IOM			
27/03/43	Hurricane		Burtonwood	Tipped on nose on runway		
28/03/43	P-38	AF-108	Warton		Chesley H Robertson	

Date	Aircraft	Serial	Location	Cause	Crew	Unit
3/04/43	Walrus I	X9482	Kirkbride	Ground looped		41 OTU
6/04/43	Mustang I	AG363	Timperley, Cheshire	Engine cut, crashed	P/O R A Duff	
8/04/43	Anson I	EG361	Keswick	Flew into Hillside	Sgt W A Dixon	195 Squadron
9/04/43	Typhoon	DN424	Over railway line at RAF Woodvale	Crashed		30 OTU
10/04/43	Wellington	DF611	Newhaven			
11/04/43	Hurricane I	V6884	Wigton	Flew into hillside	F/O C A Fawcett	22 OTU
11/04/43	Hurricane I	V6887	Silloth	Crashed	F/O Howett	425 Squadron
12/04/43	Wellington	BJ783	Ripley, Yorkshire	Crashed		
12/04/43	Tiger Moth I	T5143	Carlise	Forced Landing in Bad Weather		11 RS
14/04/43	Botha I	L6266	Hooton Park	Engine cut and undercarriage colapsed		
15/04/43	Hurricane I	AF984	Nicol Forest	Crashed	W/O W M Hicks	55 OTU
15/04/43	Beaufighter VI	JL566	Cardurnock	Crashed		9 OTU
16/04/43	C-47	41-19503	Burtonwood	Ran off end of runway into road.		
16/04/43	Typhoon	DN373	Beach at Warton from Woodvale	Engine Failure	P/O W McGorgan	195 Squadron
18/04/43	Bristol Beaufighter	X7887	IOM			SPTU
21/04/43	Anson I	N4953	Milestone Main St., Warton, Carnforth, Lancashire,	Broke up in air & spun into ground	Sgt Noel Leonard Pittendrigh	
23/04/43	Hurricane I	AG264	Coniston	Mid Air Collision with AG275	Sgt H M Atherton	55 OTU
23/04/43	Hurricane I	AG275	Coniston	Mid Air Collision with AG264	Sgt L T Cook	20 AFU
24/04/43	Wellington X	HE496	Solway Firth	Crashed into Sea	F/O F K Dostal	6 OTU
25/04/43	P 47C	41-6297	Horsehill Tor		John E. Coenen	63 Ferry Squadron
25/04/43	Hurricane I	AG264	Coniston, Cumbria	Flew into hill in mist		55 OTU
27/04/43	Whitley V	BD263	Silloth	Overshot		
27/04/43	Bristol Beaufighter	JL772	IOM			
27/04/43	Botha I	L6172	Hooton Park	Engine cut and hit tree		11 RS
28/04/43	Mustang	AG502	Mold, North Wales	Engine cut at low altitude & crashed		41 OTU
28/04/43	Hurricane I	P3901	Croglin	Flew into Hillside	F/Sgt P Skoblack	
28/04/43	Beaufighter	R2152	Broughton, Yorkshire, Vara Moor	Flew into high ground at night	Sgt Z Kowalski (Polish)	2 OTU
28/04/43	Defiant	T4074	Beach at Fleetwood	Engine Failure		10 AGS
3/05/43	Avro Anson	R9604	IOM			
4/05/43	Tiger Moth I	N9367	Kingstown	Crashed at Night		
7/05/43	Wellington		Silloth	Crashed		
7/05/43	Liberator	FL974	Crewe, Cheshire	Abandoned in bad weather		59 Squadron
8/05/43	Defiant	N1706	Squires Gate from Woodvale	Hit pigeons at Heysham, forced landing	Pilot Sgt Burgess	285 Squadron
8/05/43	Oxford	X7280	RAF Woodvale	Hit anti invasion pole	Sgt Duckworth	285 Squadron
11/05/43	Avro Anson		IOM			
15/05/43	Hurricane		Ireby	Crashed		
15/05/43	Spitfire II	P8267	Wrexham, North Wales, Bradley	Crashed	W/O Mieczyslaw Kos	61 OTU
18/05/43	P-47	42-7931	Speke in River Mersey	Fire in flight	Mr C B Wilson	Lockheed

Date	Aircraft	Serial	Location	Crew	Cause	Unit
19/05/43	Hurricane II	Z2978	Westlington	P/O J L A Wellenkens	Crashed	ATA
20/05/43	Fulmar	DR742	Burtonwood	1st Lt Ester	Taxiing accident	42 OTU
21/05/43	Magister I	T9835	Barrow in Furness	Cadet K G Caserson	Engine Failure	
21/05/43	Oxford	R6271	Waterhouses			
21/05/43	Swordfish	W5861	In Sea	S/L S Boardman	Flying in haze at 600ft, crashed into sea	741 Squadron
23/05/43	Avro Anson	EF903	IOM		Crashed	
23/05/43	Beaufighter Ic	T4763	Brampton	Sgt D Mason	Crashed, Spin/Stall	
26/05/43	SPITFIRE Vb	AD564	Near Newport	John woods	Hit Sea	
26/05/43	Typhoon	DN438	Irish Sea of Lytham St Anne's, from Woodvale	P/O Robert Ralph Walters		198 Squadron
27/05/43	Anson I	L6290	Silloth		Crashed	11 RS
27/05/43	Botha I		Hooton Park		Engine cut on overshoot and spun in	
27/05/43	Hurricane I	P3039	Silloth		Crashed	55 OTU
28/05/43	Anson I	AX407	Millom	Sgt M S McQualter	Crashed into Sea	
31/05/43	Anson I	DJ239	Maryport	Sgt S P James	Mid Air Collision	
31/05/43	Wellington VIII	HZ637	Maryport		Mid Air Collision	
31/05/43	Anson I	LT778	Barrow, Cumbria, 3 miles W of		Collided with Martinet HP303 & crashed	116 Squadron
31/05/43	Hudson III	V9197	Kirkbride	F/O P Freugh	Take off Accident	
6/06/43	Oxford	R5974	RAF Woodvale	Sgt S F Hetherington	Undercarriage collapsed	
9/06/43	Anson	N9642	Warton, BAD2	Walter A Burns		
9/06/43	Anson	N-9642	Warton, BAD2	Walter A Burns		
15/06/43	L-4	43-1404	Warton, BAD2			
15/06/43	UC-61A	43-14487	Warton, BAD2	Emanuel Flegel		
16/06/43	Wellington Ic	HE982	Silloth		Overshot	22 MU
16/06/43	Hurricane Iic	LB612	Silloth		Hit by HE982	
17/06/43	Beaufighter XI	JM129			Crashed	
17/06/43	Anson I	K8791	Northwich, Cheshire		Broke up in air	CNS
20/06/43	A-20B	41-3385	Warton, BAD2			
23/06/43	Hurricane IIb	BE489	Cumwhinton	Alvin R New	Mid Air Collision with Z2687	
23/06/43	Hurricane IIb	Z2687	Cumwhinton	Sgt P M Clark	Mid Air Collision with BE489	
28/06/43	Wellington Ic	HE258	Silloth	W D Graves	Crashed	6 OTU
30/06/43	L-4	43-708	Warton, BAD2	Sigmund E Hausner	Forced Landing	
1/07/43	Master	DK912	Thorncliffe		Crashed	17 PAFU
2/07/43	Hurricane	66-3757	Warton	Thomas E Smith	Undercarriage collapsed	
4/07/43	Beaufighter XI	JM223	Croglin Fell	P/O H J Carver	Flew into Hillside	1 OTU
7/07/43	B-26	41-31883	Warton, BAD2	Melvin E Jarvin		
8/07/43	Hurricane V	EG137	Aspatria		Engine Failure	55 OTU
8/07/43	Avro Anson	FN225	IOM			
8/07/43	Grumman Wildcat		IOM			

Date	Aircraft	Serial	Location	Remarks	Crew	Unit
11/07/43	Beaufighter	X8036	Wigton	Crashed		9 OTU
12/07/43	Halifax	DG404	Pateley Bridge, Yorkshire	Flew into high ground		1663 HCU
13/07/43	Beaufort I	JM589	Kirkbride	Take off Accident		ATA
16/07/43	Beaufighter Ic	T3352	Cumwhinton	Crashed		9 OTU
16/07/43	Beaufighter	T5335	Irthington	Crashed		
18/07/43	Lancaster I	W4947	Off Bootle, Cumbria	Crashed into Sea		1661 HCU
19/07/43	Master II	AZ729	Wrexham, North Wales	Lost prop blade & crashed		17 PAFU
21/07/43	Anson		Kirkbride	Crashed into Sea		
21/07/43	Avro Anson	EG548	IOM			
23/07/43	Vickers Wellington		IOM			
23/07/43	Wellington X	HE305	RAF Silloth	Crashed		
23/07/43	Tiger Moth II	T6498	Westlington	Crashed		
24/07/43	Spitfire		Kirkbride	Hit by Z7214		
24/07/43	B-17E	41-9132	Burtonwood	Take off accident, rolled through perimeter	Robert M Knox	
24/07/43	Proctor III	Z7214	Kirkbride	Swung of runway		
29/07/43	A-20B	43-3370	Keevil	Undercarriage Collapsed		9 OTU
3/08/43	Wellington	L9819	Silloth	Crashed		
4/08/43	Beaufort I	L9963	Longtown	Tail chopped off		
4/08/43	Beaufighter Ic	DJ275	Longtown			
8/08/43	Anson		Lake District, Cam Scout, Cumbria	Flew into high ground in bad weather		100 AFU
9/08/43	Anson I	DJ222	Green Gable	Crashed		10 AFU
9/08/43	Anson I	DJ275	Scafell	Flew into Hillside		10 AFU
9/08/43	Oxford	HM833	RAF Woodvale	Lost control		285 Squadron
9/08/43	Anson I	LS986	Heskit	Flew into Hillside		4 AFU
9/08/43	Anson I	M5053	Great Dodd	Flew into Hillside		10 AFU
9/08/43	Anson I	N5053	Matterdale, Cumbria, Watsons Dodd, Great Dodd	Crashed into mountain		100 AFU
11/08/43	Master II	DL195	Wettenhall, near Tarporley, Cheshire	Collided with Master DL405 & crashed		17 PAFU
16/08/43	Tiger Moth	DE-932	Squires Gate			
16/08/43	Mosquito III	HJ929	Dethick, near Matlock, Derbyshire	Abandoned after tail flutter & spun into ground	John E Harriss	410 Squadron
18/08/43	Anson	LT767	Millom	Engine Failure		
19/08/43	Hellcat I	FN355	RAF Woodvale	Emergency landing	F/O Flinterman	
20/08/43	P-47D	42-8468	Warton, BAD2	Crashed into Sea	Fred W Glover	6 Squadron
20/08/43	Wellington Ic	X3986	Silloth			9 OTU
22/08/43	Beaufighter Ic	T4721	Warwick Bridge	Crash Landing		
24/08/43	Spitfire		RAF Woodvale		P/O Van Bergan	322 Squadron
24/08/43	Beaufighter VI	EL362	Scaleby	Crashed		9 OTU

Date	Aircraft	Serial	Location	Event	Name	Unit
25/08/43	Spitfire		RAF Woodvale	Belly landing	Robert H Wehrman	322 Squadron
25/08/43	P-47C	41-6577	Warton, BAD2	Engine failure	Sgt Bollard	285 Squadron
25/08/43	Martinet	MS507	Harrington Barracks, Formby	Landing Accident		ATA
26/08/43	Hurricane V	KZ579	Kirkbride			
27/08/43	Beaufort		Solway Firth	Crashed into Sea		
27/08/43	B-24H	42-7467	Crashed Aspull, Near Wigan, from Burtonwood	Propeller contol failure	1st Lt Richard L Hester	Burtonwood Flight Test
27/08/43	L-4B	43-692	Burtonwood		Arron Z Bessant	8th AFSC
27/08/43	Tiger Moth	DE-939	Kirkham, Lancashire	Spin	William P Cassedy	
27/08/43	Avro Anson	R3410	IOM			
29/08/43	Oxford I	DF471	Dent, Yorkshire	Flew into hill		
30/08/43	B-24H	42-7468	Battery Cob, Sutton, Nr St Helens from Burtonwood	Struck earth work after take off	2nd Lt Merle F Tompkins, 0-740004	427 Squadron
30/08/43	B-24H	42-7568	Burtonwood		Tompkins Merle F	
30/08/43	Anson	R9587	Squires Gate	Crash landing	Sgt S Brooks	
31/08/43	Hurricane		Silloth	Landing accident		
2/09/43	Anson	LT140	1.5m N of Morecombe Bay Light	Engine Failure		
3/09/43	Martinet T1		Silloth			
3/09/43	Beaufort I	DX132	Longtown	Mechanical Failure		
5/09/43	Vickers Wellington	X3564	IOM	Crashed		
5/09/43	P-47D		Uttoxeter Derbyshire	Prop Ran away	Gilbert G Ross	
7/09/43	Swordfish	DK689	Fleetwood, Preesall Sands			11 RS
9/09/43	Barracuda	DN641	1.5 miles off Rossall Point			
11/09/43	Spitfire Vb	BL920	?	Fatal Accident	2nd LT Ivan R Henry	
14/09/43	Wellington	LS133	Silloth	Belly Landing		
15/09/43	B-17	42-8464	Keswick	Flew into Hillside	Diltz, Sodbury	
16/09/43	Botha	W5132	Hooton Park	Forced Landing		
16/09/43	B-17F	42-3411	Prestwick Scotland		Peter D Dustman	
16/09/43	P-47	42-7973	Warton, BAD2		Ralph "Kidd" Hofer	
16/09/43	Master II	AZ698	Wrexham, North Wales	Collided with Wellington X3807 & crashed	Frank D Gallion	17 PAFU
17/09/43	P-47C	41-6329	Warton, BAD2		Nagorka, H.J.	
17/09/43	B-17F	42-30030	1.5 miles NE Seahouses, Northumberland			
17/09/43	C-78	42-58513	Warton, BAD2		Caliphor J Sellers	
18/09/43	Beaufort I		Kirkbride	Undercarriage Collapsed		
23/09/43	Chesapeake	AL919	RAF Woodvale	Engine Failure	Midshipman Bushby	776 Squadron
23/09/43	Albacore	BF609	In Sea	Flew into sea at night	S/L A J Patterson	766 Squadron
23/09/43	Wellington	HZ251	Bradley, near Cross Hills, Yorkshire	Lost wing & crashed		60 OTU
23/09/43	Anson I	N9718	Millom			
27/09/43	P-47C	41-6620	Warton, BAD2	Crashed into Sea	Ronald S Evans	

Date	Aircraft	Serial	Location	Crew	Remarks	Unit
28/09/43	Anson	EF865	Kirkinner, Scotland	Sub Lt Mogridge	Crashed	3 SGR
30/09/43	Chesapeake	AL950	RAF Woodvale		Damaged airscrew	776 Squadron
30/09/43	Avro Anson	AX539	IOM		Structural Failure	
1/10/43	Spitfire	AD235	Kirkbride		Engine Failure	41 OTU
2/10/43	Hudson III	AG442	Silloth		Abandoned after engine cut	
3/10/43	Mustang I	MB238	Burleydam, Cheshire	Sub Lt Eric Roy Almond	Spun in	791 Squadron
5/10/43	Seafire	AZ593	2m South of RNAS Burscough		Crashed during aerobatics	17 PAFU
5/10/43	Master II	HR727	Wrexham, North Wales		Ran out of fuel	
9/10/43	Halifax II	42-5846	Ashop Moor, Derbyshire	Walter O West		
9/10/43	P-47	42-8577	Warton, BAD2	1st Lieutenant Donald K Cameron	Emergency Landing	87 Transport Squadron
10/10/43	P-47D		River Mersey, Lancashire. Offshore from Speke		Undercarriage Collapsed	
11/10/43	Warwick I	BV415	Kirkbride		Engine Failure	
13/10/43	Martinet TT1	JN657	Grune Point	P J Garner	Mid air collision with Mosquito	87 Transport Squadron
13/10/43	Mosquito	42-74642	Warton	Pilot Robert L Eckert	Mid air collision with P-47	
13/10/43	P-47D	HJ617	Near Speke, ferry flight from Warton to Burtonwood	F/O Gavner	Crashed into river after engine cut	
14/10/43	Mosquito	FX919	2 miles from Speke			60 OTU
14/10/43	Mustang III		Speke, Merseyside, In Mersey	Mr John Patrick Wakelin Topham	Crashed	Lockheed
19/10/43	Anson I	R9780	Whitehaven			
20/10/43	Oxford	LX518	Margery Hill	Denis Kyne	Engine Failure	21 PAFU
23/10/43	Hampden I	P2113	Westnewton			ATA
25/10/43	Barracuda	BV758	In Sea		Ditched in sea & sank	747 Squadron
26/10/43	Anson	N5256	Squires Gate		Take off accident	
28/10/43	Hurricane IIc	LE262	St Bees Head	J H M Lawrence	Crashed	
28/10/43	Spitfire		?Preston	F/O L W J Kelly	Engine trouble, force landing	322 Squadron
28/10/43	Wildcat	FN109	15 miles West of Blackpool, from Speke	S/L J N Wardill	Crashed into sea carrying out practise attack	1832 Squadron
3/11/43	Tiger Moth	DE-560	Warton, BAD2			
6/11/43	Spitfire		RAF Woodvale	James M Hood	Crash landing	322 Squadron
6/11/43	B-26	40-1372	Irish Sea			
6/11/43	P-47	41-6245	Warton, BAD2	Robert E Clague		
6/11/43	P-47D	42-6245	Warton, BAD2	Robert E Clague	Taxiing accident	
6/11/43	Handley Page Halifax	W1251	IOM			
7/11/43	P-47D	42-75087	Hitcham			
10/11/43	Hurricane XII	JS392	Silloth	Harry V Dulick	Undercarriage Collapsed	
11/11/43	Seafire	LR693	Clock Garage, Yealand Redmayne, 2.5 miles N of Carnforth, Lancashire, from Burscough	Sub-Lieutenant (A) R A Colbeck	Collided with Seafire NM929 & crashed	886 Squadron

Date	Aircraft	Serial	Location	Cause/Description	Name	Unit
11/11/43	Seafire	NM929	Clock Garage, Yealand Redmayne, 2.5 miles N of Carnforth, Lancashire, from Burscough	Collided with Seafire LR693 & crashed	Sub-Lieutenant (A) Eric Alwyn Philpott	808 Squadron
13/11/43	Hurricane I	Z4875	Cockermouth	Crashed		55 OTU
14/11/43	DB-7A	AH-517	Burtonwood	damaged on test flight, Landing	William T Maier	
14/11/43	Beaufighter	EL444	Dearham Bridge	Crashed		9 OTU
15/11/43	Beaufighter VI	EL285	Wolf Craggs	Flew into Hillside		9 OTU
15/11/43	Oxford I	LX464	RAF Woodvale	Hit obstruction, whilst taxing	Sgt Burgess	285 Squadron
16/11/43	Beaufighter	JL814	Crosby	Engine Failure		
16/11/43	Wellington	Z8799	Anglezark Moor, Lancashire	Crashed		307 Ferry Squadron
17/11/43	P-51B	43-12423	Warton, BAD2		Robert S packer	
18/11/43	P-38F	41-2371	Burtonwood		Robert T Schwabe	
19/11/43	Beaufort I	JM583	Little Brampton	Crashed		
20/11/43	Halifax		Crosby	Mechanical Failure	Ronald L Garkie	
23/11/43	B-17G	42-39913	Millom	Flew into Hillside		
23/11/43	B-17	9913	Millom	Crashed		
23/11/43	Halifax	DT578	Great Whernside	Dived into ground out of cloud in bad weather		1 FPP
25/11/43	Beaufighter	LZ536	? Cronton Mapley, Lancashire			
28/11/43	Avro Anson	LT175	IOM	Taxiing accident		310 Ferry Squadron
29/11/43	P-51B	43-6365	Speke en route to Warton, BAD2	Take off Accident	Eugene S Rybaczek	
29/11/43	Tiger Moth II	DE531	Kirkbride	Undershot at night		285 Squadron
29/11/43	Oxford	LX462	RAF Woodvale	Overshot	P/O Smith	
30/11/43	Wellington		Silloth			5 AOS
30/11/43	Anson I	EF909	Lake Dulyn, North Wales	Flew into high ground in cloud		
1/12/43	Beaufighter Ic	T5108	Crosby	Undercarriage Collapsed		12 PAFU
2/12/43	Blenheim I	L1196	Sharps Field, Hungerton Hall, Near Poynton Heath, Lancs	Crashed on take off		
2/12/43	Hampden I	P4347	Kirkbride	Hit Post		
3/12/43	Beaufort I	JM584	Kirkbride	Engine Failure		1691 flight
3/12/43	Martinet I	MS554	Askrigg, Yorkshire	Missing, later found crashed on high ground	Henry A Nolte	
8/12/43	P-400	BX-204	Burtonwood	Brake failure		310 Ferry Squadron
8/12/43	Beaufighter X	KW286	Kirkbride	Belly landed rwy 15		
9/12/43	P-47D	42-22780	Burtonwood	Crashed	Ist Lt Harvey H Chapman	
9/12/43	Beaufighter Ic	LZ146	Silloth	Flew into hill		53 OTU
10/12/43	Spitfire II	P7883	Chapel en le Frith, Derbyshire	Taxiing		
11/12/43	B-17G	42-31268	Warton, BAD2	Crash Landing	Rex P Robinson	310 Ferry
11/12/43	P-38J	42-67480	Crockstone Grange, Nr Longnor, Staffordshire Squadron	Belly landing	1st Lt G A Senesac	
12/12/43	Blenheim	AZ877	RAF Woodvale			12 PAFU

Date	Aircraft	Serial	Location	Circumstances	Name	Unit
14/12/43	Supermarine Spitfire	EN856	2 miles S of Snaefell, IOM	Flew into hillside in bad weather	F/O S. Podobinski	303 Squadron
16/12/43	P-47D	42-75208	Woodford from Burtonwood	Hit Lancaster	Charles B Congdon	
16/12/43	Lancaster II	DS779	Hunsingore, Yorkshire, near Knaresborough	Flew into high ground in cloud		
16/12/43	Halifax V	EB208	Whixley, Yorkshire	Crashed		1663 HCU
18/12/43	Wellington		Silloth	Engine Failure	George H Charno	
18/12/43	PB4Y-1	63934	Broken Ground, Near Mossley	Abandoned in bad weather over Lincolnshire		
18/12/43	P-400	AH-597	Burtonwood	Crash Landing	Paul s Martin	
19/12/43	Hurricane	66-3757	River Ribble Estuary	Lost formation at night & crashed	Frank L Levings	
20/12/43	Barracuda	P9828	Ambleside, Cumbria, Skelwith Bridge, High Arnside Farm		S/L G F Hopewell	747 Squadron
21/12/43	B-17G	42-37937	Warton, BAD2	Crashed	Vivian L Rees	
22/12/43	Vickers Wellington	HE681	IOM			
24/12/43	Oxford	BM837	Winter Hill, Lancashire	Flew into high ground		
26/12/43	P-47D	42-75549	Burtonwood	Overshot on landing.	1st Lt Harry V Dulick	311 Ferry Squadron
26/12/43	Swordfish	HS556	?	Off course & flew into hillside	S/L R B Cassells	766 Squadron
27/12/43	Hurricane I	AG175	Carlisle, Cumbria, 10 miles SW of	Collided with V7010 & crashed		55 OTU
28/12/43	Hurricane I	AG175	Dalston	Mid air collision with V7010		55 OTU
28/12/43	Mosquito II	DZ751	Newton, Cheshire	Flew into ground		60 OTU
28/12/43	Hurricane I	V7010	Dalston	Mid air collision with AG175		55 OTU
30/12/43	Avro Anson	N5026	IOM			
31/12/43	P-400	BX-407	Burtonwood	Crashed	Chandler R Brown	
31/12/43	Beaufighter VI	KW152	Bootle Fell	Struck Hillside	Lieutenant D.E. Harris	Burtonwood Flight Test
3/01/44	B-17	42-31581	Edgeworth, Near Bolton		First Lt Lloyd D Bingham Junior	Warton Flight Test
4/01/44	P-51B	43-12415	Irish Sea, 6 miles out from Blackpool, from Warton			
6/01/44	Miles Martinet	JN448	IOM			
6/01/44	Miles Martinet	JN492	IOM			
9/01/44	P-47D	42-75584	2m SE West Kirby, near Saughall Massey, Wirral from Burtonwood	Crashed in bad weather	2nd Lt Jay Fredrick Simpson	Burtonwood Flight Test
10/01/44	Beaufighter VI	KW152	Millom, Cumbria	Flew into hill	John P Willett	
11/01/44	B-17G	42-38029	Warton, BAD2			301 FTU
11/01/44	Avro Anson	N9751	IOM			
13/01/44	Blenheim V	AZ877	RAF Woodvale	Belly landed		
18/01/44	P-38J	42-67896	Burtonwood	Right engine dead.	Lt Robert W Hedler	
19/01/44	B-17G	42-31708	Warton, BAD2		Edwin R Anders	

Date	Aircraft	Serial	Location	Remarks	Crew	Unit
20/01/44	Anson	EF969	Irish Sea Point of Ary	Fuel supply problem	Whittaker	
21/01/44	P-38	42-75597	Burtonwood		John P Willet JR	
21/01/44	P-51B	43-12469	Warton, BAD2			
21/01/44	Wellington	BJ652	Smerrill			27 OTU
21/01/44	Wellington	BJ658	Mayfield			27 OTU
21/01/44	Avro Anson	MG671	IOM			
21/01/44	Vickers Wellington	Z1339	IOM			
22/01/44	Anson I	EG321	Warton, Lancashire	Flew into ground in bad weather		3 SGR
23/01/44	B-17G	42-97463	Warton, BAD2	Taxied into crane	Charles W Bradshaw	
24/01/44	B-17E	41-9089	Warton, BAD2	Taxied into crane	Milton H Shoesmith	
24/01/44	Halifax II	JP182	Braithwaite, Cumbria, Eel Crag	Flew into high ground		ATA
24/01/44	Beaufighter I	T4772	Bewcastle	Flew into Hill Side		
25/01/44	Wellington XIV	NB686	Silloth	Overshot Runway		SPTU
30/01/44	Anson I	EG640	Satterthwaite, Cumbria	Crashed in forced landing		
30/01/44	Anson	MG393	Cleator Moor, Cumbria, at Starling Dodd	Flew into hill breaking cloud after fuel ran out		
31/01/44	Anson	DG931	Cark, Cumbria	Flew into ground		SPTU
31/01/44	Whitley	LA765	Dilhorne			81 OTU
3/02/44	Avenger	FN821	Pwlliago, North Wales, near Llanygnog, Snowdonia	Flew into high ground in bad weather	S/L E H Green	848 Squadron
4/02/44	Beaufighter VI	JL774	Crosby	Engine Failure		
5/02/44	Wellington	42-22758	Silloth	Overshot Runway		
6/02/44	P-47D	42-8621	Pendle Hill, Nr Burnley, Lancashire	Crashed due to weather	Flight Officer John R Runnells T	
6/02/44	P-47D	42-100331	Nr Grange Farm, Freckleton Marsh	Collision with ground in bad weather	Captain Charles Francis 0-660131	
7/02/44	B-24J	43-6556	Nr Blackpool Tower, Lancashire	Mid air collision	Jack B Knight	Warton Flight Test
7/02/44	P-51B	BB320	Nr Blackpool Tower, Lancashire	Mid air collision	Robert J Murtha	Warton Flight Test
7/02/44	Halifax	43-12469	Blakeley Lane Cellerhead			1662 HCU
9/02/44	P-51B	LR412	Warton, BAD2			
9/02/44	Mosquito IX	N4919	Aran Fawddwy, North Wales	Flew into high ground	Robert J Murtha	540 Squadron
10/02/44	Anson I	MG107	Tarnbrook,Trough of Bowland	Forced landing		2 AFU
11/02/44	Avro Anson	42-68031	IOM			
11/02/44	P-38J	HS615	Burtonwood			
12/02/44	Swordfish	43-6840	Morecambe bay	Ditched in sea	Delbert E Harris	766 Squadron
14/02/44	P-51B	BB278	Warton, BAD2		S/L D Meats	
16/02/44	Halifax II	43-6635	Solway Firth	Crashed in Sea	Kelly R Moutray	1674
18/02/44	P-51B	43-6623	Knowsley Safari Park	Stall during approach, spun in	Flight Officer Eugene Stanley Rybaczek (T-190748)	310 Ferry Squadron
18/02/44	P-51B	HE747	Speke en route to Warton, BAD2	Stalled on take off	2nd Lieutenant Langhorne S Gee	310 Ferry Squadron
18/02/44	Wellington I		Silloth	Crashed		6 OTU

Date	Aircraft	Serial	Location	Incident	Pilot	Unit
19/02/44	Beaufort I	L9948	Crosby	Undercarriage Collapsed		9 OTU
20/02/44	Beaufighter V	JL570	Crosby	Engine Failure		9 OTU
20/02/44	Beaufighter	JL616	Anglesey, North Wales, Trewan Sands	Spiralled into ground out of control		
21/02/44	P-38H	42-66637	Near Warton, BAD2	Mid air collision	William H Vallee	9 OTU
21/02/44	Wellington III	BK506	Cliburn	Flew into Hill Side		
23/02/44	Wellington III	BK156	Solway Firth	Crashed in Sea		
23/02/44	Anson	R9638	Cark, Cumbria, Applebury hill	Ran out of fuel on overshoot & crash landed		SPTU
25/02/44	P-47	42-76398	Warton	Landing Accident	Edwin Meltzer	
25/02/44	Beaufighter I	T5106	Crosby	Undercarriage Collapsed		9 OTU
25/02/44	Beaufighter VI	X8070	Crosby	Undercarriage Collapsed		
26/02/44	P-47D	42-75561	Warton, BAD2	Take off accident	Robert G Peres	
1/03/44	P-47D	42-8418	Tarleton	Crash landing	Burtie Orth	Warton Flight Test
3/03/44	Lancaster II	DS650	Byrness, Northumberland		Calder, R.G.	
3/03/44	Botha I	L6463	Hooton Park	Tyre burst, swung and tipped up		11 RS
6/03/44	Spitfire		Squires Gate	Landing accident	1st Officer Wozulanis	ATA
8/03/44	Skua	L4457	Irish sea off Southport	Crashed		776 Squadron
10/03/44	Beaufighter VI	JM115	Crosby	Undercarriage Collapsed		9 OTU
11/03/44	B-24H	41-29484	Balderton	Engine Failure		9 OTU
11/03/44	Beaufighter I	T4655	Crosby	Collided with T4712	Joseph R Saviske	9 OTU
11/03/44	Beaufighter I	T4712	Crosby	Collided with T4655		9 OTU
12/03/44	Oxford	LX745	Shining Tor	Flew into high ground	C. S. G. Wood	17 PAFU
13/03/44		42-67469	Hooton Park		Hammack, Donald E	27ATG
13/03/44	Beaufighter VI	T5271	Crosby	Engine Failure		9 OTU
16/03/44	P-47D	42-8414	Burtonwood, Mary Ann's Bridge	Stalled	Jessie H Oswalt	Burtonwood Flight Test
18/03/44	P-38H	42-66637	Sand dunes west of RAF Woodvale	Crashed after go around	Lt H W Vallee	Warton Flight Test
18/03/44	Martinet TT1	HP274	Firbank Fell, Mossfoot	Flew into Hill Side		
18/03/44	MOSQUITO	MM340	Warton, BAD2		Charles W Himes	Warton Flight Test
20/03/44	Hurricane I	AF970	Castle Carroch, Cumbria	Flew into hill in cloud		2 TEU
20/03/44	Anson	DJ680	Hollingworth			2 PAFU
20/03/44	Anson I	EG686	Coniston, Cumbria	Flew into hill		SPTU
21/03/44	Spitfire LFVb		RAF Woodvale	Forced landing due to engine trouble	Sgt Kowalski	316 Squadron
21/03/44	L4-B	43-677	1m NW of Burtonwood	flipped over, damaged engine in field	Captain Bruce R Riley	
21/03/44	Spitfire V	W3569	Congleton, Chesire	Engine Fire		316 Squadron
24/03/44	Mosquito PRXIV	MM385	Burtonwood			
25/03/44	P-38J	42-47469	Burtonwood			

Date	Aircraft	Serial	Location	Name	Cause	Unit
27/03/44	P-38J	42-104203	Overton, Flintshire	Howard N Pearson	Crashed on landing	3 STT
28/03/44	Tiger Moth	BB809	Warton, Lancashire		Wings came off in dive & crashed	57 OTU
28/03/44	Master III	W8640	Wrexham, North Wales			
30/03/44	B-26C	134956	Warton, BAD2	John E asmussen		
30/03/44	Hudson	AM686	Squires Gate		Landing accident	ATA
30/03/44	Albemarle	P1463	Haven Hill			42 OTU
31/03/44	Beaufighter	JM128	Crosby		Undercarriage Collapsed	
31/03/44	Beaufort I	L9963	Crosby		Undercarriage Collapsed	9 OTU
6/04/44	Wellington XII	MP682	Solway Firth		Crashed in Sea	6 OTU
6/04/44	Beaufighter VI	T5349	Crosby		Engine Failure	
9/04/44	Beaufighter VI	JL820	Great Orton		Ran out of Fuel	
9/04/44	Beaufighter VI	T5104	Crosby		Undercarriage Collapsed	
11/04/44	Bristol Blenheim	L6674	IOM			
11/04/44	Spitfire XIV	NH700	Rothbury, Northumberland	Van Hamel, J		9 OTU
12/04/44	B-24H	41-10038	Warton, BAD2	John J Collins		285 Squadron
12/04/44	P-47	42-25530	Felton, Northumberland	Serapiglia, A.L.		42 OTU
12/04/44	B-24H	42-94994	Warton, BAD2	Robert T Reed		9 OTU
12/04/44	Halifax Mk II	BB310	10 miles E Penrith, Cumbria	Brookes, S.		
13/04/44	P-47D	42-8669	Calveley	Martin J Chaves	Nose Up	
13/04/44	Anson I	DJ564	Solway Firth		Crashed in Sea	
13/04/44	Beaufighter I	T5103	Solway Firth		Crashed in Sea	
14/04/44	Oxford I	LX642	RAF Woodvale	S/L G F Harris	Undershot	
15/04/44	Albemarle	V1609	Hartford, Cheshire		Hit high chimney	
16/04/44	Beaufighter VI	KW293	Caldbeck, Cumbria		Control lost in bad weather & crashed	
17/04/44	P-51	42-106847	Warton, BAD2	Kenneth L Inman	Collided with civilian truck	
19/04/44	Wellington XIV	HF	?		Crashed	310 Ferry Squadron
20/04/44	P-51C	42-103308	RNAS Burscough	James L Planchard	Forced Landing	12 PAFU
20/04/44	Blenheim V	AZ948	RAF Woodvale		Crashed on landing	30 OTU
21/04/44	Wellington	BK347	Whernside		Crashed into hillside	
22/04/44	MILES MASTER	DL-679	Speke			
23/04/44	Beaufighter VI	T5108	Crosby		Mechanical Failure	
27/04/44	Beaufighter VI	T5217	Silloth		Engine Failure	311 Ferry Squadron
28/04/44	P-51	42-103306	Warton, BAD2	Algee M Hill		
28/04/44	Botha I	L6220	Hooton Park		Crashed on Landing	11 RS
28/04/44	Botha I	L6741	Hooton Park		Undercarriage jamed and crash landed	11 RS
1/05/44	B-24	41-29520	Warton, BAD2	Walter L Williams	Taxiing accident	
2/05/44	Martinet	JM127	Seascale		Crashed	
4/05/44	Beaufighter VI		Crosby		Undercarriage Collapsed	
6/05/44	Halifax V	DK138	? Stawanden, Cheshire		Engine caught fire & crashed	1663 HCU

Date	Aircraft	Serial	Location	Cause	Name	Unit
6/05/44	Mosquito	DZ747	Penley, North wales, near Wrexham, in grounds of military hospital.	Crashed into ground	J R Milne	60 OTU
6/05/44	Halifax II	JN919	?Lonesome Hill Farm, Yorkshire	Engine caught fire & abandoned & crashed		102 Squadron
10/05/44	P-38	42-67207	Tintwistle	Engine failure	F/O Hugh Jones	
10/05/44	Hawker Hurricane	L1917	IOM			
16/05/44	Reliant	X9596	Squires Gate	Landing accident	G/Cpt Harston	650 Squadron
17/05/44	Martinet I	EM556	Seascale, Cumbria	Engine fire & prop fell off & crashed		
18/05/44	Halifax V	EB200	Norton le Clay,Yorkshire	Crashed after control lost	W/O Feliks Teofil Wares	1664 HCU
19/05/44	Spitfire	X4173	Prestatyn, North Wales	Collided with Spitfire R7127 & crashed into sea		61 OTU
21/05/44	Spitfire		Ainsdale	Spun and crashed into houses	F/O Storey	63 Squadron
24/05/44	P-38J	43-28738	Moss Bank Village, nr St Helens	Engine Faliure	2nd Lt John E Austin	Burtonwood Flight
27/05/44 Test	Stirling	LK502	Cliffe Park, Leek	Spun in	Sub Lieut.	1654 HCU
28/05/44	Firefly	Z1906	Rufford from Burscough		Maurice Walton Williams	1771 Squadron
29/05/44	Martinet	B129	Crosby	Overturned		
2/06/44	P-47D	42-75522	Burtonwood		Jesse H Oswalt	27ATG
2/06/44	A-20G	43-9388	Little Walden			
4/06/44	B-17	43-37573	Burtonwood	Collision of aircraft with ambulance		
5/06/44	DH Mosquito CB-24D	DD733 785	IOM		Henry A Podgurski 1st Lt. Lennox, George W Reynolds	
7/06/44	B-24	42-51202	Heston	Flew into hillside		
8/06/44	P-61A J	42-5548	Lower summit of Snaefell, IOM	Landing accident		422nd Night Fighter Squadron
9/06/44			Speke		James E Morgan Jr	Burtonwood Flight Test
10/06/44	P-47	42-26473	3 miles N Chester from Burtonwood	Forced landing with engine failure		
10/06/44	A-20G	43-9712	Gosfield			
11/06/44	A-20G	43-9703	3 mile North station 165 little Walden			
11/06/44	A-20G	43-9946	4 mile North station 165 Little Walden			
12/06/44	B-17G	42-97110	Warton, BAD2	Nosed over on runway	William S Buhler	
12/06/44	B-17G	44-13403	Warton, BAD2		2nd Lt Bill Clearwater	Warton Flight Test
12/06/44	P-51D	EG233	River Ribble estuary			
12/06/44	Avro Anson		IOM			
13/06/44	P-47D	42-26677	Burtonwood	Spun in	Clifford M Glaze	

Date	Aircraft	Serial	Location	Cause	Name	Unit
	Anson I		Boscobel?, North Wales,			
14/06/44	UC-78	43-7778	Moel Hebug / Burtonwood	Flew into Hill Side	Woirol, Warren S	22 OTU
16/06/44	Wellington X	43-9679	Keswick	Flew into hill in cloud		22 OTU
16/06/44	A-20G	HZ715	Boreham, Essex			9 OTU
16/06/44	Wellington	42-40552	Buttermere, Cumbria		Jacob J Conrad	
17/06/44	CB-24	HZ715	Warton, BAD2	Stall practising evasive action & dived into grnd.		
17/06/44	Beaufighter	JM173	Crosby			
17/06/44	Beaufighter XI	MM310	Bewcastle, Cumbria	Electrical Failure,	Keefe, E.F.	Warton Flight Test
17/06/44	Mosquito XVI	JL572	Warton	Undercarriage Collapsed	Charlie Himes	9 OTU
19/06/44	Beaufighter VI	43-9378	Crosby			
20/06/44	A-20G	44-13593	Little Walden	Crashed	2nd Lt. Burtie Orth Gardiner	Warton Flight Test
21/06/44	P-51D	LJ628	Cadley, Preston			1654 HCU
21/06/44	Stirling	43-21460	Upper Commons Grove, Berkshire			
25/06/44	A-20J	AZ884	RAF Woodvale	Landed with undercarriage up		12 PAFU
25/06/44	Blenheim I	HF155	Silloth	Crashed		
26/06/44	Wellington X	Z1947	Clevelys, In sea 1.5 miles W of,	Crashed into sea attempting to pull out of dive	S/L H Gabutt	1772 Squadron
26/06/44	Firefly	HK119	IOM			
27/06/44	DH Mosquito	W1707	Hooton Park, Merseyside			
28/06/44	Anson I	42-51133	Warton, BAD2	Engine cut on approach, F/L on mudbank, Submerged		11 RS
29/06/44	B-24J	42-93541	Burtonwood	Landing accident	Jacob C Eckert	
30/06/44	C-47A	43-10194	1 mile North of Cottesmore Field	Take off accident		
30/06/44	A-20G	AZ957	RAF Woodvale			12 PAFU
3/07/44	Blenheim V	44-23224	Burtonwood	Crashed on take off.	George V Bartley	Burtonwood Flight Test
4/07/44	F-5E	41-35791	IOM	Missing		
5/07/44	B-26 Marauder	41-6187	Warton, BAD2	Take off accident	Gregory P Thomas	
6/07/44	P-47D	42-50762	North Barrule IOM	Flew into hillside	Capt. Lynch	12 PAFU
6/07/44	B-24	BA753	RAF Woodvale	Swung into ground		
6/07/44	Blenheim V	BA783	RAF Woodvale	Overshot		
6/07/44	Blenheim V	JL825	Crosby	Undercarriage Collapsed		
8/07/44	Beaufighter VI	JL945	Silloth	Engine Failure		9 OTU
	Beaufighter II	42-31321	Adjacent to RAF Towyn	Overshot and struck air raid shelter		
9/07/44	B-17	42-51280	Warton, BAD2		Arthur E Ford	
11/07/44	B-24J	42-5533	3 miles NW of Nantwich	Unkown failure	Pilot Edgar E Merriman	310 Ferry Squadron
11/07/44	P-61	43-12411	Barton-On-Humber		Slade, William C Jr.	
11/07/44	P-51B	43-9189	Parkhold Farm, Gosfield			
11/07/44	A-20G					

Date	Aircraft	Serial	Location	Description	Name	Unit
11/07/44	Miles Martinet	MS502	IOM	Flipped onto its back by B-24 prop wash	Walter H Malmiak	
14/07/44	Tiger Moth		Warton, BAD2	Nosed Over		
14/07/44	B-17G	42-5900	Burtonwood		Bertram Astrove	
14/07/44	Handley Page Halifax	LW115	IOM			
15/07/44	P-51D	44-13765	Warton, BAD2	Collided with C-45		
16/07/44	B-17	310	Burtonwood	Collision		
16/07/44	UC-78	42-37664	Burtonwood	B17 taxied into aircraft		
16/07/44	C-45	43-35664	Burtonwood	Collision		
16/07/44	UC-64	43-5310	Burtonwood			
17/07/44	P-51	43-13610	Warton, BAD2			
17/07/44	P-51D	44-13610	Warton, BAD2			
17/07/44	P-51D	44-13873	Warton, BAD2			
17/07/44	Anson	EG447	1m off St Annes		Kenneth G Kirkhuff	
19/07/44	P-47		On or near Burtonwood			
19/07/44	P-47		On or near Burtonwood			
21/07/44	Stirling	LJ628	Upper Commons, Peak District	Flew into ground desending in cloud		1654 HCU
22/07/44	P-38J	42-67707	Warton, BAD2 from Burtonwood		Kenneth L Inman	
23/07/44	Beaufighter II	JM163	Crosby	Belly landing		
24/07/44	Whitley		Weston Underwood			
24/07/44	B-17E	41-9132	Burtonwood			
25/07/44	Avro Anson	N9606	IOM			
27/07/44	Hurricane	V6793	Fleet Green			4 PAFU
28/07/44	Martinet	HP311	High Duddon	Flew into Hill Side		
29/07/44	Firefly	Z1956	Southport, In sea, 17 miles W of	Collided with Z1958 & crashed into sea	Lt M J C Wright	1772 Squadron
29/07/44	Firefly	Z1958	Southport, In sea, 17 miles W of	Collided with Z1956 & crashed into sea	L/C A H D Gough	1772 Squadron
30/07/44	Lancaster	PB304	Langley Road, Pendleton, Salford	Dived into ground in cloud	F/L Peter Lines 112751	
31/07/44	Warwick I	BV471	Squires Gate	Overshot emergancy landing		281 Squadron
1/08/44	Anson	EG437	2 miles North of Laxey IOM	Flew into high ground		
2/08/44	B-17G	42-102390	Burtonwood	Explosion in flight	W/O De Courcey	
3/08/44	Wellington X	HF470	Cark	Engine Failure	Lewis D Chase	
5/08/44	Vickers Wellington	Z1667	IOM			
7/08/44	Fairey Barracuda	LS844	IOM			
8/08/44	Anson	EG325	1 mile South of Ballacrack, IOM	Flew into high ground		
9/08/44	Blenheim V	BA246	Bleasdale Moor, Lancashire	Flew into hillside at night	F/L E F H Bent	12 PAFU
13/08/44	Blenheim V	BA104	RAF Woodvale	Belly landed		12 PAFU
14/08/44	UC-64	43-5540	Speke enroute from Warton, BAD2	Minor accident with a P-47	2nd Lieutenant James R Peele	310 Ferry Squadron

Date	Aircraft	Serial	Location	Cause	Crew	Unit
14/08/44	P-47D	44-19565	Speke	Minor accident with a UC-64		310 Ferry Squadron
14/08/44	Mosquito XX	KB269	?Egerton, Yorkshire	Controls locked, abandoned in spin		1655 CU
16/08/44	A-20G	43-9902	Burtonwood	Landing Accident	Albert R Sitzer	
17/08/44	Mustang I	AG443	Clitheroe, Lancashire	Flew into hill in bad weather	F/O Charles William Haythornthwaite	41 OTU
17/08/44	Oxford	PH235	Holmes Chapel, Cheshire	Cause unknown		14 FPP
18/08/44	Oxford	MP346	Kingsley, Cheshire	Flew into ground at night, cause unknown		11 PAFU
19/08/44	Sea Hurricane Mk1A	BW855	Hepple, Northumberland		Medd, P.N. MBE	
21/08/44	Martinet I	JN554	?Middleton Sands, Lancashire	Flew into ground in turn		650 Squadron
22/08/44	B-24J	42-51530	Warton, BAD2		Thomas S Krepps	
23/08/44	B-24H	42-50291	Holy Trinity School, Freckleton	Caught in violent downdraught	Lt John Bloemendal	Warton Flight Test
24/08/44	P-38	42-68151	Burtonwood	Hit by B-17 43-38251		
24/08/44	B-17G	43-38251	Burtonwood	Collision	Ray D Lohr	
24/08/44	B-17	43-38347	Warton, BAD2	Taxiing	Walter Zaier	Warton Flight Test
24/08/44	Swordfish	HS346	Inskip, Lancashire	Engine failed on take off & force landed & crashed into hedge	S/L G D Brierly	766 Squadron
24/08/44	Beaufighter	NE825	Burtonwood	Collision		
25/08/44	Martinet		Solway Firth	Crashed in Sea		
28/08/44	B-17G	43-38315	Warton, BAD2	Collision	Paul E Oberdorf	Warton Flight Test
28/08/44	P-51D	44-14304	Warton, BAD2			
30/08/44	B-24J	44-10614	Warton, BAD2	Landing accident	Lester V Smith	
30/08/44	B-24J	44-10614	Warton, BAD2	LANDING	Smith, Lester V	
30/08/44	Anson	EC428	Squires Gate	Collision		
30/08/44	Mosquito VI	LR263	? Burton Marsh, Cheshire	Caught fire during flare drop & crashed		60 OTU
31/08/44	P-38J	42-104269	Warton, BAD2		Clarence H Kadow	Warton Flight Test
31/08/44	P-38J	43-28455	Warton, BAD2			Warton Flight Test
31/08/44	Beaufighter	T5207	Squires Gate	Landing accident		1656 HCU
3/09/44	Halifax II	JD417	Yr Eifl, North Wales	Flew into mountain	S/Lt L Terry	
7/09/44	Barracuda	LS841	In sea 2-3 miles off St Annes	Crashed inn to sea		60 OTU
10/09/44	Mosquito VI	HJ816	Banks, Southport	Broke up recovering from dive, Banks Ranges, Southport		
14/09/44	Wellington X	HF200	Silloth	Crashed		6 OTU
16/09/44	Wellington X	HF179	Solway Firth	Crashed in Sea		
16/09/44	Mosquito XVI	NS-635	Warton, BAD2	Landing accident, hit hole	Pilot Robert L. Lee	
17/09/44	P-51D	44-14350	Speke		Craig C More	
17/09/44	Fairey Barracuda	LS701	IOM			

Date	Aircraft	Serial	Location	Incident	Name	Unit
21/09/44	Airspeed Oxford	V3816	IOM		Elmer H Stuchell	
23/09/44	P-51D	44-14197	Warton, BAD2	Taxied into parked truck	Robert S Backer	
23/09/44	P-47D	44-20063	Warton, BAD2	Electrical fire		
24/09/44	B17		Burtonwood			
25/09/44	Stirling Mk III	EE972	Cheviot Hill, Northumberland		Verrall, H.J.	
26/09/44	B-24H	42-51209	Warton, BAD2		George M Wilson	
26/09/44	P-51D	44-14361	Warton, BAD2		George M Wilson	
26/09/44	P-51D	44-14600	Warton, BAD2		George M Wilson	
26/09/44	P-51D	44-14671	Warton, BAD2		George M Wilson	
26/09/44	P-51D	44-14838	Warton, BAD2		George M Wilson	
27/09/44	P-51D	44-14738	Beese, Cheshire		Thomas A white	
30/09/44	P-47D		Warton, BAD2	Belly landing		
30/09/44	P-47D	42-8967	Warton, BAD2	Belly landing, gear stuck	Jess H Edwards	10 AGS
30/09/44	Anson I	LT532	Barrow, Cumbria	Hit tow cable in flt. control lost on approach		
2/10/44	B-17G	44-8204	Burtonwood			
2/10/44	B-17G	44-8350	Burtonwood			
4/10/44	Lancaster X	KB745	Cheviot Hill, Northumberland		Duncan, G.R.	
5/10/44	P-51	41-4608	Warton, BAD2	Ran out of runway	Malcom A Stewart	
5/10/44	B-24J	44-40466	Warton, BAD2	Ran out of runway		
5/10/44	A-20K	44-561	Warton, BAD2			
6/10/44	P-47D		Burtonwood			
6/10/44	P-47D		Burtonwood			
6/10/44	P-47D	44-20099	Burtonwood	Overshot into road	Edward Johnson	
6/10/44	Helldiver	JW121	Preesall Sands	Crashed		
9/10/44	B-24	42-94841	Twizzle Head Moss			
11/10/44	B-24J	42-52003	Mill Hill, Near Hayfield, Yorkshire from Burtonwood	Crashed into Hillside	Lt Haopt	310 ferry Sqn
13/10/44	A-20B	41-3371	Warton, BAD2			
14/10/44	P-47D	42-28991	Cuerdley near Widnes	Spun in	William H Powers	109 OTU
15/10/44	Halifax	BB116	Marvins Pike	Flew into Hill Side		
15/10/44	Halifax Mk V	DK116	Kielder, Northumberland		Haddrell, H.G.	
17/10/44	B-17G	43-38707	Burtonwood		Thomas A White	
17/10/44	P-47D	44-20087	Burtonwood	Take off, ran of end of runway	Thomas A White	
17/10/44	Halifax VII	NP745	Penruddock, Cumbria	Iced up & abandoned. Crashed		408 Squadron
18/10/44	B-24	42-50347	near Arrowe Park on the Wirral, en En route to Burtonwood	Broke up in bad weather		
18/10/44	P-38J	43-28528	Warton, BAD2		Fred W Rue	
18/10/44	Anson	EG210	1/2 mile SE of Squires Gate	Engine failure	P/O H G Greenwood	
18/10/44	Oxford	V3873	Nr Lingwood, Liverpool	Crashed in forced landing		577 Squadron
19/10/44	Anson	EG209	Squires Gate	Overshot	P/O Atkinson	

Date	Aircraft	Serial	Location	Description	Name	Unit
22/10/44	Halifax V	LL505	Coniston, Cumbria, 3 miles NW of	Flew into high ground		1659 HCU
22/10/44	Mosquito XVI	PF395	Saddleworth Moor, Dean Rocks	Flew into high ground breaking cloud		571 Squadron
23/10/44	P-51D	44-14923	Warton, BAD2			
24/10/44	P-51D	41-4996	Warton, BAD2		Joseph M Bosworth	740 bomb Squadron
25/10/44	B-24	41-29411	RAF Woodvale	Dragged wing	1st Lt D J Cheffer	
27/10/44	AT-6D	42-85163	Warton, BAD2			
27/10/44	Hawker Hurricane	NF726	IOM			
1/11/44	B-17G	44-8257	Burtonwood	Wheel bogged down and aircraft swung into a ditch	Pilot George H Pritchard	
1/11/44	Wellington XII	MP680	Silloth	Crashed		6 OTU
1/11/44	Mosquito II	W4088	Mynydd Mawr, North Wales	Flew into mountain		51 OTU
3/11/44	Warwick I	BV474	Burtonwood	Swung into ditch on landing		281 Squadron
3/11/44	Oxford I	HN429	Ashe Edge, Buxton Derbyshire	Flew into high ground		11 PAFU
5/11/44	Wellington		Burtonwood	Swung off runway and undercarriage collapsed		
6/11/44	Fairey Barracuda II	MD777	IOM			1689 Flight
9/11/44	Hurricane II	HW684	? Harrendale Farm, Yorkshire	Collided with Halifax DK149 & crashed		
10/11/44	Fairey Barracuda	MX538	IOM			
12/11/44	C-47A	348473	Snowdonia en route to Burtonwood	Crashed into hillside	2Lt William George Gough	86th Transport Squadron
13/11/44	Anson Mk.1	AX177	north face of Cronk-ny-Arrey-Lhaa, IOM	Flew into hillside	Flt.Sgt. McDonald	1 AFU
14/11/44	Proctor		Field near Singleton	Force Landed		
14/11/44	CB-7A	AH517	Burtonwood		William T Maier	15 FTS
14/11/44	Tiger Moth II	T6828	Bewcastle	Flew into Hill Side		
15/11/44	Anson	LT578	Squires Gate	Collision	W/O Hollis	
15/11/44	Anson	NK161	Squires Gate	Collision	F/Lt Walsh	
15/11/44	Halifax	W7771	Blackpool, Lancashire, Squires Gate	Crashed in forced landing		1656 HCU
16/11/44	P-51D	44-15584	Warton, BAD2			
16/11/44	Avro Anson	EG416	IOM			
16/11/44	Fairey Barracuda	MD848	IOM			
17/11/44	Anson	MG464	Long Craggs, Griesdale Pike, Cumbria	Flew into high ground in cloud at night		
17/11/44	Swordfish	NF337	Inskip, 100 yds N of airfield	Crashed in flames	P/O P H Nelson	766 Squadron
19/11/44	Spitfire V	AA933	Wrexham, North Wales	Dived into ground		61 OTU
20/11/44	Wellington	MF509	Scrin-y-Giedd, North Wales	Flew into mountain at night		22 OTU
22/11/44	Anson	EG267	Squires Gate	Landing accident	W/O Spiers	
23/11/44	C-47	43-93508	Warton, BAD2			

Date	Aircraft	Serial	Location	Description	Name	Unit
23/11/44	Mosquito XX	KB232	Birkdale, Lancashire	Crashed in forced landing		
25/11/44	B-17G	44-8445	CEDDINGTON 3 MI W, UK from Burtonwood	Hit object in flight	Jimmie Mah	ATA
27/11/44	Mosquito V	NT147	Kirkbride	Crashed		
29/11/44	A-26	43-22298	River Ribble estuary	Mid air collision		
29/11/44	A-26	43-22336	River Ribble estuary	Mid air collision		
30/11/44	Swordfish		Foreshore at Squires Gate	Force Landed		
30/11/44	Harvard	FT442	Shining Tor			5 PAFU
1/12/44	L-4J	44-80557	Warton, BAD2 from Burtonwood			
1/12/44	Spitfire V	EP518	Askerton	Flew into Hill Side		
5/12/44	Fairey Barracuda	MD743	IOM			
6/12/44	Wellington XII	HF199	Cold Fell	Flew into Hill Side		
6/12/44	Dakota III	KG639	IOM	Crashed		
7/12/44	Fairey Barracuda	LS906	IOM			
8/12/44	Fairey Barracuda	LS956	IOM			
10/12/44	A-26B	41-29236	Warton, BAD2			
11/12/44	Anson I	N9853	Edale, Derbyshire, 3 miles NW of, Edale moor	Flew into ground in bad visibility	Chelstowski	16 FTS
12/12/44	Fairey Barracuda	MD880	IOM			
15/12/44	Fairey Barracuda	LS895	IOM			
16/12/44	B-17	44-6504	Cheviot Hill, Northumberland		Kyle, G.A. Jnr	
17/12/44	P-38J	42-67402	Warton, BAD2			
17/12/44	P-38J	43-28745	Warton, BAD2			
20/12/44	P-51K	44-63201	Prestwick			
21/12/44	Fairey Barracuda	MX633	IOM			
22/12/44	C-47	41-38608	6 Miles S of Macclesfield, Bosley (Burtonwood)	Crashed and burned out,	Theodore A Rogers	
22/12/44	Wellington Mk.X111	MF174	northern slopes of South Barrule, IOM	Flew into hillside	W/O Piasecki	
23/12/44	Spitfire	JK940	Blackburn	Fuel shortage		
24/12/44	Fi103 (V-1)		Cut Gate, Featherbed Moss	Ran out of fuel in fog & abandoned	F/O A R Butler	17 FTS
24/12/44	Lancaster	PD420	Kirkham, Lancashire	Overshot on landing,		
26/12/44	P-47	42-75549	Burtonwood	Crashed		
26/12/44	Barracuda	P9925	Coniston, Cumbria	Crashed		785 Squadron
27/12/44	Tiger Moth		Kingstown			
27/12/44	Anson	EG211	Squires Gate	Collision		
27/12/44	Anson	EG391	Squires Gate	Collision	F/L D Kerr	
27/12/44	Fairey Barracuda	LS866	IOM			
28/12/44	A-20G	43-9366	Warton, BAD2			
29/12/44	B-26G	44-67896	Burtonwood			
30/12/44	P-47	42-8535	Burtonwood	Fire on ground-run up.	John E Kicher	

Date	Aircraft	Serial	Location	Emergency Landing	Name	Unit
31/12/44	Stirling	AX538	Squires Gate			1665 HCU
31/12/44	Avro Anson	MH109	IOM			
31/12/44	Avro Anson	MX543	IOM			
1/01/45	Fairey Barracuda					310 Ferry Squadron
2/01/45	B-24J	42-100322	Burn Fell, Trough of Bowland	Struck Hillside	Lt. Holt	
2/01/45	B-17	43-38944	Birchenough Hill		Donald J. Decleene	
3/01/45	Anson I	T7411	Corney Fell	Flew into Hill Side		
3/01/45	P-47		Flash			
3/01/45	A-20G	43-9958	6 miles ssw of Buxton			
3/01/45	Lancaster	NF908	The Roaches	Landing accident	W.V.W Allamby	467 Squadron
7/01/45	Proctor	BV551	Squires Gate	Flew into hill in cloud	F Pecho (Polish)	ATA
8/01/45	Anson I	EF935	Tebay, Cumbria, 2 miles SE of			10 AFU
8/01/45	Fairey Barracuda	MD850	IOM			
8/01/45	Fairey Barracuda	MD892	IOM			
9/01/45	B-17G	8608	Burtonwood	Left wing tip caught covered ammunition hanger	1st Lt W L Miller	
9/01/45	Anson	EG428	Foreshore at St Annes	Engine failure	W/O Hopkinson	
9/01/45	Oxford	LB537	Cornel, North Wales	Flew into hillside		
10/01/45	B-26		Burtonwood	Collision		418 Squadron
10/01/45	C-45F	43-35762	Burtonwood	Collision	Lt Harry L Oberholtzer	
10/01/45	C-47	9186	Burtonwood	Collision	1st Lt T L Perdue	
10/01/45	B-24H	42-94889	Warton, BAD2	Landing Accident	Guy M Webb	
11/01/45	P-51K	44-11632	Near Spurstow, Calverly Cheshire	Unknown	1st Lt Leonard D Johnson	310 Ferry Sqn
13/01/45	Typhoon IB	RB210	North Charlton, Northumberland		Hall, R.W.	
14/01/45	P-38L	44-24633	Burtonwood	Take off accident	1st Lt Nick P Bebaeff	
14/01/45	Halifax III	MZ466	?Stoon Hall, Yorkshire	Flew into ground descending in cloud at night		425 Squadron
16/01/45	Avenger	JZ390	Wastwater Screes, Cumbria	Flew inland from coast at low altitude & hit hill	S/L B J Kennedy	763 Squadron
17/01/45	P-47	19742	Burtonwood	Collision		
17/01/45	B-17G	42-31185	Burtonwood	Collision, brake failure	Charles R Dodge	
17/01/45	P-47D	44-19742	Burtonwood		Charles R Dodge	
17/01/45	B-26	44-67988	Burtonwood			
17/01/45	B-26	46988	Burtonwood	Collision		
17/01/45	Wellington	NC706	?Walton, Lancashire	Engine cut, stalled & crashed		29 OTU
19/01/45	Anson	MG862	Squires Gate	Flying control failure	F/O Kymersley	1510 flight
19/01/45	Tiger Moth I	N9160		Mid air collision		
19/01/45	Tiger Moth II	T5960		Mid air collision		
21/01/45	C-47A	42-93683	Manchester 20 Miles SE		Rockman, Lloyd H	
22/01/45	Fairey Barracuda	MD754	IOM			
27/01/45	Fairey Barracuda	LS954	IOM			

Date	Aircraft	Serial	Location	Cause	Crew	Air Service Command
28/01/45	YP-80A	44-83026	Union Bank Farm Cottage, Bold, Nr St Helens from Burtonwood	Internal fire burnt tail off aircraft	Major Frederic Austin Borsodi	
28/01/45	B-24	869	Burtonwood	Collision		
28/01/45	B-17	9113	Burtonwood	Collision		
28/01/45	Halifax III	LL576	Pateley Bridge, Yorkshire	Engine cut after T/O, Flew into high ground in cld. blown off course	2nd Lt W A Palmer	1664 HCU
1/02/45	B-26		Glyders Hills, Caernarfon, Wales			
1/02/45	Master II	AZ309	Runcorn, Cheshire, Randle Island	Flew into ground in turn	W/O Stanislaw Sowinski	61 OTU
2/02/45	Avro Anson	MG354	IOM			
2/02/45	Hawker Hurricane MkIIC	PG472	Hampson's Pasture, Belmont, Nr Bolton	Mid air collision with PZ848	Flight Sergeant Thomas Stanley Taylor	11 PAFU
2/02/45	Hawker Hurricane MkIIC	PZ848	Horrocks Fold Farm, Smithalls, Nr Bolton	Mid air collision with PG472	Warrant Officer Norman Thomas Huckle	11 PAFU
3/02/45	Hurricane		Squires Gate	Overshot	Major H M Powers	
3/02/45	B-17	1410	Burtonwood	Collision		
3/02/45	B-17	34	Burtonwood	Collision		
4/02/45	Barracuda	PM859	Timperley, Cheshire	Unauthorised low flying crashed into house		
5/02/45	Wellington X	ME978	Knutsford, Cheshire, wood at Lower Peover	Iced up in cloud & abandoned?	F/O R Williams	14 FPP / 14 OTU
6/02/45	Hawker Hurricane	LF693	IOM			
10/02/45	Mosquito XII	HK141	Helvellyn, Cumbria	Flew into mountain in cloud		51 OTU
10/02/45	Beaufighter	RD210	Aran Fawddwy, North Wales	Flew into mountain in cloud		
13/02/45	Mosquito		RAF Woodvale	Crashed	F/L Smith	
13/02/45	Hawker Hurricane	PG607	IOM			
14/02/45	Mosquito	FX931	RAF Woodvale	Crashed	S/L Cowper	61 OTU
14/02/45	Mustang III		High Bentham, Lancashire, Thornber Farm	Dived into ground out of cloud	Sgt Pawel Struniewski	61 OTU
14/02/45	Mosquito FB6	TA525	Rountree Park, Castle Bolton, Yorks	Flew into high ground, presumed control lost in cloud - 1 killed		13 OTU
15/02/45	Mustang	KH838	Nr Wigan	Pilot fell from aircraft	3rd Officer Albert Edward Fairman Stock, M.B.	ATA
17/02/45	Halifax Mk III	NR126	Alwinton, Northumberland England		Charles B Congdon	
18/02/45	A-20G	43-10187				
19/02/45	B-24	42-50668	Black Hameldon, Nr Burnley, Lancashire	Struck Hillside	First Lieutenant Charles Goeking	854 Bomb Sqn
19/02/45	P-47D	44-33282	Newton, Wirral, Cheshire		William T Maier	
22/02/45	Hurricane	PZ765	Tintwistle, Didsbury Intake, Derbyshire	Flew into high ground in formation in haze		11 PAFU
22/02/45	Hurricane	PZ851	Tintwistle, Didsbury Intake, Derbyshire	Flew into high ground in formation in haze		11 PAFU

Date	Aircraft	Serial	Location	Cause	Crew	Unit
22/02/45	Hurricane	PZ854	Tintwistle, Didsbury Intake, Derbyshire	Flew into high ground in formation in haze		11 PAFU
24/02/45	A-26B	41-39220	Warton, BAD2		Wilton B Hidges	31 ATG
28/02/45	Beaufighter Mk VI	ND226	Hexham, Northumberland		Harvey, J.M.	
1/03/45	Avro Anson	DG939	IOM			
2/03/45	Mosquito	KB206	Cheddleton Heath			
2/03/45	Fairey Swordfish	NF409	IOM			
4/03/45	Halifax III	HX332	Knaresborough, Yorkshire	Shot down by intruder		10 Squadron
4/03/45	Oxford	NM683	Edale, Derbyshire	Flew into hill descending in cloud		
5/03/45	Proctor III	MM324	Buxton Derbyshire, 3.5 mile NE of	Flew into hill in bad visibility		
5/03/45	Halifax III	MZ454	Little Ouseburn, Yorkshire	Control lost due to icing & crashed		425 Squadron
16/03/45	A-26A	43-22656	Warton, BAD2			
23/03/45	B17G	43-38856	South face of North Barrule, IOM	Flew into hillside		
24/03/45	Wellington X	NC691	Millom	Crashed in Sea		
26/03/45	Mustang		Kingstown	Engine Failure		
26/03/45	Tiger Moth II	T5362	Kingstown	Crashed		
27/03/45	Vickers Wellington	HE687	IOM			
31/03/45	A-26C	43-22636	Warton, BAD2			
4/04/45	Harvard	FT442	Shining Tor, Cheshire	Flew into high ground		5 PAFU
4/04/45	Oxford I	L4601	Shining Tor, Cheshire	Flew into high ground at night in bad weather		17 SFTS
5/04/45	P-51D	44-72985	Warton, BAD2			
6/04/45	B-17	43-37667	Meltham Moor	Engine caught fire at night & crashed	Winston Johnson	709 Bomb Squadron
6/04/45	Harvard IIB	KF284	Farndon, Cheshire, near Wrexham	Crashed		11 PAFU
12/04/45	Tiger Moth	T6164	Chew Brook	Wing hit water in turn & crashed	M A O'Connell	24 FTS
13/04/45	Wellington X	LP981	Fleetwood, Lancashire, in sea			10 AGS
14/04/45	B-17G Fortress	42-37840	IOM			
14/04/45	Oxford	L4601	Shutlingsloe			17 FTS
15/04/45	Mustang	SR434	Inglewhite, Lancashire	Wing broke of in dive & spun into ground	Sgt Romauld Stefan Zywicki	61 OTU
16/04/45	Avro Anson	MG652	IOM			
18/04/45	Fairey Barracuda	AA920	IOM			
18/04/45	Spitfire Mk VB	43-38856	Longhorsley, Northumberland		Pannett, E.K.	
23/04/45	B-17G Fortress	44-89885	IOM			
224/04/45	P-47D	KJ562	Burtonwood			
25/04/45	Mitchell	42-39676	Kirkbride	Engine Failure		
29/04/45	P-61B		Burtonwood		Robert G Simpson	310 ferry Sqn

Date	Aircraft	Serial	Location	Incident	Crew	Unit
29/04/45	Harvard IIB	KF205	Wrexham, North Wales	Control lost in snow storm & abandoned		11 PAFU
2/05/45	Anson I	LT741	Black Coombe, Cumbria	Flew into rock face in cloud	W/O Thomas Price	10 AGS
4/05/45	Hurricane	LF652	Irish sea off Southport Pier, from Woodvale	Crashed		577 Squadron
4/05/45	Fairey Swordfish	NS134	IOM			
12/05/45	Grumman Avenger	JZ471	IOM			
15/05/45	P-51B	42-106570	Warton, BAD2			
15/05/45	P-38J	42-67422	Warton, BAD2	Belly Landing	Pete Manaserro	
15/05/45	P-47D	42-75151	Warton, BAD2			
15/05/45	P-51D	44-15335	Warton, BAD2			
15/05/45	P-51D	44-63864	Warton, BAD2			
15/05/45	P-51D	44-73200	Warton, BAD2			
17/05/45	A-20K	44-187	Irish Sea	Crashed into sea	John M. Allen	310 ferry Sqn
17/05/45	B-17G	44-8683	Kettlewell	Hit hill in flight	Cole, Harry J.	
18/05/45	A-20		Irish Sea	Mid air explosion		
18/05/45	Lancaster	KB993	James Thorn	Flew into high ground	F/O Anthony Arthur Clifford	
20/05/45	Short Sunderland	NJ186	IOM			
24/05/45	Fairey Firefly	MB498	IOM			
24/05/45	Fairey Firefly	DK443	IOM			
24/05/45	Firefly	MB498	In Sea	On fire & ditched immediately in sea	Lt P A Toynbee	1790 Squadron
26/05/45	Firefly	DK448	Blackpool, in sea 7 miles off.	Believed dived from 1000ft into Irish sea	S/L I A C Jamieson	776 Squadron
28/05/45	Wellington	HE226	Conistone	Crashed into hillside		17 OTU
29/05/45	P-51D	44-64084	Glossop en route to Speke	Crashed whilst letting down through clouds.	1st Lt Barnaby M Wilhoit	336th Fighter Squadron
29/05/45	P-51D	44-72181	Cudworth Pastures, Cattleshaw,	Crashed whilst letting down through clouds.	1st Lt Harold H Fredericks	336th Fighter Squadron
29/05/45	Spitfire V	BL688	Cob House Farm, Walmsley Nr Bury, Lancashire	Contol lost in cloud		58 OTU
29/05/45	Hurricane	LE391	Higher Carden, Cheshire, near Chester	Hit house		11 PAFU
1/06/45	Dakota III	KG633	Crosby	Taxiying accident		
5/06/45	Vought Corsair	MD982	IOM			
15/06/45	Fairey Barracuda		IOM			
16/06/45	B-24D	41-23737	Warton, BAD2	Taxiing accident	Howard E Day	
16/06/45	C-47A	42-100499	Warton, BAD2	Collision	Gunn Robert G	
19/06/45	B-17G	42-97280	Valley, North Wales	Brakes failed - Scrapped	Robert A Pfluger	
19/06/45	A-20K	44-077	Burtonwood	Landing accident		
25/06/45	Tiger Moth II	DE215	Ullswater	crashed in lake		
26/06/45	Spitfire V	W3765	RAF Woodvale	Undercarriage collapsed	Patterson, Melton D.	577 Squadron

Date	Aircraft	Serial	Location	Cause	Name	Unit
29/06/45	B-24J	42-50607	Warton, BAD2	Ran out of runway	Ellis R Vanhossen	
1/07/45	Mustang		Crosthwaite	Engine failure		
5/07/45	P-47D	42-25719	7 M NE of Liverpool from Burtonwood	Engine failure		310 ferry Sqn
9/07/45	Hellcat	FN377	In Sea, 1 mile from Bar lightship	Crashed into sea in heavy thunderstorm		889 Squadron
12/07/45	Fairey Barracuda	PM668	IOM			
14/07/45	Fairey Barracuda	MD878	IOM		Francis E Kurtz	
17/07/45	B-24J	42-51523	Warton, BAD2	Landing gear failure		
17/07/45	A-20G	43-9384	Warton, BAD2	Collision		
17/07/45	A-20G	43-9394	Warton, BAD2	Hit by B-24 that was taxing		
17/07/45	Fairey Barracuda	MD883	IOM			
18/07/45	Avro Anson	MG808	Millom			
24/07/45	Miles Martinet		Shelf Moor Nr Glossop, Derbyshire	Engine failure	George L Johnson	
24/07/45	C-47	42-108982		Flew into high ground		
28/07/45	Fairey Barracuda	LS713	IOM			
28/07/45	Fairey Barracuda	LS872	IOM			
29/07/45	Barracuda	MD963	Redbrook Clough			
29/07/45	Mustang III	SR411	Darwen	Hit high ground	Herbert Noga	316 Squadron
7/08/45	Fairey Barracuda	PM766	IOM			
9/08/45	F-5E	44-24226	IOM in Irish Sea	Forced landing	BAIRD, JAMES A.	
9/08/45	Fairey Barracuda	LS713	IOM			
9/08/45	Avro Anson	MG192	IOM			
17/08/45	Firefly	MB688	Holmeswood, Lancashire	Control lost, stalled in tight turn, spun into gnd		816 Squadron
20/08/45	C-87	43-30617	Burtonwood	Crashed on take off. Fatal Crash	Carl N Stitzel	
28/08/45	P-47D	44-89932	Southport at Sea from Burtonwood	Engine failure soon after take off, crashed in F/L	Billie M Taylor	
28/08/45	Martinet	PW958	Woodvale, 1 mile south of airfield			776 Squadron
1/09/45	P-47D	44-89903	Burtonwood	Belly landing	William P Cullen	
4/09/45	Fairey Barracuda	MX845	IOM			
4/09/45	Handley Page Halifax	NA277	IOM			
11/09/45	F-5E	44-24229	Aberystwyth	Hit ground in flight		
12/09/45	P-47D	44-33864	Thurleigh from Speke	Forced landing		
18/09/45	P-47D	44-33739	Villacoublay, france from Burtonwood	Take off accident	Eugenedes, Xenophon F. Lijewski, Edwin J. William W Kellog	310 ferry Sqn
28/09/45	Fairey Barracuda	LS925	IOM			
28/09/45	Fairey Barracuda	MD626	IOM			
2/10/45	Avro Anson	NK723	IOM			
8/10/45	Fairey Barracuda	MD821	IOM			

Date	Aircraft	Serial	Location	Name	Details	Unit
11/10/45	Supermarine Spitfire	MD169	IOM	K A Rodgers		714 Squadron
17/10/45	Barracuda	P9744	Scarisbrick, Lancashire, Wyke Thorn farm		Force landed on ploughed field & overturned	
5/11/45	Halifax II	JN886	Blackley, Manchester		Engine cut & lost height & crashed	1666 HCU
5/11/45	Lancaster	PA571	Ilkley, Yorkshire		Flew into hill in cloud	429 Squadron
5/11/45	Lancaster B1	RA571	Beamsley Beacon, 4M N of Ilkley, Yorks		Flew into hill braking cloud on air test - 4 killed	429 Squadron
23/11/45	Anson C11	NL185	The Cloughs, Edale, Derbyshire		Flew into hill in bad visibility	24 FTS
28/11/45	Tiger Moth	N6879	Queensferry, Cheshire		Crashed after collision with N9250	
29/11/45	Avro Anson	MG451	IOM		Engine cut, belly landed on sand	
14/12/45	Spitfire LF5	W3828	4.5M SW of Humphrey Head, Morecambe Bay	J R Cromer	Crashed	769 Squadron
15/12/45	Barracuda	DR306	Ingleton, Yorkshire			
18/12/45	Avro Anson	EG178	IOM			
28/12/45	Anson I	DJ441	Kingstown		Overshot	
28/12/45	Oxford I	HN594	Derbyshire, Brown Knoll near Edale	Edward Croker	Flew into high ground in cloud	12 PAFU
3/01/46	Avro Anson	MG445	IOM			
3/01/46	Anson mk.1	MG445	Slieu Ruy, above Laxey, IOM		Flew into hillside	
10/01/46	Mosquito NF30	NT544	2M W of Aygil, Yorks	Flt.Sgt. Wladyslaw Beller	Flew into high ground during night training flight	54 OTU
11/01/46	Oxford	LX673	WincleMinn Clough, Derbyshire		Flew into hill descending in cloud	21 PAFU
3/02/46	Dakota III	KG502	Castle Carrock, Cumbria, Cold Fell		Flew into Hillside	
4/02/46	Tiger Moth T2	DE834	Ellesmere Port Football ground		Ran short of fuel while lost, hit hut in forced landing	2 FPP
11/02/46	Dominie	X7453	Wimboldsley, Cheshire		Collided with Seafire ?SW822 & crashed	782 Squadron
14/02/46	Mosquito IV	TA525	Castle Bolton, Yorkshire		Flew into high ground	13 OTU
18/02/46	Firefly		Bootle, Liverpool, from Burscough		Baled out	
4/04/46	Anson I	NK442	Skiddaw, Cumbria		Crashed in forced landing in bad weather	47 MU
10/05/46	Halifax B7	PP349	Tancred Farm, Whixley, Yorks		Caught fire in air & dived into ground - 7 killed	1665 HCU
1/07/46	Wellington X	LP764	Irish Sea	F/O R Grey	Ditched into sea	10 AGS
2/07/46	Anson I	MG437	Irish Sea		Stuck mast of fishing boat	10 AGS
8/07/46	Warwick I	HF944	Silloth		Engine failure	41 FPP

Date	Aircraft	Serial	Location	Crew/Pilot	Unit
12/07/46	Seafire 17	SX315	At sea opposite Derby baths, Blackpool, North of North Pier	Sub Lt (A) J.W.Byers	Flew into sea
23/07/46	Warwick 1	HG136	The Cheviot, Northumberland	Wyett, K.F	Dived into ground
24/07/46	Wellington III	BJ895	?Abley, Yorkshire		Flew into Hillside	782 Squadron
30/08/46	Dominie	X7394	Scafell	Slt S K Kilsby	
2/09/46	Avro Anson	MG366	IOM			6 FTS
5/11/46	Harvard IIB	KF239	Copster Green, Lancashire, near Blackburn		Belly landed out of fuel, lost at night	6 FTS
22/11/46	Harvard II	KF992	Malpas, Cheshire		Control lost at low altitude	6 FTS
20/12/46	Wellington II	NC445	Kirkbride		Overshot	6 FTS
16/01/47	Harvard T2B	KF570	Postern Hill, Derbyshire		Crashed in forced landing at night	47 Squadron
13/02/47	Halifax	RT922	Grindon Moor, Staffs, 8 miles S of Leek		Flew into ground in snow	
13/02/47	C-45		Black Combe		Flew into Hillside	
20/03/47	Supermarine Spitfire	TB330	IOM			
19/06/47	Miles Martinet	EM524	Bigrigg		Mechanical Failure	631 Squadron
21/07/47	Spitfire F21	LA211	Irish sea off Rossall, from Woodvale	F/O Robert Ivor Reid	Engine failure	6 AACU
10/10/47	Proctor	LZ598	Silloth		Overturned	
9/11/47	Spitfire FR.14	TZ125	2m from Ringway, in farm yard.		Engine Failure	613 Squadron
20/11/47	Spitfire LF16	SL611	Ill Crag, Scafell Peak, Cumbria		Flew into mountain on navex, not found until 01.05.48	603
22/12/47	Hornet F1	PX274	Bacup, Lancs.		Flew into high ground descending through cloud	64 Squadron
9/03/48	Spitfire		Silloth		Ran of runway	
16/03/48	Spitfire 21	LA193	Woodvale, Lancashire, on airfield		Throttle jammed open, wheels up landing	602 Squadron
8/05/48	Spitfire XIV	RN210	Freckleton from Woodvale	F/O Robert Hugh Price Griffiths	Spun in	612 Squadron
3/06/48	Spitfire F21	LA193	RAF Woodvale		Bellylanded on approach	602 Squadron
20/06/48	Spitfire F.14	RM861	Ringway		Landed tail first and overturned	613 Squadron
3/07/48	Spitfire IX	MH814	Kirkby Stephen, Cumbria		Abandoned in cloud & crashed	611 Squadron
3/07/48	Spitfire XIV	NM814	Kirby Stephen, Westmoreland	F/O Geldart	Baled out	611 Squadron
31/07/48	Mosquito	TV982	Snowdon, North Wales	Lt J I Green RN	Broke up in cloud	502 Squadron
20/09/48	Barracuda V	RK555	Anthorn	Loran D Briggs	Crashed on to beach	
29/10/48	B-29A	42-93889	Burtonwood	Captain Landon P Tanner	Belly Landing	372 bomb Sqn
3/11/48	RB-29A	44-61999	Higher Shelf Stones, Wig Point Nr Glossop enroute to Burtonwood		Crashed	
26/11/48	Dakota IV	KK153	Kirkbride	Sgt F Wilkinson	Oil pressure dropped	42 Squadron
12/12/48	Spitfire F.14	RM851	Ringway		Overshot	613 Squadron
13/12/48	Mosquito NF36	RL197	Great Whernside	P/O A.G. Bulley	Crashed into hillside	228 OCU
20/12/48	Lancaster	PA411	Rhodes Hill	Jack Sherwood Tompson		230 OCU

Date	Aircraft	Serial	Location	Remarks	Crew	Unit
7/01/49	C-54	45-0543	Stake House Fell en route to Burtonwood	Crashed into hillside		
19/03/49	Spitfire F.14	RM924	Hooton Park	Undercarriage failure		611 Squadron
22/04/49	Meteor F4	VT233	Off Thorney Island	Abandoned in inverted spin during aerobatics		222 Squadron
22/06/49	Tiger Moth	T5952	Kirkbride	Forced Landing		
29/06/49	Blackburn Firebrand	EK848	IOM			
3/07/49	Spitfire	PK521	St Georges School, Formby		R A Bailey	611 Squadron
16/07/49	Seafire	SP314	Wildboarclough			1831 Squadron
16/07/49	Seafire F.Mk.17s	SP325	Wildboarclough			1831 Squadron
16/07/49	Seafire F.Mk.17s	SX314	Wildboarclough			1831 Squadron
16/07/49	Seafire	SX325	Wildboarclough			1831 Squadron
3/08/49	Anson 19		Silloth	Engine failure		
4/08/49	Harvard T2	KF387	Ringway	Swung on take off		
29/08/49	Vampire FB5	VZ114	Duxbury, Nr Chorley	Crashed	F/O Richard H Clyno	613 Squadron
16/09/49	Master III	DL609	Hebden Bridge, Yorkshire	Flew into high ground in cloud		
16/09/49	Master T2	DL981	Hebden Bridge, Yorkshire	Flew into high ground in cloud		
5/01/50	Mosquito B35	VP199	Mickle Fell, Yorks	Flew into hill in cloud - 2 killed		109 Squadron
12/02/50	Seafire	SX129	Adjacent to Common End, Addlington, Nr Chorley	Mid air break up.	Lt(A) Geoffrey Alan Beaumont RNVR	
3/03/50	Oxford	HN176	Kirkbride	Engine failure	J Jurby	230 OCU
15/03/50	Meteor F4	RF511	Carvedd, North Wales, near Bethesda	Flew into mountain descending in cloud		
29/03/50	Meteor F4	VW277	Off Thorney Island	Lost formation & hit mud flats during formation aerobatics - 1 killed		56 Squadron
1/404/50	Lincoln	RE232	Silloth	Crashed on take off	F/Lt R L Ducan	
6/05/50	Kirby Cadet 2	VM645	Samlesbury Lancs	Spun in	Kenneth Lovett Brandwood	182 Gliding School
15/07/50	B-29	44-33919	Burtonwood	Engine failure	KESTING, WILBUR F	
26/07/50	Sea Fury II	TF960	Anthorn	Flew into Hillside	Lt P J Busby RN	
20/08/50	B-50D	49-275	Burtonwood		John W Rapp	
20/08/50	Spitfire 22	PK595	Skipe Scar, 3M S of Hackworth, Cumbria	Flew into Hillside	E A Carter	607 Squadron
24/08/50	Valetta C1	VW826	Kirkbride	Port Undercarriage failed	J S Luby	19 RFS
24/09/50	Tiger Moth T1	K4291	Hooton Park, Cheshire	Overturned on landing		
6/11/50	KB-29A	44-86420	Burtonwood		Thomas W Podbesek	
8/12/50	Meteor	RA487	Hagg Side	Flew into Hillside		66 Squadron
12/01/51	Vampire F1	VF273	Millom	Flew into Hillside		
8/02/51	Tiger Moth II	NM213	Stainmoor		Sgt B J Cundall	203 AFS
5/04/51	Vampire FB5	WA371	Cottam, Yorks	Spun into ground whilst practising stall turns	F/O W S Bateson	203 AFS

Date	Aircraft	Serial	Location	Crew/Pilot	Cause/Notes	Unit
12/04/51	Meteor	VZ518	Sliddens Moss		Flew into high ground	66 Squadron
12/04/51	Meteor	WA971	Sliddens Moss		Flew into high ground	66 Squadron
6/06/51	Tempest TT5	JN807	Low Heskit, Cumbria		Engine cut, Bellylanded in fields & broke up	
19/06/51	Meteor F4	VT239	Ribble Head, Yorks		Dived into ground, cause not known - 1 killed	205 AFS
3/07/51	Chipmunk	WB579	Arnfield Moor	Harry Bate Wright	Flew into high ground	2 RFS
10/07/51	Meteor F4	Vz418	Clapham, Yorks (NR Settle)		Flew into hill in dive, Cause obscure - 1 killed	205 AFS
22/07/51	Meteor F4	VT121	Over Kellett, Lancs	Sgt T A R Price	Dived into ground out of cloud	611 Squadron
25/07/51	Vampire	WA400	Moscar Top		Collided with Wellington PG367 & spun into ground	102 Squadron
13/08/51	Martinet TT1	NR570	2M W of Richmond, Yorks		Collided with Martinet NR570	228 OCU
13/08/51	Wellington	PG367	2M W of Richmond, Yorks		Engine problem	
14/12/51	Chipmunk T10	WB552	RAF Woodvale		Hit by nose of P2V Neptune that broke away	228 OCU
4/01/52	C-47		Burtonwood		Crashed short of runway and nose broke off	ULAS
	P2V Neptune		Burtonwood			
14/01/52	Harvard T2B	FT415	Kinder Scout, Derbyshire	Brian Farley	Followed railway on navex into tunnel, hit hill attempting to climb out - 1 killed	22 FTS
25/03/52	Canberra 2	WD991	Cottam, Preston	F/Lt Thomas Evans	Crashed	BAC Ltd
21/04/52	C-97A	48-403	Burtonwood		Aircraft Spun in	
4/05/52	Spitfire PR19	PM549	RAF Woodvale	F/O K G S Hargreaves	Flew into high ground in cloud - 2 killed	THUM Flight
7/08/52	Meteor T7	WF793	Leyburn, Yorks			228 OCU
11/08/52	Anson C19	VM407	Snowdon, North Wales		Flew into mountain in cloud	
1/09/52	Chipmunk	WB576	Barton		Undershot	23 MU
17/10/52	Wellington	MF627	Ughill		Ran out of fuel & crash landed in field	2 RFS
21/11/52	Meteor F4	VT341	1.5M N of Middleton, Lancs			215 AFS
20/12/52	Chipmunk T10	WD320	South of Formby		Carb Icing	19 RFS
20/12/52	Chipmunk T10		Great Altcar, Lancs	F/O Limpett-Low	Engine cut, turned over in forced landing	19 RFS
21/01/53	Vampire FB5	WA339	Liverpool Bay		Crashed in sea, cause unkown - 1 killed	202 AFS
5/02/53	Supermarine Attacker FB.1	WA535	Lower Alder Root Farm, Winick, Nr Warrington	Commissioned Pilot R.E. Collingwood	Dived in	767 Squadron
22/02/53	Vampire FB5	VV604	8M NW of Harrogate, Yorks		Dived into ground, cause not known	613 Squadron

Date	Aircraft	Serial	Location	Description	Name	Unit
30/05/53	Wellington X	HE553	Reeth, Yorkshire	Flew into hill in cloud returning from Wuppetal		432 Squadron
27/06/53	Chipmunk T10	WD326	Waltham Moor, Skipton	Crashed	F/O K B Wallace	MUAS
17/07/53	Firefly T7	WJ158	Grasmere	Broken throttle linkage		
21/07/53	Meteor F4	VT138	Leyburn, Yorkshire	Flew into ground in cloud		215 AFS
9/06/53	Avro Anson	VM418	IOM			
2/10/53	Sky Raider	132350	Banner Fell	Flew into Hillside	Lt/Jg T E McDonald	USN
14/11/53	Meteor F8	WH383	1M N of Edgeworth, Lancs	Flew into hill in cloud		610 Squadron
14/11/53	Meteor F8	WH384	Edgeworth, Lancashire	Flew into hill in cloud		610 Squadron
26/01/54	Washington	WF495	In Irish Sea, 16 miles W of Lancaster	Crashed into sea during heavy icing conditions		35 Squadron
22/02/54	Airspeed Oxford	NM576	IOM			
4/03/54	Spitfire PR19	PM628	Church Pulverback, Salop	Engine failure	F/L Tommy Heyees	THUM
24/03/54	Meteor Mk II	WD778	9 miles NE	Flew into Hillside	Briggs, J.D	
11/04/54	Auster T7	WE588	Appleby-in-Westmorland, Cumbria 6.5M E of Cester, Cheshire	Hit fence on take off from precautionary landing		663 Squadron
11/04/54	Meteor T7	WF850	2M S of Hooton Park	Force-landed and hit pond on approach to single-engined landing		611 Squadron
1/05/54	Vampire FB5	VV602	Macclesfield, Cheshire	Lost control in bad weather		613 Squadron
22/06/54	Harvard T2B	KF954	Woodvale, Lancashire, on airfield	Swung on landing & Undercarriage collapsed		
8/07/54	Anson C12	PH760	Woodvale, Lancashire, on airfield	Undercarriage collapsed on take-off		
20/07/54	Chipmunk T10	WB747	Flint, North Wales, in Dee Estuary	Spun into sand bank in river		THUM
22/07/54	Spitfire PR19	PS853	Calverly, Cheshire	Carb problem		
22/07/54	Sabre F4	XD707	Kinder Scout, Derbyshire	Flew into hill in cloud		66 Squadron
22/07/54	Sabre F4	XD730	Kinder Scout, Derbyshire	Flew into hill in cloud		66 Squadron
18/09/54	Meteor F8	WH302	Hooton Park, Wirral	Dived into ground during aerobatics		610 Squadron
20/10/54	Venom FB1	WR347	Top Farm, Whitby, Cheshire	Became inverted in cloud, control lost, abandoned		
28/10/54	Anson	PH722	Kirkbride	Crash Landing		
28/10/54	Anson 12		Carlisle	Crashed - struck by lightning	Flt Lt Green	
16/11/54	Vampire FB5	VV659	In Sea, off Anglesey	Abandoned in spin & crashed into sea		7 FTS
22/11/54	Hawker Sea Fury	VR922	IOM			
22/11/54	Hawker Sea Fury	VW664	IOM			
14/12/54	F-86E	19234	Black Hill, Holme Moss	Flew into high ground		
17/12/54	F-86 Sabre	19234	Holme Moss			
24/12/54	Spitfire PR19	PS915	RAF Woodvale	Canopy failure	Patrick V. Robinson	THUM
1/01/55	Spitfire PR19	PM652	Near RAF High Ercall, Salop	Engine Failure	John Formby	THUM

Date	Aircraft Type	Serial	Location	Cause	Crew	Unit
11/01/55	Harvard T2B	KF160	Woodvale, Lancashire, on airfield	Swung on landing & ground looped		MUAS
12/02/55	Vampire FB.5	VZ123	Ringway	Undercarriage failure		613 Squadron
23/03/55	Meteor NFII	WD650	Masham, Yorkshire	Crashed after abandoning		228 OCU
12/05/55	Meteor	WE904	Millthorpe	GCA approach to Leeming		211 FTS
14/05/55	Beaufighter	RD783	Bromborough GC, 3M WNW of Hooton Park	Yawed on approach, due to power loss & bellylanded		5 CAACU
25/10/55	WB-29A	44-61600	Lupton Fell, Kirby Lonsdale	Ran out of fuel, engine failure	Captain Major Benjamin S Hilkeman	53rd Weather Recon Sqn
20/01/56	Canberra PR7	WT505	Ponsonby Fell, Nr Calder Bridge	Flew into high ground	W/Cdr D De-Villers	58 Squadron
6/02/56	Canberra	WM715	Haverigg	Technical Difficulties		BAC Ltd
22/03/56	F-86F	52-5355	Burtonwood	Ran out of fuel. Flame out	Captain James M Hambrick	45 FDS
22/03/56	F-86F	52-5373	Moss Vale Farm, Billinge, Nr Wigan diverting to Burtonwood	Ran Out of fuel, Flame out		45 FDS
6/04/56	Harvard T2B	FX459	Woodvale	Swung on landing, U/C leg collapsed	1st Lt Wenbell Berg Stockdale	LUAS
15/04/56	Chipmunk T10	WD351	Down Holland, Nr Lydiate, Lancs	Crashed	S/L L J Cook	LUAS
23/10/56	Vampire Fb4	WR555	Silloth	Engine failure	F/O R Marks	
5/12/56	Beaver	26145	Devil's Elbow			
7/12/56	Shackleton	WR970	Foolow			
6/01/57	Auster AOP6	VF546	Dorfold Farm, 1.5M WSW of Nantwich, Cheshire	Lost outer wing and dived into ground		663 Squadron
29/01/57	Mosquito TT35	TK604	Woodvale	Undercarriage jammed, bellylanded		Thum
4/03/57	Venom Mk 4	WR557	Alston, Northumberland	Elevators jammed, flew into hill on approach	Marshall, W.F	
7/08/57	Vampire	XE866	Stanage Edge	Flew into ground descending in cloud		4 FTS
8/08/57	Hunter F4	XE866	Hathersage, Derbyshire			4 FTS
20/09/57	Varsity Mk 1	WL640	Falstone, Northumberland	Belly landing	Garlick, T.	
23/10/57	Mosquito T35	TK604	RAF Woodvale		Pilot Eric Richard Schooling, B.W	76 Squadron
14/02/58	Hunter F6	XG236	Kielder Forest, Northumberland	Crashed after rocket exploded at 45,000 feet	Flight Lieutenant Peter de Salis	
9/04/58	Canberra B6	WT207	Monyash, Derbyshire			
26/05/59	Avro Anson	VM322	IOM	Flew into Hillside	F/O R G Starling	421 Squadron
29/06/59	Sabre 6	23380	Iron Cragg	Engine caught fire & abandoned		228 OCU
29/09/59	Javelin FAW7	XA662	Leyburn, Yorks			
1/10/59	English Electric Lightning		IOM			
9/03/60	Javelin 8	XH988	Durdar	Engine failure	Pilot Sgt K Mitchell	41 Squadron

Date	Aircraft	Serial	Location	Description	Name	Unit
5/09/60	Meteor F8	VZ521	Woodvale	Tyre burst on takeoff, swung off runway		5 CAACU
16/12/60	McDonnell Douglas F101A Voodoo		IOM			
23/01/61	Hunter F4	XE882	Aysgarth, Yorkshire	Abandoned in spin		1 FTS
3/02/61	F-101	41456	Solway Firth	Crashed into sea	1st Lt R S Nishibayshi	
20/02/61	Avro Anson	VL312	IOM			
24/04/61	Vampire T11	XK584	Angelsey, North Wales	Abandoned in spin & crashed		7 FTS
26/05/61	Pembroke	VW737	North Berwick			
4/09/61	Vampire T.II	XD592	Acklington, Northumberland	Fuel shortage	Lambert, G.D	
2/01/62	DH Chipmunk		IOM			
12/04/62	Anson 19	TX219	Carlisle	Undercarriage collapsed		1 FTS
23/01/63	Vampire T11	XE882	Aysgarth, Yorks	Abandoned in spin		1 FTS
29/01/63	Canberra PR7	WJ824	High Pike, Caldbeck, Cumbria	Flew into ground in bad visibility	F/Lt L Broughton	58 Squadron
18/04/63	Jet Provost T4	XP635	2 miles east of Netherwitton, Northumberland		Shadbolt, B	
29/04/63	Jet Provost T3	XM368	Pateley Bridge, Yorks	Abandoned in spin		2 FTS
31/07/63	Lightning P1B	XG311	Ribble Estuary, Lancashire	Crashed into river		BAC Ltd
25/11/63	Whirlwind HAR2	XD164	In Sea, off Anglesey	Engine cut & ditched in sea		CFS
17/09/64	Jet Provost T3	XN583	Hill Top Farm, 2.5M S of Harrogate, Yorks	Flew into wood during aerobatics - 1 killed		7 FTS
8/07/65	Lightning T4/T5	XM966	Whithaven in Sea	Structral Failure		
15/11/65	Jet Provost T4	XP621	Catterick Camp, Yorks	Abandoned after false fire warning	J Dell,	3 FTS
22/12/65	Chipmunk T10	WP968	Winter Hill, Nr Bolton, Lancs	Flew into hill descending in cloud		MUAS
26/04/66	Chipmunk T10	WB555	Woodvale	Stalled on landing & hit ground, not repaired		LUAS
7/03/67	Lightning T55	55-710	Warton	Landing accident	J L Dell	BAC Ltd
24/07/69	Super Sabre F100		IOM			
15/08/69	Hunter F6	XG204	Angelsey, North Wales, near Rhosneigr	Flew into ground after take-off from Valley		4 FTS
30/01/70	Super Sabre F100		IOM			
6/05/70	Phantom	64-1018	Near Dronfield (Chesterfield)	IOM	Donald Tokar	10 TRW
4/01/72	Hawker Siddeley Buccaneer					
10/08/72	Hunter F6	XF384	Angelsey, North Wales	Collided with XF387 & crashed		4 FTS
10/08/72	Hunter F6	XF387	Angelsey, North Wales	Collided with XF384 & broke up		4 FTS
21/11/72	Phantom FGR2	XV477	Thack Moor	Flew into Hillside		6 Squadron
22/07/73	Bulldog T1	XX618	Birkdale, Lancs	Control lost in spin, abandoned	F/Lt C M Haynes	YUAS

Date	Type	Serial	Location	Remarks	Crew	Unit
5/05/75	F-111	F081	Shap Fell	Bird Strike		41 Squadron
17/12/75	Phantom	XV463	Off Maybray Nr Silloth	Crashed into Sea, contol lost		233 OCU
19/01/76	Harrier GR3	XV745	Wardle, Nantwich, Cheshire	Collided with XV754 during practice attack		233 OCU
19/01/76	Harrier GR3	XV754	Wardle, Nantwich, Cheshire	Collided with XV745 during practice attack		
21/04/76	Hunter F6	XG185	Angelsey, North Wales	Abandoned after fire warning		4 FTS
22/07/76	Bulldog T1	XX632	Ainsdale Beach	Crashed		YUAS
29/07/77	Jaguar GR1	XX148	1.5m SE Whittingham, Northumberland	Dived in	Hinchcliff, J.	
1/06/78	Jet Provost	XN598	Gouthwaite, Pateley Bridge	Wing hit water low flying over reservoir		1 FTS
12/06/79	Tornado,	XX950	In Irish Sea 44 M off Blackpool	Flew into sea in mist during loft bombing trails		BAC Ltd
3/07/79	Jet Provost T5A	XW371	10M E of Lancaster, Lancs	Flew into ground in bad weather on low-level navex		7 FTS
9/12/82	Jet Provost T5A	XW417	Lake Thirlmere, Cumbria	Dived into trees beside lake		7 FTS
13/04/83	F-104 Starfighter	D-8337	3 miles west of Alwinton, Northumberland	Dived in	Sasbrink-Harkema, M. (dutch)	
24/06/83	Hawk Mk.1T	XX166	Clagh Ouyr, IOM	Flew into hillside	Flt.Lt. Lane	4 FTS
21/11/83	Jet Provost T3	XM453	2M SSE of Ribblehead viaduct, Ingleton, Yorks	Hit birds & abandoned & flew into hill		3 FTS
7/10/85	Jaguar GR1A	XX728	Hartside Pass, Alston, Cumbria	Collided with XX731 in formation and abandoned		6 Squadron
7/10/85	Jaguar GR1A	XX731	Hartside Pass, Alston, Cumbria	Collided with XX728 in formation and abandoned		6 Squadron
24/10/85	Tornado ECR	4145	Falstone, Northumberland	Flew into the hillside in poor visibility.	Schimpf, H-J. (ger)	
7/01/86	Phantom FGR2	XV434	West Burton, 12M SW of Richmond, Yorks	Became uncontrollable on low-level ex.& abandoned		29 Squadron
17/06/87	Jaguar GR1A	XZ116	Walla Crag, Keswick, Cumbria	Collided with Tornado ZA493 & abandoned - 1 killed		41 Squadron
17/06/87	Tornado GR1	ZA493	Keswick, Cumbria	Collided with Jaguar XZ116, abandoned		20 Squadron
2/03/88	Bulldog T1	XX712	Southport Beach	Crashed	Acting P/O Mark F Davies	MASUAS
9/08/88	Tornado GR1	ZA329	Blencarn, Penrith, Cumbria	Collided with ZA593 at night & crashed - 2 killed		
9/08/88	Tornado GR1	ZA593	Nr. Milburn, Cumbria	Collided with ZA329 at night & crashed		
25/04/89	Bulldog T1	XX517	Great Langton, 3M ESE of Catterick, Yorks	Control lost after entering cloud, abandoned		617 Squadron
30/01/90	Tornado GR1a	ZA394	Corbridge, Northumberland	Mid air collision	MacLean, I	1 FTS

Date	Aircraft	Serial	Location	Incident	Pilot / Crew	Unit
11/06/93	Hunter	G-BTYL / XL595	Broomhead Moor	Engine lost power, crashed in forced landing		10 AEF
28/07/94	Chipmunk T10	WB697	Scarisbrick, Lancs	Rolled after overshoot from Squires Gate, abandoned		Bae
28/09/96	Tornado F3	ZE759	Off Blackpool, Lancs	Crashed on take off.	S/L Mike Murphy	MASUAS
21/07/97	Bulldog T1	XX710	RAF Woodvale	Hit ground in bad weather	Wright, R.A.	15 Squadron
14/10/99	Tornado GR1b	ZD809	Stocksfield, Northumberland	Dived into ground in turn & hit barn,		100 Squadron
22/10/99	Hawk T1A	XX193	Shap, Cumbria			
18/10/00	Hawk T.1A	XX282	Haggerston, Northumberland	Bird strike	Berris, D	Warton Flight Test
Unknown	B-17	Unknown	Squires Gate from Warton	Ran off runway	Jack Knight	776 Squadron
Unknown	Martinet	Unknown	Ainsdale, Lancashire, in sea	Spun into sea		
Unknown		Unknown	Standish, Nr Wigan	Ran out of Fuel ?		
Unknown		Unknown	Lowton, Nr Wigan			
Unknown	Tiger Moth	Unknown	Hindley, Nr Wigan	Force Landed		
Unknown	Spitfire	Unknown	Westhoughton, Nr Bolton	force landed		
Unknown	Wellington	Unknown	Holland Moss, Nipe Lane	Force landed		
Unknown		Unknown	Sutton, Nr St Helens, enroute to Burtonwood ?	Crash landing		
Unknown	B-17F	42-30071	Warton, BAD2	Landing gear failure	Joseph A Claffy Jr	
Unknown	B-17G	43-37862	Burtonwood			
Unknown	Mohawk	AR664	Ringway			
Unknown	MILES MASTER II	AZ600	Warton, BAD2	Collision		
Unknown	Hotspur 2	BT488	Near Ringway Aerodrome			
Unknown	Barracuda	F9661	Nr Ringway			
Unknown	Wildcat IV	FN243	Kirkbride	Swung of runway		
Unknown	Botha	L6288	Squires Gate	Landing accident	M/Ship D J McDonald	
Unknown	DH 86A	L7596	Kirby in Furness	Forced Landing		
Unknown	Swordfish	NF300	Speke	Engine trouble and force landed safely	F/O Miss Cholmondley (Australian ATA)	12 FPP
Unknown	Mosquito 6	NS829	Ringway Airport Manchester			
Unknown	Tiger Moth	T7174	Barton			
Unknown	Hurricane	V7001	Dovenby	crashed		601 Squadron
Unknown	Hurricane	V7539	Keswick, Cumbria	Hit mountain in blizzard	Sgt Much	
Unknown	Dominie	X7394	Scafell, Cumbria	Flew into mountain		782 Squadron
Unknown	Albacore	X9152	Inskip, Lancashire			
Unknown	Firefly	Z1960	RNAS Burscough	Belly landing		
Unknown	Whitley II	Z9362	Solway off Saltcoates pier	crashed into sea	F/O J C N Lewis 109536	24 OTU

THE RAF MILLOM AVIATION & MILITARY MUSEUM

The RAF Millom Aviation & Military Museum is home to probably the finest collection of aviation memorabilia and militaria in the Northwest. The museum project originated in a very small way in 1992, however due to a great deal of hard work by volunteers and ex-servicemen and women of the old RAF Millom, the collection has all but outgrown the present buildings it occupies and is looking to the future with plans for a major extension project to accomodate the exhibits. These include several aero engines, including; Rolls-Royce Merlin, Kestrel, Griffon and Avon, Bristol Hercules, Junkers Jumo, and more. There are a number of airframes and cockpits on display at the museum including Vampires, Tornado, Whirlwind and two Flying Fleas, including a faithful recreation of the unique military version used by the French resistance. Also many items that have been recovered by excavating wreck sites including a striking display relating to the C4 "Time Team" dig that was carried out on two A-26 Invaders, with two of the aircrafts' massive engines, complete with their dramatically twisted and scarred propellers.

The museum operates in partnership with the Lancashire Aircraft Investigation Team and Peak District Air Crash Research and the collections of these groups are displayed in their own building at the museum. Displays cover the aviation and military history of the Northwest, including Lancashire, Cumbria, Merseyside, Greater Manchester, North Cheshire, North Wales and the Peak District. Material includes; an extensive Home Front collection, complete with an original Anderson Shelter, the National Collection of the Mountain Rescue Service, as RAF Millom had a pivotal role in the birth of what is today the RAF Mountain Rescue Service. Also a large military collection with a special emphasis on the Cold Stream Guards, including a collection of wartime firearms and more recently the beginnings of what promises to be an extensive collection of military vehicles. The museum has a growing archive section, including over 4000 photographs from the wartime era when the North-west was a busy training & maintenance area and including a large number of personal collections of memorabilia and ephemera. Histories of the airfields in the North-west and are extensively covered and the museum specialises in the Dominion, Polish & Czech aircrews who served in the RAF. This represents only a small amount of what the museum holds, as there are currently five original wartime buildings accessible to visitors, each one packed with displays, plus outside display areas, not to mention much further material in storage, making it the leading independently funded collection in the region.

The museum is open 363 days a year and is located at:

The RAF Millom Aviation & Military Museum
Bank Head Estate
Off North Lane
Haverigg, Millom
Cumbria
Website: www.rafmillom.co.uk

Curator: Glynn Griffith
21 Holborn Hill,
Millom,
Cumbria,
LA18 5BH
Tel: 01229 772636
Email: curator@rafmillom.co.uk

BIBLIOGRAPHY

Freeman, Roger A. *The Hub Fighter Leader*, Airlife, 1988

Hobbs, D. *Aircraft Carriers of the Royal and Commonwealth Navies*, Greenhill Books, 1996

Smith, Claude. *The History of the Glider Pilot Regiment*, Leo Cooper, 1993

Ramsey, Winston G. *The Blitz, Then and Now Vol. 2. After the Battle*, 1988

Brew, Alec. *The Defiant File*, Air Britain Historians Ltd, 1988

Thompson, Scott. *Douglas A-26 and B-26 Invader*, Crowood Press, 2002

Lansdown, John R.P. *With the Carriers in Korea*, The Naval and Military Press, 1998

Earl, David W. *Hell on High Ground Volumes 1 & 2*, Airlife 1995, 1999

Bader, Douglas. *Fight for the Sky*, Sidgwick & Jackson, 1973

Leslie, S.C. *Bombers over Merseyside*, Scouse Press, 1998

Smith, David J. *Action Stations: Vol. 3*, Patrick Stephens, 1981

Various RAF forms 1180 & 78, Unit ORBs, Combat Reports, individual Pilot's Service Records and Board of Inquiry reports.

Various USAAF Reports of Aircraft Accident Files, Individual Aircraft Record Cards and Individual Deceased Personnel Files.

Australian National Archives file 1163/118/512 (Defiant N3328)

United States Air Force Reserve 403rd Wing, 53rd Weather Reconnaissance Squadron Factsheet.

Halton Borough Council press releases 05/11/1998 & 15/03/2000 (HeIII Werke No 2989)

Various Newspaper / Journal Articles from: *Air Pictoral, Bristol Express, Burtonwood Beacon, Daily Mail, Ealing Recorder, The Gazette, Lancashire Evening Post, Lancashire Evening Telegraph, Lancaster Guardian, Liverpool Echo, Warrington Examiner, Warrington Guardian, Westmoreland Gazette, Widness Weekly News.*

INDEX

14th Troop Carrier Squadron - 131
15th Troop Carrier Squadron - 131
17th Troop Carrier Squadron - 131
296th Combat Engineer Battalion - 88
310th Ferry Squadron - 84, 87,
328th Bombardment Squadron - 91
329th Bombardment Squadron - 91, 98
330th Bombardment Squadron - 91
409th Bombardment Squadron - 91
48th Troop Carrier Squadron - 131
53rd Strategic Reconnaissance Squadron – 141, 147
53rd Troop Carrier Squadron - 131
56th Fighter Group - 18
576th Bombardment Squadron - 93
577th Bombardment Squadron - 93
578th Bombardment Squadron - 93
579th Bombardment Squadron - 93
641st Bombardment Squadron - 172
829th Bombardment Squadron - 91
852nd Bombardment Squadron - 67
853rd Bombardment Squadron - 67
854th Bombardment Squadron - 67
855th Bombardment Squadron - 67

A
A.V. Roe & Co. - 12
Abbotsinch - 26, 115
Accrington - 70
Adams, Sgt. R.T. - 77
Airborne Interception (A.I.) Radar – 102, 150
Akin, S/Sgt W.C. - 142
Ambrus, S/L J.K. – 163 - 166
Andrews Field, Essex - 52

Arandorra Star, Troopship - 42, 60
Armstrong, T/Sgt. R. - 97
Aspull, Wigan - 35

B
Bae North West Heritage Group - 22
Baedeker raids - 42
Bailey, Lt. F.D. - 115
Barnoldswick - 103, 104
Barrage Balloons - 151 - 154
Barton Hall - 17
Barton, F/L W.S. - 124
Base Air Depot 1 (BAD1), Burtonwood - 67, 69, 70, 74, 84, 91, 92, 94, 96, 99, 116, 117, 130, 132- 134, 141
Base Air Depot 2 (BAD2), Warton - 15, 16, 18, 20, 22, 51, 73, 84, 85, 87, 91, 172, 173, 176, 181
Base Air Depot 3 (BAD3), Langford Lodge - 91
Battery Cob - 94, 95
Battle of Britain - 13, 164, 166
Battle of the Bulge - 68
Bee, Sgt. E.H. - 164
Begonsky, Sgt. S.C. - 174
Bell, F/O V.R. - 96, 97
Berchtesgaden, Germany - 53
Bergevin, Capt. J.R. - 142
Bergstrom AFB, Texas - 131
Berlin, Germany - 129, 138
Berlin, Hptmn. W. - 149, 151, 152, 154, 155
Birkenhead - 75, 149, 159
Blackpool - 11, 20, 42, 44, 51, 66, 87

Bock, 1st Lt. F.E. - 72
Bodien, Sgt. H.E. - 101
Boeing Company - 140
Bold - 12, 96
Boscombe Down - 115
Bou, De La Cruz, T/Sgt. J. - 142, 144
Bradley, Col. Mark - 15
Bradley, Warrant Officer - 17
Brater, 2nd Lt. E.R. - 72
Bretigny, France - 172
British Aviation Archaeological Council - 14
British Commonwealth Air Training Plan - 123
British European Airways - 161
Burdekin, Capt. H.W. - 69
Burnley - 70, 72
Burscough - 45, 46, 48
Bury - 12

C

C.W.G.C. - 112
Campbell, 2nd Lt. W.H - 92
Church, nr. Accrington - 11
Clearwater, 2nd Lieut. W.T. - 16
Cody, Col. Samuel F. - 11
Collingwood, Mr. R - 112 - 122
Comerford, F/L H.A.G. - 163, 165 - 167
Culceth, Warrington - 27
Cunningham, Sgt. J.D.H. - 78

D

Dalton in Furness – 165, 169
Daly, 1st Lt. J.F. - 142, 144
Danilo-Sniezkowski, Plt. R. - 60
Darling, F/L D.F.W. - 101
Darwen - 51, 53, 54, 58
Davidson, P/O J.S - 101
Davis, Capt. G.R. - 68
D-Day landings - 43, 68
Deblin, Polish Air Force Officers School - 42, 65
Denham, T. Sgt. H.E. Jr. - 69, 72, 73

Diem, Uffz. X. - 149, 152, 154, 155
Ditton - 156
Dollin, Hugh - 28
Douglas Aircraft Co. - 84, 172, 182
Dropsonde - 142
Dunkirk, France - 45, 65, 125
Dunsop Bridge - 60, 62, 126
Dvorak, P/O - 163

E

Eindhoven, Netherlands – 24, 160
EOD - 178

F

Fairweather, Sgt. S.J. - 101
Falcon Flights - 141
Firearms Act - 42
Fizell, AC2 J.F - 164
Fleet Air Arm Museum - 112
Ford Motor Company - 93
Freckleton - 18, 24, 27, 28, 172
Froelich, 2nf Lt. B.H. - 92
Fulwood & Cadley County Primary School - 16, 22

G

Garstang - 132
Gilhooley, P - 156
Gillam, F/L D.E. AFC - 163
Gleaston - 165
Glen Niven, Queensland - 103
Glider Pilot Regiment - 33
Gloster Aircraft Co. Ltd. - 46
Goeking, 1st Lt. C. A. - 69 - 74
Golborne, Colliery - 36
Gosney, George - 73, 74
Goulter, F/Sgt. H.M. - 103
Goulter, F/Sgt. J.L. - 102 - 109
Grace, LAC. R. - 86
Gravenor, S/L H.N. - 102
Green, 2nd Officer A.E. - 60
Griffiths, F/O R.H.P. - 24 - 33
Griffiths, F/O W.P. - 33
Ground Controlled Approach - 143

Ground Controlled Interception
  Radar - 150
Groupe de Chasse I/5 - 166
Guy, Cpl. J.F. - 173 - 186

H
Halsall - 78
Haney, 1st Lt. C.N. - 68
Hanzlicek, Sgt. O. - 163
Hardwick, Norfolk - 91
Haworth, Rev. F.W. RAF - 158
Hendrix, 1st Lt. L.E. - 68
Herek, A/2C V.A. - 142
Hester, 1st Lt. R.L - 92
Hilkeman, Maj. B. - 141 - 143
HMS Ameer - 25
HMS Blackcap - 114
HMS Daedalus - 113
HMS Empress - 26
HMS Fulmar - 114
HMS Gannet - 114
HMS Seahawk - 114
HMS Shah - 26
HMS Theseus - 114
Hornsby – Smith, S/L F.C. – 154,
  158
Hoyle Bank - 163
Hubbard, 2nd Lt. K.E. - 173 - 186
Humphreys, P/O J.D. - 164
Hyett, Sgt. R.E. - 72

I
II Gruppe, Kampfgeschwader 54 -
  77
II Staffel, Kampfgeschwader 806
III Gruppe, Kampfgeschwader 26 -
  149
Isigny sur Mer, France - 43

J
Jackson, AC2 A. - 164
Jamieson, P/O A.M. - 158
Johnson, T.Sgt. L.E. - 72, 73
Jonas, Sgt. D.E.C. - 101

K
Kampfgeschwader 55 - 148, 149,
  151, 155
Kirby Lonsdale - 144
Knight, Ted - 88
Knowsley Park - 85, 88 - 90
Korean War - 114
Kutznik, Fw. L. - 149, 152, 154, 159

L
L'Escadrille des Cigognes - 163
L'Escadrille Guynemeyer - 166
Lancashire Engineer Volunteers
  (2nd) - 94
Lancaster - 164
Latham, Hubert - 11
Lend – Lease Agreement - 51
Liverpool - 12, 34, 42, 70, 75, 77,
  131, 132, 148, 159
Lockheed Aircraft Corp. - 84, 87,
Lofgren, Capt. M.A. – 94, 97
Long, Capt. W.M. – 68, 69
Longland, E - 94
Loran Navigation receiver - 141
Lovasik, T/Sgt. L. - 97 - 99
Ludwinski, Fw. H. - 149, 152, 154,
  158
Lunecliffe - 60
Lytham - 20
Lytham & District Wildfowlers
  Association - 172

M
Maddock, Cpl. - 153
Majchrzyk, Sgt. - 34
Malcolm Canopy - 15, 52
Maloney, 2nd Lt. E.V. - 96, 97
Manchester - 11, 12
Marlatt, F/O S.P. - 123 - 128
Martin, Warrant Officer - 158
McKenzie, 1st Lt. D.W. - 68
McKeown, Capt. J. C. - 68
McKnight, 2nd Lt. W. - 97
Mcmullen, F/L D.A.P. - 101

McNair, Sgt. R. – 151 - 153 , 160
Mohlenrich, Sgt. R.R. Jr. - 72
Morgan, Sgt. J. J. - 26
Murphy, T/Sgt. W.F. - 94
Murphy, T/Sgt. W.F. - 96, 97

N

National Fire Service - 95, 96
Nawrocki, Sgt. T. 60 - 64
No. 6 A.A.C.U. - 87
No. 1 A.A.S. - 102
No. 7 A.G.S. 54
No. 10 A.G.S. - 102 - 105
No. 334 Battery AA - 157
No. 8 E.F.T.S. - 102
No. 25 E.F.T.S. - 86
No. 3 F.P.P. - 54
No. 9 Group, Fighter Command 17
No. 20 M.U. - 52
No. 22 M.U. 51
No. 29 M.U. - 46
No. 39 M.U. - 24
No. 48 M.U. - 85
No. 55 M.U. - 65
No. 75 M.U. 66
No. 2 O.A.F.U. - 64
No. 6 O.T.U. - 166
No. 409 R.S.U. - 24
No. 16 S.F.T.S. - 54, 87
No. 22 S.F.T.S. - 113
No. 20 (Training) Group RAF - 86
No. 1 Squadron - 46
No. 3 Squadron - 160
No. 4 Squadron - 124, 125
No.12 Squadron - 103
No. 24 Squadron - 33
No. 28 squadron - 167
No. 29 Squadron - 163
No. 41 Squadron - 166
No. 137 Squadron - 160
No. 141 squadron - 100
No. 148 Squadron - 33
No. 151 Squadron - 25, 100, 101, 102
No. 239 Squadron - 25

No. 245 Squadron - 160
No. 245 Squadron - 42
No. 247 Squadron - 160
No. 249 Squadron - 160
No. 256 Squadron - 76, 77, 78
No. 26 Squadron – 25, 126
No. 65 Squadron - 52
No. 74 squadron - 161
No. 87 Squadron - 160
No. 93 Squadron - 150
No. 96 Squadron - 76, 151, 152
No. 264 Squadron - 150, 151
No. 271 Squadron - 65
No. 302 Squadron - 43
No. 303 Squadron - 42
No. 306 Squadron - 53, 61
No. 307 Squadron - 60
No. 308 Squadron - 34, 42, 43, 76
No. 309 Squadron - 53
No. 310 Squadron - 162, 166
No. 311 Squadron - 162
No. 312 Squadron - 76, 162, 163, 164, 166, 167
No. 313 Squadron - 166
No. 315 Squadron - 53, 60, 61, 64, 65
No. 316 Squadron - 51, 52,
No. 317 Squadron - 43, 64, 65
No. 539 Squadron - 45, 46, 49
No. 604 Squadron - 150
No. 611 Squadron - 24, 26
No. 738 Squadron FAA - 114
No. 759 Squadron FAA - 114
No. 766 Squadron FAA - 113
No. 767 Squadron FAA - 114, 115
No. 803 Squadron FAA - 115
No. 804 Squadron FAA 25
No. 807 Squadron FAA - 114
No. 919 Balloon Squadron - 76
No. 921 Balloon Squadron - 76
No. 922 Balloon Squadron - 153, 154, 158
Noga, Plt. H. - 53 - 59
North American Aviation - 15
North Pickenham - 69

O

Oglet - 163
Omaha Beach - 43
Operation Bodenplatte - 160
Operation Livery - 26
Operation Market Garden - 68
Operation Matador - 25
Operation Sankey - 25
Operation Vittles - 129, 135, 138
Orth, 2nd Lieut. B.L. - 16 - 23
Over Kellet - 165

P

Paley, F/O B. 34 - 44
Pandora aerial minefield - 150
Panta Air Base, India - 167
Pendle Hill - 62
Pennine Aviation Museum - 56, 64
Personal effects - 107, 109
Ploesti raid - 98
Pound, Capt. J.E. - 132
Powell River, British Columbia - 123
Preston 16, 17, 22, 62, 143
Prestwick - 143
Procita, F/O G. - 72
Protection of Military Remains Act 1986 - 14
Public Record Office, Kew - 112
Pucek, F/O W. - 64 - 66
Purple Heart - 186

R

RAF Acklington - 45
RAF Air Intelligence - 157
RAF Barrow - 105
RAF Belfast - 87
RAF Binbrook - 103
RAF Cark - 87
RAF Chailey - 43
RAF Clifton - 125, 126
RAF Coltishall 53
RAF Cranage - 76, 151, 152
RAF Digby - 104, 167
RAF Fazakerly - 76

RAF High Ercall - 76
RAF Hooton - 155
RAF Hucknall - 87
RAF Llanbedr 76
RAF Manby - 103
RAF Millom Museum - 14, 169, 187
RAF Newton - 87
RAF Padgate - 86
RAF Speke - 76, 84, 85, 162, 164, 167
RAF Squires Gate - 76, 77, 78
RAF Syerston - 113
RAF Tern Hill - 76
RAF Valley - 76
RAF Warton - 28
RAF Weeton - 66
RAF West Malling - 25
RAF Woodvale - 26, 27, 34, 43, 60 - 64, 66, 76
RAF Wrexham - 76
Rainhill - 118
Rathberger, Capt. W.A. - 133
Redhead, Special Constable - 95, 96
Reid & Sigrist Ltd. - 102
Reynolds, S/Sgt. H.S. - 142
Rhein-Main AFB, Germany - 130, 131, 138
Richfield, Kansas 19
RNAS Culdrose - 114
RNAS Gannet - 114
RNAS Lee on Solent - 113
RNAS Lossiemouth - 114
RNAS Stretton - 114 - 116
Robinson, F/O D.A. Jr. 72
Rootes Securities Aircraft Factory - 51, 75, 84, 163
Ross, Sgt, W. - 77, 78
Rossendale - 12
Royal Aero Club - 11
Rybaczek, F/O E.S. - 84 - 90

S

Sadler, James - 11
Sadler, William Windham - 11

Sayre, Maj. L.V. - 142
Sbrogna, A/1C R.H. - 142
Schwartz, T/Sgt. H. - 94, 97
Scorton - 137
Single, Oberfw. K. - 149, 152, 154, 155
Skinner, Stf. Sgt. H.C. - 132
Sly, Sgt. O.K. - 164
Smith, 1st Lt. G.H. Jr. - 72, 73
Smith, T/Sgt. R. -142
Spilsbury, J - 124
SS Malakand - 75
SSSI Site designation - 175
St. Andre de L'Eure, France - 77
Stalag Luft III - 44
Stehlik, Sgt. J. - 163
Stenton, F/Sgt. J. - 77, 78
Stevens, P/O R.P. – 101, 102
Stevens, Sgt. R.E. - 164
Stewart, Mr. A. - 112
Stone, Pvt. R.E. - 131, 133, 134
Strain, 1st Lt. D.B. - 68
Sunder, 1st Lt. E.L. - 69

T

Tadeusz Kosciuszko Polish Army Camp, Canada - 86
Tarentum, Pennsylvania - 97, 99
Tarnbrook, - 62, 63
Terryville, Connecticut - 86, 87
Theis, Cpl. N.H. - 131, 133
Thompson, Miss M. - 137
Thorpe Bay, Essex - 112, 113
Timewell, Sgt. Plt. R.S. - 45 - 50
Tomkins, 2nd Lt. M.F. - 96, 97
Turbinlite - 45, 46, 150

U

Usson, France - 33

V

V-1 Rocket - 43, 52
Van Horn, Capt. - 117
Vasatko, P/O A. - 163
Vickers Armstrong Ltd. - 24, 34, 115, 167
Victory parade, London - 55
Vybiral, P/O T. - 165, 166, 167

W

Walker, 2nd Lt. J.B. III - 72
Warplane Wreck Investigation Group - 167
Warth Mills POW Camp, Bury - 155
Watkins, Sgt. B.J. - 133
Wegner, A/1C W.D. - 142
Wendling, Norfolk - 93, 99
West, F/L D.R. - 77
Wheaton, 1st Lt. L.A. Jr. - 133
Widnes - 153, 155, 161, 163
Wigan - 12
Williams, F/Sgt. B.C. - 49
Wilson, C.D. Warden. R. - 95, 96
Winchester Repeating Arms Co. - 146
Wood, Sgt. A.D. - 78
Woodward, 2nd Lt. D.E. - 68
Worswick, Bill - 63
Wurgel, 1st Lt. R.M. - 131, 133

Y

Yalta Conference - 55

Z

Zbigniew, F/L C. - 65
Zemke, Col. Hubert - 18
Zeppelin - 12
Zuber, 2nd Lt. N. - 173 - 186